W9-CEJ-630

To PEARL

[signature]

11/19/16

TWO WHEELS THROUGH

T E R R O R

TWO WHEELS THROUGH

T E R R O R

Diary of a South American
Motorcycle Odyssey

GLEN HEGGSTAD

ECW Press

Copyright © Glen Heggstad, 2010

Published by ECW Press
2120 Queen Street East, Suite 200, Toronto, Ontario, Canada M4E 1E2
416.694.3348 / info@ecwpress.com

Hardcover edition first printed in 2004,
Whitehorse Press, Center Conway, New Hampshire.

All rights reserved. No part of this publication may be reproduced, stored in a retrieval
system, or transmitted in any form by any process — electronic, mechanical, photocopying,
recording, or otherwise — without the prior written permission of the copyright owners and
ECW Press. The scanning, uploading, and distribution of this book via the Internet or via any
other means without the permission of the publisher is illegal and punishable by law. Please
purchase only authorized electronic editions, and do not participate in or encourage electronic
piracy of copyrighted materials. Your support of the author's rights is appreciated.

LIBRARY AND ARCHIVES CANADA CATALOGUING IN PUBLICATION

Heggstad, Glen
Two wheels through terror : diary of a South American motorcycle
odyssey / Glen Heggstad.

ISBN 978-1-55022-922-6

1. Heggstad, Glen—Travel—South America. 2. Heggstad, Glen—Travel—
Central America. 3. Kidnapping victims—Colombia—Biography. 4. Ejército
de Liberación Nacional (Colombia). 5. Motorcycle touring—Central America.
6. Motorcycle touring—South America. 7. Central America—Description
and travel. 8. South America—Description and travel. I. Title.

F2225.H44 2010   918.044   C2010-901251-8

Cover design: Rachel Ironstone
Typesetting: Mary Bowness
Photos: Glen Heggstad
Printing: Lake Book Manufacturing   3   4   5

PRINTED AND BOUND IN THE UNITED STATES

ECW PRESS
ecwpress.com

Dedicated to Joe Gallagher

My passport photo when originally issued in 1997.

My passport photo in December 2001 after five weeks with the ELN.

Table of Contents

ATLANTIC
OCEAN

Gulf
of
Mexico

MEXICO

HONDURAS
GUATEMALA

EL SALVADOR
NICARAGUA
COSTA RICA
PANAMA
COLOMBIA
ECUADOR

PERU

BRAZIL

BOLIVIA

PARAGUAY

CHILE

PACIFIC
OCEAN

URUGUAY
ARGENTINA

0   500   1000 Miles

0   500   1000 Kilometers

Preface

I am vacillating in and out of a restless dream that lacks definition. It's the kind of awkward departure from slumber experienced when traveling and waking up with furrowed brow in a strange hotel — unable to recall where I had gone to sleep or where I am. There are familiar beeping and buzzing noises. It sounds like dozens of pagers and cell phones ringing somewhere in a cloud of semiconsciousness. I open my eyes and focus on my surroundings — groggy but acutely aware of intense itching from head to foot. On reflex, I slap and brush my face to rid myself of hundreds of tiny feet crawling across my skin. As my head begins to clear, I realize that the beeping and buzzing is a choir of insects beating their wings or rubbing their legs together, as they creep and fly around into my ears and eyes.

Suddenly alert, I jolt upright, interrupting a stream of tiny ants marching into my nose. Inside my soggy clothes I sense armies of prickling legs and stingers at work feasting on the flesh of this unwitting intruder. I'm covered by a variety of species of insects that invade the evenings of the Colombian wilderness. It's their turf and I'm fair game. As I tear off my shirt, whisking a hundred gnawing critters from my welted torso, I recall that I am not alone. From the jungle floor, I look slowly up from a pair of black knee-high rubber boots planted firmly in the damp earth, to a menacing face. It's a face connected to a black-uniformed soldier pointing an AK-47 submachine gun down at my head.

"Hey, gringo — *vamos!*" he gruffly commands in an unfamiliar Castellan accent. Then he waves his weapon to one side toward a trail at the end of this small clearing. There are a dozen others similarly dressed, methodically untying hammocks, cleaning weapons, and stuffing gear into backpacks. A young woman with a rifle slung over her shoulder gathers used plates and cups. Others warily stand guard around the camp perimeter with weapons at ready and cold distant stares. Slowly emerging from the haze of my fading dream — dismally recalling events leading to this stomach-burning moment — I return to the savage nightmare of reality. It's true. I'm here in the mountains of Colombia, a prisoner of a violent Marxist terrorist army, deep in the chilly wilds far from the people I love, people who don't yet know that I am missing. Images of a happy life in California flicker into the back of my mind as I now must focus on a moment-to-moment struggle to stay alive. The motorcycle adventure of a lifetime has become two wheels through terror. Now I sit trying to remember how this all started out.

Statistics state that white guys like me tip over around the eighty-year mark. If true, that meant more than half the show was over. A gap was closing and I was faced with a dilemma. What next? Play it safe? Take no chances? Be happy that I had navigated life's curves so far without being hit by a train or contracting some unpronounceable disease? Maybe sit home and watch TV and let the media sort it all out for me? Or should I get off my butt, roll the dice and find out what's really going on in the world as well as in my own head?

Every day had become the same. I could point to a calendar and tell how my day would begin and end. Lines separating the days grew obscure. Television news seldom varied; the stock market fluctuated and another politician got caught lying. And then there were hurricanes or a few minor earthquakes to tease us about the big one coming. Even when something did go wrong, there was insurance to cover it. The only mystery was how much the company would pay.

This Nerf-ball world was becoming so painfully predictable there was little left to relieve the monotony of existing. It was a good life — a nice home, great friends, and a successful career behind me. But something was missing. I had reached all the goals I had set earlier in life and struggling toward goals was what always kept me feeling alive.

After retiring from martial arts competition in 1999, I moved out to the country to seek inner peace as a mild-mannered judo instructor. Life was decelerating at a pace that I feared was grinding to a halt. I still kept a motorcycle for primary transportation and lightweight thrills but seldom ventured out of California anymore. I craved one last hoorah, a journey somewhere into the unpredictable to wake me up. It was time to swap the drumming of my fingers for a firm grip on my destiny.

Since returning from living in Asia a decade before, I had often pondered what it would be like to ride a motorcycle through South America, top to bottom. I was thinking of it more often, until — why not now? If not now, when? It's easy to make excuses when faced with a difficult challenge. My choice became now or never, otherwise there would always be an excuse not to go. To find what I was after, I would have to depart from a typical American comfort zone.

Until two years ago, I was always busy with work, my school, relationships, or an upcoming competition. Yet in my off-time I still managed some backpacking through the Third World on everything from elephants through Thailand and Burma, to a bicycle across Laos. While living in Southeast Asia during the eighties, I trekked the Himalayas twice and wandered the rest of the continent by bus, jeep, and riverboat from Beijing to Bali. Most thrilling was a 6,000-mile motorcycle ride across Thailand, Malaysia, and Singapore. On that ride, I spent three months rolling through monsoon storms, past ancient temples and senses-rocking cultures where yes means no, one and one is three, and a smile defines a hundred different moods.

A bus ride would have been more comfortable and provided a chance to relax along the way, but I would have missed merging into the exotic surroundings and forgone the constant challenge of figuring out the next move. Actually, I would have gone mad had I chosen any other means of transportation. Motorcycles are in my blood.

My motorcycle addiction began at age fifteen while riding to school on a little Honda 50, and ever since, I have never been without a bike. Like others in my generation, I was captivated by the sixties cult film *Easy Rider*, a story of two men riding cross-country on Harley-Davidson choppers.

For me, the brand of machine was irrelevant as long as it had two wheels. It was torture to travel by car, which dedicated riders refer to as a cage. There is no single excuse for why people get strung out on motorcycles; reasons range from "a motorcycle is the ultimate expression of freedom" to "it's a drug-free escape from reality," or even that "it's an instrument of rebellion." My reasons were all of the above, combined with a passion to explore the world.

I first caught the travel bug in high school while reading Jack Kerouac's novel *On the Road*, which I hardly finished before setting out to hitchhike from California to New Orleans. Three weeks later I returned on fire with travel fever, and was barely able to finish my senior year before scrounging together enough stray dollars to buy my first real motorcycle, one big enough to travel on Interstate highways, a Triumph 650.

That same afternoon I blasted down the Pacific coast for a year of roaming the western U.S., drifting from town to town with only an extra change of clothes and a sleeping bag. Friends were off in college warning me on the dangers of motorcycling — I was never so content.

One accepts numerous risks when embarking on the two-wheeled path to salvation. We learn to tolerate unmerciful weather, from painfully blazing heat to tooth-clacking freezing cold. For the most part, we're invisible to other drivers, who run us over then claim, "Sorry, I didn't see the guy." If that's not enough, as we lean blissfully through mountain curves, there's that nagging threat of what's around the next bend. Water, sand, or gravel spell loss of traction and an abrasive body-to-pavement slide as the layers of protection disintegrate, starting with our clothing, down to skin, meat, and bone.

On the other hand, the wind in our face combined with blood draining from our brains under hard acceleration toys with our reasoning. Or maybe it's being swept under the influence of inertia and centrifugal force in a fast hard lean through the curves of a well-engineered banked turn that keeps us gasping for more. Winding out through the gears on a high-performance motorcycle is rapture.

But adventure travel on a motorcycle is more subdued. And although it can be a roller coaster ride of surging adrenaline, that's due more to the danger of unpredictable consequences — like exploring regions and countries where little makes sense to the uninitiated and sometimes unwelcome.

Riding off the beaten path through the developing world is a numbers game — within a certain number of miles a rider will experience misfortune. We take our chances. It's considered bad luck to talk about motorcycle wrecks, yet the awareness is always there — we could end up as organ donors or vegetables.

At one time or another, everyone fantasizes about faraway exotic places, usually without consideration of how to get there. Bikers fantasize about riding motorcycles to those faraway exotic places. We discover shortly after the first time crossing a state line on two wheels that it is not the destination but the journey. There's seldom T-shirt weather. It's mostly too hot or too cold, but we have equipment to contend with that, maps to keep us on track, and an attitude that whatever happens, it's not so bad. It's all part of the journey that provides experience for fresh perspectives. I give myself plenty of time when traveling so I can stay off the main freeways and always take the head-clearing, long road.

In the past, the long road in the U.S. took me along dusty country highways and beside small slow rivers next to quiet little towns too tiny to be counted. What made it more interesting were the people I met along the way, the ones who didn't get out much and seldom had reason to go beyond the next county line. The long road is a refreshing contrast to efficiency, high-tech solutions, and deadlines. A two-wheeled sojourn is a journey back to simplicity that develops patience and discipline. It's a path to clarity that books cannot reveal.

My time had come. The challenge of navigating across fifteen Third World countries, through some of the roughest geographical terrain and volatile political landscape on earth, was too much to turn down. The next eight months would be dedicated to living a lifetime dream, engaging in the perils and pleasures of wanderlust while seeking the pulse of mankind.

Introduction

"Security is mostly a superstition. It does not exist in nature, nor do the children of men as a whole experience it. Avoidance of danger is no safer in the long run than outright exposure. Life is either a daring adventure, or nothing." — Helen Keller

EVE OF DEPARTURE
September 30, 2001
● ● ● ● ● ● ● ● ● ● ●

Warriors claim that battles are won in the preparation. This is a personal battle for which I am preparing—a battle to survive the adventure of a lifetime: riding the road from Southern California, through Mexico, Central America, and down the west coast of South America to the tip, across the Straights of Magellan to the island of Tierra del Fuego, and back up the east coast — on a 650cc dual-sport motorcycle. A 25,000-mile ride through blazing deserts, freezing mountain passes, sub-Antarctic wilderness, and steaming tropical rain forests.

The pathway is composed of mud, gravel, and poorly paved roads. There's not much to slow me down except aftermaths of earthquakes, hurricanes, breakdowns in social order, military police states, drug cartels, and civil wars. One can only guess if the natives are friendly. My command of Spanish is minimal, but I practice daily.

The journey is all via motorcycle, alone and unarmed. My weapons are determination, life experience, and a fervent desire to be amongst the people who live there. I will taste their love, joy, suffering, and anger. Deep inside I feel that I am one of them. The locals don't always receive me well, yet I've learned in the past that it's possible to break the ice of mistrust with a big hearty *Buenos dias* and a warm smile from my heart. I also know, in times of hostility it is most often best to be silent and wait. I've coaxed both cops and soldiers alike into smiling like children and treating me as a friend when situations began unfriendly.

The U.S. State Department travel warnings claim that regions of Guatemala, El Salvador, and Nicaragua are in states of social disorder. There are 3,000 kidnappings a year in civil war–ravaged Colombia, with half the country now under the domination of Marxist rebels or cocaine warlords. Argentina is edging toward economic collapse and Venezuela's left wing strongman Hugo Chavez is on the verge of being toppled by the military. It has only been three weeks since the September 11 attacks and it is clear that Americans are targets wherever we travel, and now wherever we live. Yet if I cancel this trip, terrorists win.

Late at night, I wonder how I will react to hostile forces or armed bandits. How will I survive the freezing mountain passes of the Bolivian Altiplano or the fiery heat of the driest region on earth, the Atacama Desert of northern Chile? The Patagonian wilderness will test my skills at navigation as I travel along the *Camino Astral*, backtracking the route of Charles Darwin into the barren tundra of southern Argentina and Chile where eighty-mile-an-hour crosswinds regularly thunder in from Antarctica.

In Latin America, geographic boundaries can change as highways disappear in bad weather or border conflicts. If the road ends at a river, I will find a boat to carry me across, or ride off road through the jungle until a better path appears. A global positioning satellite device will display my latitude, longitude, and direction. The primary direction, however, is into the unpredictable.

How does one prepare for the unpredictable? I pack medical supplies of injectable antibiotics, bandages, anti-inflammatories, and enough sutures to patch me up with in the event of involuntary street surgical procedures or motorcycle mishaps. To be visible in the lunacy of Latin American driving, a friend painted my helmet fluorescent orange, and my multi-colored motorcycle is so bright it's painful to the eyes. All my equipment is heavy duty, from tires and drive chains to luggage, brakes, and electronics. Yet this doesn't guarantee anything.

A close friend and judo student, Jimmy Weems, is a master motorcycle mechanic, who has gone over the bike from top to bottom, rewelding, reinforcing, and installing new support brackets and heavier suspension. He has modified the carburetor to perform reliably from sea level to an anticipated wheezing 17,000 feet in the Andes.

Jimmy owns the largest motorcycle shop in town and should really be busy building expensive custom Harley-Davidsons for his exclusive clientele, but he shuts down his business to focus on this project.

Fabricating motorcycles from sheet metal and blocks of aluminum is what he's famous for. His workmanship is his signature for my journey. Believing my safety is in his hands, he loses more sleep over this undertaking than anyone. He insists I road test every modification.

To be at the top of my game, I practice high-speed braking maneuvers with heavy loads on windy mountain roads and probe stability in the harsh crosswinds of Coachella Valley desert passes. Next, I ride over ruts, rocks, and every type of terrain to evaluate the limits of my suspension and handling capabilities. My foul-weather gear, from insulated nylon riding suit and waterproof deerskin gloves to electrically heated grips, is evaluated and dialed in. South America attacks overland travelers with every type of extreme weather condition imaginable and seldom on schedule. No matter the effort, Murphy's Law prevails.

The plan is to stay on the road eight months; one can only imagine the difficulties in scheduling life at home to proceed on autopilot without direct input from me. Property taxes, insurance bills, and expenses must be paid a year in advance. My mail is forwarded to Susan Aldrich to open and use her own judgment on how to deal with whatever "situation" lurks inside. My top students, Daniel and Anthony, will take over the teaching at my judo school and a friend has rented my house. A support team of loyal friends in California is ready for anything, including a series of secret codes to use over the phone if disaster strikes and we must communicate with bad guys listening.

For whatever reason, from a critical motorcycle injury to being thrown in jail or succumbing to tropical disease or maybe just falling in love with a person or place, the possibility exists that I might not return as scheduled. Those issues put tremendous strain on my friends. To set them at ease and to share the adventure with the world, we decide to create a web site so I can upload journals and digital photos from my laptop. From capital city Internet cafés, I will chronicle the journey almost in real time.

Using every available resource, I research this project by studying the journals and warnings of other similar travelers. Seven months before, I took a thirty-two-day, 8,000-mile shakedown ride through Mexico, Guatemala, and Belize for a taste of what's in store. More experienced travelers have told me that South America would be far more intense and that few ride there and back. True or not, I believe I am the most prepared man on earth. Half of my friends are terrified of what lies ahead — others enviously egg me on.

For the last year and a half, I've lived and breathed this upcoming odyssey. I am about to jump into an icy river that I know will be cold, but I won't know how cold until I'm floundering in the chilling current, swimming to remain afloat. If I encounter a problem too big to resolve, just knowing I will be alone with little chance of rescue will keep me alert and alive.

September 30, 2001, on the eve of departure, I stare distantly at the maps pinned on my office walls, reflecting on the hundreds of hours of painstaking preparation, convincing myself I am finally ready to charge into the merry chaos of Latin America.

THE VIKING STRIKES OUT

Adventure begins when events stop going as planned.

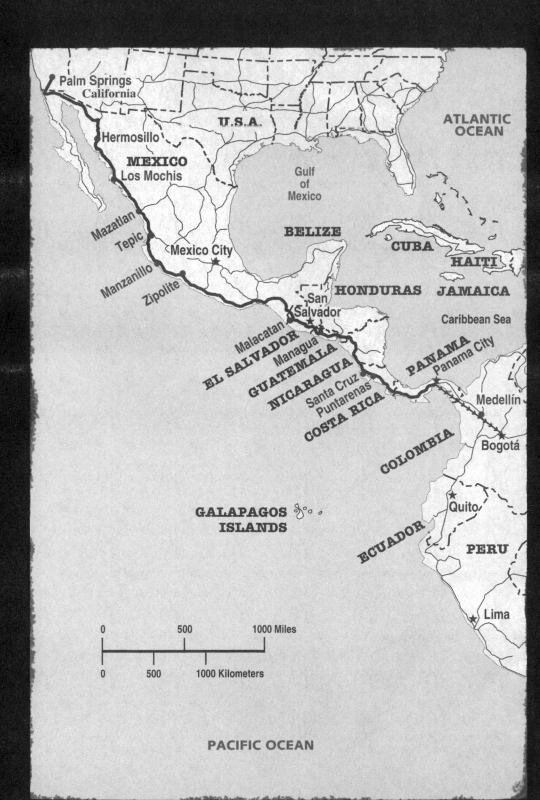

MEXICO

● ● ● ● ● ● ● ● ● ●

After double-checking my lengthy checklist of supplies and equipment, and dealing with last-minute bits of business, I sat spacing out on my loaded-down motorcycle. Finally, after sufficient procrastinating I fired up my engine to head south across the desert on Interstate 10 for the border at Mexicali. The year-long countdown has ended and my adventure begins with a taste of anxiety over the safety and comfort I leave behind and the unknown about to swallow me. The past no longer exists. The odyssey is in control. Once out on the road, I am deliciously beyond the point of no return. Security is as uncertain as the tumbleweeds blowing aimlessly across the parched desert ahead. Soon, varying degrees of wanderlust and perseverance will be my only guides. There is no turning back. The only direction for the next eight months, no *matter* the consequence, is forward.

If my timing is right, I'll be sleeping 500 miles down the road tonight in Hermosillo, the capital of Sonora, Mexico. Only the miles behind me will clear the residue of trepidation and cement the determination necessary to achieve my goal. The cactus-strewn desert plains are hair-dryer hot but the roads are lightly trafficked straightaways with cattle safely fenced away. Clear visibility whisks out for miles in all directions. Enormous electrical towers line the highway, appearing as ghostly steel skeletons grimly frozen in long even lines to the horizon.

13

When friendly Mexicans at the first gas stop ask where I'm heading, I have trouble convincing them, and myself, "to the tip of South America — and back."

WAITING ON A HURRICANE
October 3, 2001
Hermosillo, Mexico (24,400 miles to go)
• •

Since leaving Palm Springs, I've been monitoring weather reports on the CNN web site. For the first 800 miles south, temperatures range from 110 to 115 degrees. Riding during daylight hours guarantees dehydration in the fiery Sonora Desert heat — I'll sweat it out faster than I can replace it. Yet traveling at night, because of the dangers of stray animals, poorly maintained roads, or bandits, is as problematic as heat stroke. Roll the dice, the adventure has begun.

It's just me and a few overcrowded, speeding buses overtaking lumbering double-trailer semitrucks creeping across the fresh dawn landscape. Saguaro cactus and trash strewn along the roadside decorate the early morning sunrise. Multicolored shards of broken bottles backlit by refracting sunbeams turn the otherwise monotonous Sonora Desert into a beach of shimmering emeralds, diamonds, and amethysts. Nothing can deter me today; even garbage is beautiful.

And good fortunate is with me as Hurricane Julia has just finished tormenting my scheduled stopover cities a few days ahead. The weather abruptly turns cool enough to wear a jacket without breaking a sweat as high swirling clouds shield me from a scorching sun that yesterday choked livestock and nearly melted asphalt.

Checkerboard fields of multi-shaded green from a season of sultry summer rains line the road on either side. Under such ideal circumstances it's difficult to be light on the throttle yet I manage to honor a pledge to someone important to me who placed a sticker on my speedometer ordering, SLOW DOWN. Every time I read it I see her smiling face.

At the last two gas stops, I've been hearing rumors that the road to the coastal city of Guaymas on the Sea of Cortez is closed because of a washed out bridge. The only alternate route is a narrow winding mountain road out of my way by hundreds of miles. Before I left Palm Springs, Jimmy set up my carburetor vent hoses with enough clearance to allow passage through two feet of water as long as it is not flowing fast. In an effort to keep moving, I opt to chance it and attempt to cross the flooded washes ahead without a bridge.

Soon enough, I discover the road out of Hermosillo is backed up with cars and semitrucks waiting for construction crews to repair a series of hurricane-damaged bridges. No one knows when the bridges will be fixed and there is conflicting opinion whether the bridges in question are located before Guaymas or past it, closer to Los Mochis. The only way to be sure is to continue.

An hour later, I discover the washed out bridges are well past Guaymas, by ten miles. I plead my case to bored *Federales* stopping traffic, who only respond with commands to return to Guaymas until the bridges can be fixed. Stories are flying — it could take only a few days or maybe a week, everyone has a different theory. I can't be sure until I get there.

Tomorrow, I'll try again; maybe the water level will be lower. A new hurricane, Lorena, is slowly spinning up the Pacific Coast so I must get moving quickly or be stuck here for weeks. Although Guaymas is a relaxed little fishing town with plenty of friendly locals, there are far too many tourists. I spent a few days here six months ago on my shakedown ride; it's less exciting the second time around. New experiences will begin once past the Guatemalan border heading down into El Salvador and Nicaragua, places I've only read about and visited in my imagination. News reports vary on the civil war situation in Colombia and there is some doubt whether customs officials will grant me a temporary vehicle import permit. Most countries have unique requirements for obtaining temporary vehicle import permits, and policies can vary border to border within the same country. Authorities worry that travelers will sell their vehicles and avoid paying the high import taxes, so they require lengthy entry procedures to guarantee people leave with what they brought.

DETERMINED
Thursday, October 4, 2001
Los Mochis, Mexico
• • • • • • • • • • •

It's total chaos this morning in Guaymas. Streets not flooded or buried in mud are clouded by a swirling powdery dust suspended in the air above the roadway, making it difficult to see or breathe. Every thick mustached, potbellied public official has different information about road conditions heading south. The bridge is fixed. The bridge is only fixed enough for light vehicles. And the bridge won't be fixed for weeks and we're all stranded. Most people I ask say it's impossible to pass. *Eemposeeblay!* That's code for me; whenever someone tells me I cannot do something, what they really mean is, they cannot, but I can.

Saddled up and cinched down, I'm ready to roll and leave the rumors behind. Just when my frustration is peaking from dealing with uncooperative *Federales*, I met an innovative Mexican in a small pickup truck who knew a way around the checkpoint. *Vamos a ver.* (Let's go see.)

Sure enough, after winding our way through the crumbling back streets of Guaymas, we arrived near another connection to the main highway south where there was a mile-long string of traffic about to be permitted through by a different team of *Federales*. Concerned over further delay, I white-line it to the front of the line and find my way back to Highway 15. The road beyond is empty, with hundreds of cars and trucks now following me far behind. It doesn't take long to see the damage. It isn't just a few washed out bridges but rather about thirty partially crumpled concrete overpasses. Work crews have been busy all night reconstructing traffic lanes around flooded gullies while others are filled with gravel. I never would have been able to cross any of these washouts on my bike. The mud is much too deep.

The original double-lane highway was built on top of elevated dirt levees designed to control seasonal rains, but clearly not capable of withstanding hurricanes. The fragile road is now being undermined by rapidly flowing water and ready to collapse at any moment. Buses too heavy for the cantilevered asphalt plunge head-first into the muddy swamp where they lie like fresh carcasses, ready to be picked clean by bandits of the night. It's chaos for a hundred miles yet Mexican repair crews juggle and divert cars from both directions to keep traffic moving.

Hopefully, the road stays passable long enough to get me to Los Mochis, my anticipated overnight. CNN weather forecasts promise that new storm; Hurricane Lorena will still be swirling in this week-end. Wherever I wind up tonight could be home for a few days.

Word must have passed that the roads are shot because once ahead of the pack, there is no traffic in either direction. Today the fresh green Mexican countryside belongs to me. I almost forgot how beautiful it is down here and how nice the people are. A simple smile or a *Buenos dias*, and everyone is my friend. They want to know where I'm coming from and where I'm going. They can't compre-hend that I'm riding to South America on this little green motorcycle so I just respond, "Southern Mexico, maybe Guatemala," and that alone is enough to shock them.

I arrived in Los Mochis by mid-afternoon, enjoyed a spicy Mex-ican dinner, and found a new twenty-dollar-a-night hotel with hot water, air conditioning, and color TV. There was just enough time to shower and search for a *Café Internet*, to send my readers a hearty *Buenas noches* from Mexico. Life is good.

GARDEN OF EDEN
Friday, October 5, 2001
Mazatlán, Mexico
• • • • • • • • • •

Awakened early by a classical Mexican alarm clock of crowing roost-ers and honking taxis, I hastily devoured four fried eggs and a liter of water. To beat another predicted storm I need to start early — already, long white clouds are curling up into giant cotton balls in the distance, threatening to turn black by noon and spoil my day. As so often happens on a motorcycle, I'm once again racing Mother Nature.

As the day unfolds, my luck changes. A hundred miles down the road, ominous cloudy skies suddenly clear and the warm tropical sun seeps down into a pleasant afternoon. Thick humidity cools this fast moving motorcyclist who is now tempted to remove his helmet and savor the sweet smelling jungle air. But a convoy of large buses and diesel trucks thundering down the road on the edge of control is a reminder to keep it on.

Rolling hillsides mixed with steep ravines reflect a rainbow of colors: varying degrees of green, speckled with fluorescent dots of red, purple, pink, and orange blurs of tropical flowers flashing by. If it were not for all the friendly people along the roadway, I would swear I'm alone in the Garden of Eden.

At the first Internet café after entering the coastal city of Mazatlán, I receive more peculiar looks than usual. A quick peek in the mirror surprises even me. Earlier today, I didn't think much about riding through an annual massive butterfly migration, even though I developed a smeared yellow crud on my helmet face shield. Upon glancing at my image in a bathroom mirror, I discover that from the front, I look as though I came in last place in a mustard fight. Color me yellow.

EL CAJONE GRANDE
Saturday, October 6, 2001
Tepic, Mexico
● ● ● ● ● ● ● ●

Little has changed in Mazatlán since my last trip here in April. A few more fast-food franchises have mushroomed. For the most part, it's downtown America, shadowed by shantytowns and squalor a few streets away from wealthy tourist luxury beach hotels and housing.

Since I already traveled the Central Highland road the previous spring, I've decided to ride the coastal route to Guatemala. There are faded roadside signs posted outside small towns warning about outbreaks of dengue fever and malaria, diseases carried by mosquitoes. Before leaving home, I was inoculated against a dozen different known viruses, but for the new strain of malaria there is a recently developed, very expensive pill to be taken daily while in infected areas. For me, that means from here to the rest of South America, a period much too long to ingest a substance so toxic.

At last, hurricane warnings have ended and the sweltering heat subsides into warm coastal breezes, so as long as I keep moving, it's comfortable. There are rows of fresh fruit stands along the way for when it's time for a break or to say "Howdy" to the locals. Late afternoon, I meet an old woman wearing a crispy-clean threadbare white dress who, while chatting in Spanish and dicing up fresh picked mango, suddenly thinks to add a drink of coconut milk to my little snack. In one smooth move, she snatches an unhusked ice-cold coconut with one hand, whips out a razor sharp machete with the other and lops off the top. She gives me her finest every-other-tooth-missing grin, pops in a straw, and hands me both treats like a magician proudly completing a trick. My tab for this heavenly treat is ten pesos, about a dollar.

Desiring a taste of reality, I depart from the smooth-surfaced *autopista* and return to the genuine Mexican driving scene — chaos in motion. At between ten and thirty cents a mile, *autopistas* are outrageously expensive but similar in quality to U.S. interstates. Compared to the broken down *camino libre* (free road), *autopistas* are much safer for a motorcyclist. It's not that Mexican drivers are rude or careless; they are just aggressive at the moments I least expect and passive when I'm braced for the worst. A little consistency would take the edge off. It would be nice to get used to one pattern of driving or the other; the unpredictability of the road conditions and drivers is the most troubling issue.

That oncoming trucker wouldn't pass a bus on a blind curve — would he? Is that farm tractor really going five mph in the fast lane of a high-speed turn? And nobody ever stops in the middle of the highway just to take a leak; that might cause an accident. At least the lurking variables sharpen my reflexes.

Latin American commercial drivers have their own signs and signals to indicate trouble ahead. Tree branches in the road are the equivalent of emergency flares and there is likely a stalled or disabled vehicle around the next bend. Oncoming truckers flash their lights to warn of problems behind them. Most confusing though is when riding blind curves. Drivers of slow moving buses or trucks often flip on their left turn signals when they think it's safe to pass them. Two problems with that procedure: what do they consider safe and what if I start to pass and they are actually signaling a left turn?

In spite of the lunacy it's a gorgeous day, T-shirt weather on a motorcycle. No matter how high the temperature, it's best to wear a long sleeve cotton shirt. This is necessary protection from long hours in the glaring solar oven or from anything else that might land on bare skin. Today, riding the fresh paved road is like water-skiing on a placid lagoon, with just enough gently banked turns through the farmlands to keep me smiling and alert. Drifting into motorcycle oblivion, while attempting to pass the second of two enormous tour buses, from out of nowhere, Brother Buzz and company pulls a sneak attack.

One moment the air is damp and sweet with the fragrance of fresh cut fields. The next it is filled with angry flying insects swarming in dark formation, obviously annoyed about running headlong into a pack of invading motorists. As they harmlessly bounce off my shirt and splatter on my helmet, I'm miraculously escaping without being stung. Suddenly, I feel a buzzing sensation of tiny furiously vibrating wings, right where I'm sitting, followed by several sharp stings in my left testicle.

The pain is incredible. Swatting the bee increases the pain. There is no shoulder to pull off on and I'm stuck between two giant tour buses trying to break the land speed record. One hand is down the front of my trousers groping through a manual checkup when the bus behind me decides to pass. I look up in time to catch an audience of fascinated tourists gawking at me, unaware of my predicament. As the bus slowly slides past, a few *senoritas* smile with a blush and men hoot while saluting with a thumbs-up.

A strip of barren shoulder appears, finally a spot to pull over and inspect the damage. So there I was, by the side of the road, with my pants around my ankles checking for stingers in a rapidly swelling section of anatomy not designed to be a rapidly swelling section of anatomy.

PUERTO VALLARTA
Monday, October 8, 2001
Manzanillo, Mexico
● ● ● ● ● ● ● ● ● ● ●

In spite of being a major seaside tourist attraction, Puerto Vallarta has managed to retain a significant portion of its old-world Mexican charm. But the number of business franchises is growing and price structures are higher than other major cities in Mexico. And the effect of tourism on locals makes them view foreigners as suckers to be hustled. It doesn't help that foreigners routinely behave foolishly. Talking down to people because they don't speak English or arrogantly making demands while flaunting wealth is hardly a way to win friends in any culture. Not every tourist is a jerk but offended locals lose the ability to tell the difference. It's always a relief to get back on the road where I'm judged as an individual — as a traveler, not a tourist to be fleeced. I love country folk.

The first two hours south out of Puerto Vallarta toward Manzanillo offer more of the same scenery as yesterday. Sprays from giant waterfalls cascading down through thick jungle terrain running along the coastal roadway provide a pleasant escape from the tropical heat. There are just enough ruts, holes, and four-foot-long, lime green iguanas to dodge in the road to keep me sharp.

Although it is difficult to understand the Mexican TV news I catch in hotel lobbies, it looks as though the U.S. will invade Afghanistan searching for terrorists involved in the September 11th World Trade Center attack. This could be the reason there's so little tourism and hardly any traffic. Mexican roads are generally crowded with pounding commercial vehicles spewing black smoke into my face, but recently the highways are as deserted as the hotels.

Mexicans are polite on political subjects but when locals find out I am American there is muffled chatter from a distance about Bin Laden and words like *Afganistán* and *terroristas*. I avoid conversation on the subject. Visions of airliners crashing into the World Trade Center Complex are too fresh in my mind to tolerate lectures.

Just before sundown, I approach the blazing hot coastal city of Manzanillo in 100-degree heat with ninety percent humidity. The moment I stop, dropping out of the wind with no breeze to dry off the sweat, I'm drenched in body water as though emerging from the sea. Forgetting my hunger or the need to find a hotel room, I begin a street-by-street search for a Laundromat.

SAILING AWAY
Wednesday, October 9, 2001
Southwest Coast of Mexico
● ● ● ● ● ● ● ● ● ● ● ● ● ● ● ●

The best part of the day is in the early morning when my mind is most alert and I'm freshly saddled up with my gear cinched down and rocketing past the last traffic signal out of some crowded Mexican town. Choking clouds of filthy exhaust fumes disappear as the sweetness of the countryside fills my soul. There is no greater feeling of freedom.

It's always a welcome relief to stop at the end of a long day's ride and relax in a friendly family-owned hotel with the promise of a refreshing shower and exotic meal. But nothing tops the exhilaration of taking to the open road before the brutal heat of day intrudes. It's like a pleasing mystery unraveling, the unknown evolving into reality as one bizarre scene after another reveals itself with as much casual grace as utter confusion.

My faithful single-cylinder iron steed smoothly pops along at a comfortable measured pace, barely sipping a gallon of fuel every fifty miles. This could go on forever. I flip up my face shield and smile with the wind in my face coaxed along by a subtle desire to know what lies beyond the next bend.

One hour out of Manzanillo, I pass the last of the neatly manicured rows of mango orchards and endless giant-leafed banana plantations that flow across the chunky coastal terrain. The jungle is so thick and tightly packed against the road, it feels like I'm riding down through a long windy corridor of luxuriant green overgrown tropical hedges too solid to penetrate on either side. Sometimes the green walls open to expose wavering grassy meadows where scattered herds of shiny brown horses and squinty-eyed donkeys graze carefree. These uninhibited creatures wander perilously across the roadway at will, enhancing my awareness. The roadside stench of mangled carcasses with mouths gaping open, rotting in the drenching heat, fouls the air for miles. Their upturned faces frozen in agony are reminders I must be vigilant, or I too will be as them. Any motorcycle mishap could spell such an end, and then it would be me lying twisted in some muddy gully, with an expression contorted in anguish and left to perish.

The jungle on the ocean side soon disappears, opening into rocky cliffs revealing a storybook landscape below. Ahead lie hundreds of miles of deserted beaches and secluded lagoons disturbed only by schools of playful dolphins and patrolling seagulls laughing in the morning's glory. Outstretched palm trees sprouting from the sand line the secret bay beyond, beckoning me to stretch out a hammock and spend the afternoon sailing away with Jack London.

Around the bay's guardian rocky point, a crystal turquoise sea foams into bubbling fists, pounding the vanilla shoreline into tranquility. I sense the ocean is as warm as the air.

I have not seen a car or human for hours. I daydream that I am the last man on earth. There is no hustle and nowhere I have to be. I can stop and dive into paradise, or continue slowly meandering, as a lazy leaf drifting down a twisting river, without worry. I can't recall what day it is; time is no longer a factor. I only think in terms of now. There is no before or after. I rejoice in the splendor of solitude, marveling with the tropical sun. It's only early fall and I will travel through winter into spring, guided by summer rains of a distant southern hemisphere.

There is no place to be, no one to meet, and much to peer into. I'm often unsure of where I am but I know I'm always where I want to be. As in a dream, so deeply alone, my only companion is the shadow beneath my wandering spirit.

SHAVING CLOSE
October 10, 2001
Somewhere on the Oaxaca Coast
• • • • • • • • • • • • • • • • • • •

In a day packed with moments of splendor, four more hours cramped inside a steamy helmet just didn't feel right. Bikers know the feeling, the need for rushing wind blowing in our faces and through our hair. We are a different breed because more than savor the wind, we crave it, and wallow in the powerful gusts of life. Bikers don't just smell the freshness in the air; we feel it flow inside our spirits. We sense the landscape, then merge with it. We become what surrounds us. Helmets, although they can save our lives in critical moments, inhibit such sensations of freedom.

An hour outside a slow moving Mexican *pueblo*, after some of the best Oaxaca roasted chicken ever, I feel that need for freedom and reluctantly yield to temptation, stopping at the side of the road to pry off that smothering chunk of plastic. It's instant relief, instant gratification, and an instant problem if things go wrong. But it is too right a moment; I should have done it an hour ago. I know the risk better than most, because helmets saved me twice in past motor-cycle wrecks. Without them, I might be typing this using a pencil in my mouth. All the warnings of danger pass through my mind as pleasantly and worry-free as the wind by my face.

I glide gracefully into turns, dipping and leaning, smiling so much I laugh out loud — thinking to myself, "It can't get any better than this." When clearing the last blind curve and blissfully rolling into the next, a biker's nightmare strikes — an oncoming vehicle in the same lane, coming straight at me. With a split second to react, I swerve but there is no shoulder. Holding my breath, I pucker up and as the panicking driver does his best to return to his lane, he almost makes it.

A painful crack and crunch later, I'm hurtling toward an open field, fighting a high-speed wobble that's tugging me to the ground. Somehow, I manage to ride it out into the adjacent meadow and slide to a stop.

I look back to see chunks of metal and scraps of plastic in the roadway, and the other driver speeding away. Red anger flares into my eyes as I spin my wheels back onto the street. While my rear tire bites into the asphalt, the front end shoots up like a bucking stallion snorting in hot pursuit.

A mixture of anger and indignation drives me to chase as I slice into turns, scraping the foot pegs and smoking down the straight-aways. It takes miles to catch him, but he knows he can't escape and finally surrenders, pulling off by the side of the road. I have no idea who he is or what I'm going to do with him. All I know is, he is going to face me, man to man. Something needs to get settled and it won't require much conversation.

As I stomp down my kickstand the same moment as jumping off the bike, I come face to face with a tall skinny Mexican teenager with eyes snapped wide open and filled with tears. It's hard to tell who is shaking more, him or me — his fear, my rage affects us both. I scream in a mixture of English and Spanish that makes no sense to either of us while he apologizes in as many ways as he can.

My anger is not about the accident but because he didn't stop to see if I was okay, and I try to explain that to him. We talk it out for a few minutes, ending with a few friendly pats on the shoulder and calmer thoughts. After all, I came to learn from these people, not beat them up. There is writing on his car door indicating it's a hotel taxi. He could lose his job over this, and Oaxaca is one of the poor-est regions of Mexico. He most likely supports a full household with his meager earnings and is probably more scared of losing his job than anything. We shake hands, exchange the Mexican embrace, and then proceed on our separate ways.

The good news is, time spent re-engineering the entire motorcycle for a single moment like this paid off. It appears that although we barely collided in a slight sideswipe, my hand guard snagged and tore his mirror off, then scraped the side of his car. Before I left California, Jimmy scrapped the stock cheap plastic hand guards for stronger ones with thick aluminum support straps inside. Without them, that driver's mirror would have ripped my hand off, instead of the other way around.

The soft saddlebags broke away as designed and suffered only mild scuffing; even the resilient plastic fasteners survived and snapped back into place. The dual-rate, progressively wound springs stuffed into the front tubes and the reinforced fork legs improved stability enough to keep me upright.

As for my body: just a few bruised ribs, knee and elbow. Apparently, as the impact on my hand guard wrenched the handlebars out of control, I overcorrected and bounced back into the side of the car, taking the body shot. After a brief inspection, I immediately launch back in the wind. If I don't do this quickly, I might sit there shaking and think about it all day. I am well aware there will be dues to pay on this ride — at least I know I've paid up for a while.

ZIPOLITE (ZEE POH LEE TAY)
October 12, 2001
Southwest Coast of Mexico
● ● ● ● ● ● ● ● ● ● ● ● ● ● ●

I now have twelve days and 2,500 miles behind me. Riding south through the seven states of Sonora, Sinaloa, Nayarít, Jalisco, Colima, Míchoacan, and Guerrero continues as a journey into bliss down the west coast into Oaxaca. Tomorrow, I drift through Chiapas, the last Mexican state bordering Guatemala. According to Internet travel reports, Central American border crossings involve ridiculous delays of bureaucratic nonsense processing temporary vehicle importation permits. Issuing these documents can consume one to six hours, depending on crowds, computer failures, or attitudes of the immigration officials, which can be influenced with *propinas* (tips). The trick is to remain patient, keep smiling, and enjoy the experience while being appreciative for the opportunity to practice Spanish.

Traffic is normally light on church days so I schedule border crossings on Sundays, early in the morning when it's cool and other vehicles have not backed up yet in the stifling heat. These are my least favorite ordeals while traveling, and I minimize the hassle with careful timing. Since I will be riding through Central America again on the way home, the plan is to hurry as much as possible to South America where I can slow down to spend more time in each country.

Progress has been slow because of my promise to take it easy, and I'm constantly reminded by the sticker on my speedometer, SLOW DOWN. Fast or slow, I'm still determined to reach Argentina and then ride back to California within eight months. But there are sometimes minor annoyances. Long stretches through the countryside are broken periodically by *pueblitos* (little towns). Most are too small to have traffic signals or stop signs, so instead, to control traffic, authorities use speed bumps called *topes*. *Alto* signs are a joke with little meaning to most drivers. Traffic laws are, at best, mere suggestions. When approaching stop signs, some slow down a bit, some ignore them completely while others actually speed up, leaving this wary rider to guess. Cops have no effect. I see one a day and he is generally parked under a tree dozing.

Since there are children, chickens, pigs, horses, goats, and cows roaming about freely through the dusty streets of Mexican *pueblitos*, there wouldn't be much left of them if citizens of those communities allowed vehicles to speed through. Truckers won't slow down unless forced and don't hesitate to thunder through villages if there is nothing to discourage them. *Topes* are the best solutions and vary in height and angle according to how much the powers that be want you to slow down. Some are so high and steep, you must creep over, others are milder, requiring only a near stop. If you misjudge the size and don't slow down accordingly, the impact will send shock waves up your spine and demolish your motorcycle's suspension.

Nearing neighborhood *topes*, enterprising Red Cross solicitors, cripples and street vendors stand ready to grab the attention of slowing drivers. Sometimes there's a little, round-faced Indian girl under a thatched-roof fruit stand peddling long spears of ice-cold papaya. I'm a sucker for these young entrepreneurs who are always good for a wisecrack in Spanish, resulting in a laugh and a giggle.

Ironically, cities with traffic signals are the most difficult to navigate because they seldom divert traffic around the center. Drivers must pass through heavily congested areas first where turnoffs are seldom marked. I use a lot of *¿Donde esta?* this and that, trying to find my way through cluttered mazes of confusion and back onto the open road.

Humidity makes a big difference too. When the weather is hot and dry, the faster I ride, the warmer I become. If the weather is hot and humid, the faster I ride, the cooler I become. To be comfortable, I just keep moving and barely notice the heat. Yet this all changes in city traffic. At the first signal, I'm immediately drenched in my own sweat. Within seconds, wet, sticky clothes cling to my overheating body. When the light turns green, whatever dirt and grime the truck ahead kicks up adheres to the moisture, coating me in pasty grime. Then as I get moving again and dry off, a light cake forms on whatever skin the wind and dust can reach. At the next signal, the process repeats, so one can imagine what a motorcyclist looks and feels like after eight hours in the saddle.

For the last several days I've avoided overnights in big touristy cities useful only for Internet access. Smaller towns are far more relaxing and cheaper with better opportunities to mingle with a local population untainted by negative experiences with foreigners.

At last, I reach the fabled seaside village of Zipolite, the "Backpacker's paradise" according to my *Lonely Planet* guidebook. This rustic tiny village of cabañas built with palm fronds and tree posts nestles on the southern Oaxaca coast of the Pacific Ocean. Three hundred permanent residents live out their dreams on a deserted two-mile strip of sunny Mexican beach. Well, it would be paradise, if not for a few scrounging parasites begging for spare change. It's quite the experience dining in the same restaurant with green-toothed sons and daughters of upper class white folks from wealthy countries stumbling around imitating Rastafarians sporting filthy dreadlocks and yellow skin. Sickly European girls with bulldog faces and greasy hair wander about in marijuana dazes mumbling hip slogans to each other while peddling matchboxes of weed. The scuzziest is queen. That's okay but I want to tell them, "Darlin' please put your top back on, I'm trying to eat."

I rode in last night unknowingly making a major fashion statement — unshaven for days and coated in road crust. Smelling like those donkeys in the ditches earned me head bobbing nods of approval while they overlooked the blunder of me brushing my teeth every day.

ATTACK!
October 13, 2001
Zipolite, Mexico
● ● ● ● ● ● ● ● ●

Although Zipolite is the most peaceful village yet, a potentially dangerous situation has been intensifying and a highly developed traveler's sixth sense warns it's time to flee. If I wait any longer it may be too late. I'm being followed. At first I think it's my imagination, but after awhile I grow positive. You know when you are being watched, you can feel the laser beam eyes focusing on you whether you see them or not. Casual eyes that spot victims. Experienced eyes that spot who is weak and vulnerable to approach. I'm being sized up for a set-up, no question about it.

While outside my hotel and in every little sandy-floored beach restaurant, the same piercing eyes are tracking me. After a while the truth comes out in the open, yet I'm not sure how to deal with it.

There's soon to be a relentless attack that could render me weakened forever.

At first I considered it coincidence because there are so many stray dogs in Mexico that look alike. But no, there is something different about this little four-legged *perrito*. He's young, about four to six months. I can tell because he still has the crystal clear brown eyes of a puppy, yet eyes that are also wise beyond his years. He is obviously an orphan, with no friends to speak of, and discreetly seeking adoption.

He is scarred up awfully bad like all the other street mutts who manage to survive the cruelty of homelessness in a poor country. He shows a few fresh wounds from brawls with other four-legged *desperados* over chicken bones and leftovers from garbage cans. A lovable little *bandito* in his own special way — with just a touch of mange.

Still, he makes every attempt to be presentable — with sort of a "I'm not like the other dogs you've met down here before" persona. With pleading little eyes, my new friend is going all out. Okay, he certainly is unique and obviously likes me, and although trying to be nonchalant, is becoming decidedly attached. Suddenly he's acting like we've known each other for a time, and like a pro he has managed to get me to talk to him. This little manipulator has a plan in mind and is going about it in a very clever manner. But he can't hide his growing anxiety.

Maybe it's because he overheard me tell a waiter that I'm riding south in the morning. That's when all the stops come out. His desperation becomes more evident as the night progresses. Time is running short.

You know how puppies can pull that following you around and laying at your feet routine? Well, this guy throws in the "plop the head on your foot with a big deep sigh" to top things off. Every place where I sit down, he runs up and lies beside my feet, quickly snuggling his mangled little head on my boot. He never begs or drools, merely politely accepts any table scraps offered in a most dignified manner. He has his pride and intends to keep it.

Then comes a double-barreled blast aimed squarely at my heart.

We all know dogs have a special way of communicating with facial expressions. Especially with those darn weeping eyes and that cute cocking of their heads. I try to warn him he's wasting his time by turning my back.

With the firmest of poise he starts in with a "Please, please, I won't be any trouble" look on his face, followed by the "I promise never to poop in the hotel room" gaze of sincerity. Then he puffs out his tiny chest and claims he is tough enough to guard my motorcycle every night faithfully and absolutely never bark unnecessarily. I think he tries to cross his heart with his little paw or something, I'm not sure.

I begin to consider it might be nice to have a companion, and maybe I could build a small platform on my gas tank where he could sit. Seeing me soften, he perks up, anticipating headway. He must be reading my mind . . .

"Please, oh please. I'll hardly eat any dog food, never chase cats or chew up your shoes. I'll never give you reason to yell or spank me."

My logic begins to prevail. He is a puppy now but there's no telling how big he'll get. "I'm sorry Paco (I've already named him), the trip is too long and too difficult, with no room for a dog. It just won't work."

He switches tactics and goes for the play-with-the-shoelace routine while wagging his scarred-up little tail, even throwing in a few polite muffled woofs of provocation.

I remain as firm as possible. "As of now, Paco, the answer is no, but let me sleep on it and we'll talk later."

The next morning I rise early hoping to slip quietly out of town unnoticed before any dogs wake up. I pack quickly, gather up my bags, open the hotel room door, and guess who is waiting patiently? How did they ever learn to plead with those penetrating eyes?

"All right Paco, we need to go have a chat." So off we march with little Paco trotting loyally by my side to the nearest taco stand.

You must be cool about feeding stray dogs in poor countries; it's offensive to the hungry people standing around that you help out a dog before them. It's a point well taken by both of us, so we are discreet and I wait until nobody is looking, then slide a bit of shredded beef his way.

There is not much for either of us to say at this point. He knows what's coming, and gives me the "Go ahead and make it easy on yourself" look while turning away. With lowered head and sagging tail, he slowly shuffles down the street and around the corner.

Abruptly, I hear a garbage can being knocked over, notice a pack of stray dogs headed in that direction and hold my breath. There is growling and snapping and high-pitched barking. A few yelps later, the pack emerges, fleeing in all directions. Moments pass until I see Paco peeking around the corner with a tasty chunk of rotted hamburger in his little pink mouth. I can't swear to it, but I think he winked as he turned and disappeared down the alley.

The damned ocean air is starting to burn my eyes, I have to get outta here. After all he is just a dog, right?

GUATEMALA

LA FRONTERA DE GUATEMALA
October 15, 2001
Melacatang, Guatemala

• • • • • • • • • • • • •

With a quick glimpse back, I bid final farewell to Mexico via a long 200-mile stretch of four-lane highway crammed with grumbling diesel trucks all aggressively converging on the Guatemalan border. I'm sad to leave the warmth and security of Mexico but alas I am about to enter a new phase.

Between this journey and my shakedown ride last spring, I've traveled through most of western and central Mexico, and although people and customs vary greatly, I always felt at home and welcome. Mexicans greeted me with open arms almost everywhere. Even when not, all it took was stumbling through a few words of Spanish and everyone soon became my friends. There was a certain security believing that someone was always watching my back in Mexico. In Central America I have little idea of what lies ahead.

Soon enough, my reluctance to leave Mexico is reinforced as I near the southern frontier. A low-lying fog, turning solid black by mid-afternoon, instantly brings near total darkness and a smothering, intense rainfall. Could this be an omen?

By the time I reach the chaotic Guatemalan border, nightfall is only hours away. All that's left to do is stand in a long line of frustrated travelers, attempting to keep my precious documents dry in the pouring rain by holding them inside my jacket. Hordes of obnoxious money changers follow me through the crowd offering the best deal while persistent teenagers tug on my sleeves promising to guide me through the maddening process for a small fee. None understand the word "No." Thoughts that my first ride in such unfamiliar territory might be in total darkness and blinding rain adds to the aggravation. Yet three hours spent wrangling through bureaucratic madness provides blackening skies a chance to empty their load and the first stormy moments into the Guatemalan countryside subside into a light, misty rain. At least I can see.

Helpful locals lead me to a pleasant, ten-room, family-owned hotel fifteen miles inside the border just as the last auburn shades of daylight dwindle into black. The twelve-dollar cubicle is cramped yet clean and, unlike my last eight nights in Mexico, has hot water.

Because it only revealed irrelevant information, I tossed my watch last week. My perception of the future has been altered. Now, time is marked by weather patterns and motorcycle maintenance schedules. Oil changes are scheduled for 4,000-mile intervals and tires swapped at 10,000. A new concept of home emerges — home is now where my front tire leads.

With luck, I'll air-freight from Panama City into Colombia in early November — then snake down through the Andes into Ecuador where the seasons will reverse as I descend into Peru just as the winter snows melt in December. The Atacama Desert in Chile is reported to be hot and dry throughout the year. The brutal crosswinds of Patagonia are always unpredictable and the steamy summer rains through Brazil's Amazon Basin hold their own mysteries. If there's time, I'll attempt to beat the springtime storms of Mexico on the return leg, but if I don't, I have a rain suit. That's the plan.

MALACATANG
October 16, 2001
Guatemala

● ● ● ● ● ● ●

Selecting this cozy courtyard hotel proved a lucky choice. With typical Latin American charm, after the second night, doting owners adopted me as family. They coordinate laundry service that uses real soap and refer me to a skillful tailor to sew zippers on the front pockets of my pants. This is to prevent vital documents from falling out, or being helped out.

While traveling internationally, if lost, documents like passport, vehicle import permit, tourist card, or driving license involve significant delays waiting for replacements. These flimsy papers must be guarded constantly and never entrusted to anyone. In developing countries, travelers without proper documents are subject to arrest or seizure of their vehicles or travel funds.

For security and the best exchange rate, I use credit cards to withdraw local currency from ATMs. Carrying too much cash at one time is risky, even my three-day-supply is well hidden from cops and robbers (they can often be one and the same). In case of banditos or pickpockets, my rear pocket contains a dummy wallet holding a few bucks and copies of my real documents. My zippered front pocket holds the treasure and to be safe, I touch it every other minute just to make sure.

But a secret pocket sewn inside the back of my pants just below the belt line hides my secret stash of emergency cash and two credit cards. This barely detectable cloth pouch will even remain unnoticed during pat-down searches. If I lose these credit cards, I could be broke within a day. Wire transfers are possible but a problem without proper credentials. Being without cash would mean living in the streets without food or shelter — the reason I brought two cards just in case one gets swallowed by the ATM or fails to work.

In the official wallet I also carry a recently expired credit card just for cops who want to shake me down and aren't satisfied with the dummy wallet. A good excuse why this won't work would be pointing to the date. The word is out, foreigners have credit cards, but hopefully the expired one would convince them I'm broke.

The first morning in Guatemala I awake to the sight of steep jungle mountains shrouded in swirling white clouds. Sharp rocky peaks poke through, glistening in the sun. I'm still gun-shy after the intensity of yesterday's downpour and decide to linger here for a while to gather information on local weather patterns. Normally rains don't begin until mid-afternoon, which allows a good six hours to ride after an early start. The trick is reaching the safety of a town with a decent hotel before the storm hits.

Throughout Latin America, road and driving conditions are seldom predictable. When asking for directions, it's more important to inquire about time frames than distances. If someone says, "it's 200 kilometers to the next town," that's meaningless as it could take anywhere from three to eight hours to arrive there. Locals know if there's a washed out bridge or a muddy road. When they say it's six hours to reach your destination, that's what matters.

Despite its run-down appearance, the little *pueblo* of Malacatang offers a distinctly hospitable atmosphere. Everywhere I walk, curious locals smile and are anxious to talk. A six-foot-three, 220-pound Viking sticks out among the sea of little brown townsfolk but they accept intruding foreigners.

An early morning stroll through the lively marketplace creates concern — hygiene is a new issue. Americans are accustomed to hospital cleanliness in the U.S., with food being stored chilled, if not frozen.

While squeezing through narrow crowded aisles of fly-infested fruit, vegetable, and meat stalls, the nose-burning stench of decay is overwhelming. No electricity and no ice. My stomach churns as I realize that this is where all the restaurants where I eat in buy their supplies.

On advice from locals, I plan a half-day ride to the mountain town of Panajachel on Lake Atitlán where vacationing locals spend weekends and foreigners enjoy the tranquil atmosphere enough to make it their homes. Two almost-overly-friendly *Guatemaltecos* invite me to spend the night in their village but as we take some photos together, one of them begins asking questions about my equipment. Since he's quickly writing down the information, including costs, red flags pop up in my head. Is he preparing a marketing plan? Traveling in poor countries carries a degree of risk but traveling alone creates a better target. With these new friends anything can happen. My logic says I could have the time of my life or end up in the boondocks looking down gun barrels while emptying my pockets. The infamous death squads from the recent civil war days are supposedly disbanded, but some of those characteristics are known to remain. With a polite smile, I take a pass.

NEW TERRITORY
Tuesday, October 16, 2001
Lake Panajachel, Guatemala
● ● ● ● ● ● ● ● ● ● ● ● ● ● ● ● ●

Two days lounging with the carefree hotel staff at Malacatang becomes comfortable. It'd be easy to stay longer but the lust to ride overcomes sentiment. So it's *"Adios amigos"* and I'm back in the saddle. While finishing my breakfast, a few *Guatemaltecos* offer descriptions of the road ahead to Lake Panajachel. They repeat, the mountains are *"muy frio, muy frio"* (very cold, very cold). I don't pay much attention to *muy frio* in the mild climate of the tropics. It usually means temperatures dropping to seventy-five degrees.

Beginning the steep ascent into the Central Highlands of Guatemala, it's soon apparent, *muy frio* has significant meaning. Temperatures plummet during the radical ascent and within thirty minutes I reach 8,000 feet and fifty degrees. An hour later, I pass two 10,000-foot summits. To a motorcyclist dressed only in a T-shirt and jacket, fast moving cold air can result in hypothermia. For high-altitude, low-temperature riding, I carry an electric vest and Jimmy has installed electrically heated handgrips to prevent frostbite on the upcoming 17,000-foot summits of the Bolivian Andes. Bitter cold weather can be dangerous because muscles cramp and become too stiff to move, reducing body control. Although I could get by with a sweatshirt and thermal rain suit, I decide to test my system's effectiveness now. Within minutes of connecting the vest, I flip the grip heater switch and almost immediately I'm breaking a sweat.

The steep winding road is lined with trudging Indians methodically traversing wooded hillsides. Dressed in traditional handwoven, bright-colored costumes decorated with ancient symbols, they stand out in stark contrast to vibrant green jungle. Men tending livestock and women carrying baskets balanced on their heads, followed by groups of scurrying children, pause and appear puzzled as I ride past. Their world ends at the edge of their village and they have no concept of where I fit into their reality.

The twisting asphalt road through the jungle is surprisingly well maintained and traffic is light. Buses and trucks outnumber cars and race each other with breathtaking driving techniques. Passenger buses barrel downhill, passing trucks on blind curves, while tilting into turns on two wheels. If someone had warned me about such madness, I would not have believed it.

To calm my pulse, I stop at a restaurant in a rustic mountain *pueblo* and break for lunch. The food is delicious: meat cooked in spicy sauces over piles of rice. Just down the street I find an Internet café and since there is no telling when I'll find another, I stop to upload journals and check for email. Often this takes several hours, as merely logging on with outdated computers is difficult in remote areas.

CNN's web site has been so jammed for the last ten days that I stop wasting time seeking news and weather reports. What more do I need to know? The terrorist situation is bad back home and it will likely rain later today. There are clips on Spanish TV about anthrax in the U.S. and dengue fever and malaria in Guatemala. That's enough information for now.

Just when thinking what a drag it would be if it rained, an icy monsoon doom, like a bucket of freezing water, smacks me square in the face. Luckily, I'm near a gas station overhang where I stop to don my insulated rain suit and am back on the road within minutes. No time to waste with a hundred miles left to ride and an hour of daylight remaining.

Although there's no traffic, the road surface is lined with potholes and the last hour of eerie darkness combined with wandering animals is nerve-racking. In Panajachel, after finding a good hotel with an armed security guard, I store my gear and hunker down for the night with a quart of chocolate milk for dinner. Tomorrow is reserved for making plans to enter El Salvador.

VISA HANG-UP
Thursday, October 18, 2001
Central Highlands, Guatemala
● ● ● ● ● ● ● ● ● ● ● ● ● ● ● ● ● ●

Over the last twenty-four hours I've been investigating a rumor that American citizens must now obtain a visa to enter El Salvador. A lengthy Internet search confirms that as of October 18, 2001, U.S. citizens must have a visa, meaning I've missed the window by one day. This now involves a trip to the El Salvadoran embassy in Guatemala City to apply in person. I consider the possibility of entering without a visa and bribing my way through. But if that fails it's a long ride back to Guatemala City, a miserably confusing maze of questionable safety. Still, I'm committed to include riding El Salvador even though a diversion through eastern Honduras is likely quicker. There are as many warnings regarding dangers of highway robbery in El Salvador as Colombia, but so far no tales of terror have materialized. Locals in Guatemala rant about bandits in nearby mountains and claim that police are involved. Everybody has a horror story to share. Maybe it's best to stay home and hide under the bed.

The lakeside *pueblo* of Panajachel turns out to be a colony of foreigners, mostly retirees from around the world. There are enough interesting people to meet with great stories about lives on other continents, but I did not ride this far to meet other foreigners. For a better opportunity to meet Guatemalans I prefer staying in remote villages under more primitive conditions. Wandering through crowded plazas, pungent markets, and lively *zócalos* (central plazas) and yakking with locals makes a traveler feel like part of the scene. Learning a new language while diving headlong into a different culture is the ultimate escape.

So far, eight hours a day of riding is sufficient. Even if trapped in pounding rain, as long as there's a warm, semi-safe place to rack out at night with a hot shower, I'm content. Each morning, I look forward to the standard procedure of buckling down my saddlebags and last glances at the map. It's similar to a pilot's preflight aircraft check; there's no margin for error. Minor slipups while jamming down the highway can cause major problems. If a frayed bungee cord pops off at high speed and gets caught in the wheel, it would instantly lock up. It's important to watch every move, forward, behind, and to the side. Once in the wind I exist on high alert, evolving into a state of hyperawareness. Trouble comes when least expected so I can't lower my guard — there's nobody around watching my back.

EL SALVADOR

CATCHING UP
Sunday, October 21, 2001
San Salvador, El Salvador
● ● ● ● ● ● ● ● ● ● ● ● ● ●

At sunrise, I roll out of Panajachel en route to the El Salvadoran Embassy in Guatemala City. The previous twenty-four hours I developed an increasing fever and headache. Feeling a mild temperature without stomach ailment, I assume it's related to altitude and will pass. It's important to score my visa and pass the border before dark for an early start to find a shortcut through a severely twisted mountain road. I have a map drawn on a paper bag by one of the old local Indians who assured me it's the shortest and quickest route out. He did stress it's bandit country and not to stop for any reason.

After farewells to a few students and merchants, I exited through the steel-gated hotel parking lot with the staff's friendly pats on the back wishing me *buen viaje* (good journey). As usual the only way to leave is to promise to return.

Incredible forested scenery unfolds as I wind back up through the steep rocky hillsides surrounding a crystal blue lake ringed by snoozing volcanoes and mountaintops hidden in the clouds. The old Indian warned that the road is rough and narrow — that was an understatement. Hairpin turns are so sharp and continuous it's impossible to shift out of second gear for almost seventy miles. The best thing about bandit country is that there's no traffic and I have the mountains to myself.

An hour into the ride, whatever sickness that has been lurking kicks in and soon I slump over my gas tank wrangling for balance. Although the mountains are chilly I get by in light gear while sweating profusely. It's better to stop and rest but I heed the Indian's warnings. In this isolated territory getting caught out alone is a bad idea.

Three hours later, once reaching the Pan American Highway south, the fever finally peaks and subsides. Still woozy, I decide to continue. The shortcut saved an hour in precious travel time and if I keep moving I'll arrive in Guatemala City ahead of schedule. Fortunately the highway leads directly to the side street where the El Salvadoran Embassy is located — phenomenal luck as it can be all-day misery getting lost in this confusing metropolis unmarked by road signs.

Unlike other Latin American offices so far, the El Salvadoran staff at the embassy are businesslike and suspicious. After I fill out a form and sign an oath to not engage in any political activity, the clerk says to come back the next afternoon and the visa will be ready. So much for border crossings today. There's also a long process at the frontier followed by an hour's ride to the first city, Santa Ana. After I punctuate my urgency with a five-dollar bill, the consular official grows suddenly sympathetic. An hour later I depart Guatemala City with a five-year visa in hand.

The fever returns, now with a gurgling stomach, but I'm going to give it a shot. Little could be worse than spending the night in the crime-ridden streets of Guatemala City. At the first fast food restaurant I stop for a quick meal to settle the growling, but I can't convince my stomach to eat. After a few Cokes, I sweat like an overworked mule and hit the road again.

The fever is growing so intense I teeter on delirium, doubling over barely able to hold my handlebars. It's foolish to be driving like this. Navigating through the suicidal madness of the Pan American Highway at rush hour on a scrawny little motorcycle dodging potholes and speeding buses requires more focus and concentration than I possess. I can only fixate on the road immediately ahead, hardly monitoring what's barreling in from the side. It's time to stop and find a hotel in a small funky border town instead of trying to cross. The first one on the right looks perfect.

After checking in, I stagger up the stairs, drop the last load of gear, and fall off the edge of the planet into a spiraling deep sleep. Minutes later, in the back of a dreamless slumber, there's a polite tapping on the door that I ignore until it turns into a persistent pounding. Finally clearing through the fog enough to open the door, I see the elderly maid and the front desk boy standing there with worried expressions and wringing their hands. They say I appeared ill and want to make sure everything is all right. I assure them I just need rest. They are not convinced and check again every hour until finally going home. Talk about being killed with kindness. This is typical of the people I've met so far, extraordinarily kind and considerate to strangers.

The lingering fever evolves into a cyclical pattern. It heats up; peaks; then I'll feel better and think the worst is over, only to have it hit harder in the next round with aching joints and muscles. Instead of waiting in bed until the fever breaks, I stumble down to load up my gear and take a shot for the border. Today, I am going to El Salvador.

It's a sparkling fresh morning on the Pan American Highway as I drift down through the sweet green mountains of Guatemala toward the border. Without a cloud in the sky, there's visibility for fifty miles into the golden plains and low rocky hills of El Salvador. Considering the tranquility of this environment and the gentleness of its citizens, it's difficult to imagine anyone raising a voice, let alone people butchering one another. Yet it's barely a decade since these countries struggled through bloody civil wars as surrogates in the Cold War. They slugged it out against tyrants and ideology they couldn't comprehend so the United States and the Soviet Union didn't have to. Was nuclear war averted by *campesinos* being slaughtered in this peaceful countryside?

Throughout Latin America, *campesinos* live in a world of their own. *Campesinos* are the hardworking people from *el campo*, the country. It's not a derogatory term; they refer to themselves as *campesinos* with dignity. Due to poor nutrition, they are generally small in stature, questionable in health, and mild in temperament, yet ferociously hearty in spirit. In their humble homes they are always willing to share a meal with a stranger in need.

If a traveler passes a remote *casita* with a *campesino* family of six and only food for five, they will insist there is a meal for seven. Their docile nature makes them prime targets for exploitation and abuse. A hard working farmer can earn five hundred dollars a year toiling on small plots of land useless to anyone else. Sadly, young *campesinos* are seldom properly educated by their governments and have little knowledge of the outside world. When conditions become so bad that their families starve, the most able-bodied from Mexico and Central America head north to *Los Estados Unidos* to pick fruit, mow lawns, and wash dishes, sending meager wages home to families in despair.

If they choose to remain on their tiny *rancheros* in their home countries, they are the first victims of civil wars. The young are recruited by leaders of radical leftist movements who promise hope and prosperity if they are willing to pick up a gun. Out of desperation, once meek *campesinos* become guerrillas brainwashed by Cuban-sponsored leaders into believing in their method of resolving issues. They have little choice; this is what happens when the world ignores the plight of the desperate. Sickening memories of television news stories involving civilian massacres and the rape of nuns jostle within my mind while I glide down into the flat lands of El Salvador.

There are no signs to indicate the frontier. The road merely ends abruptly in a solid mingling mass of jabbering humanity. I assumed I missed a turn. This appears to be the center of a marketplace, not a highway leading to an international border. Passage is clogged by hundreds of merchants with goods and trinkets spread out on blankets over the road, making it impossible to pass. I ask a policeman where the border is and he assures me this is it.

If empty of people, the road is wide enough to accommodate one bus or truck and one car coming from different directions at the same time. While weaving my way through a quarter mile of yapping vendors, I pass a dozen semitrucks and buses inching through. Some are crawling toward the border, others are creeping away from it; none are in the appropriate lane, and none of the scraggly street merchants are moving. Air horns blast as trucks back up with revving engines in nasty clouds of black soot, then move forward again to the same spot hoping to achieve something. The chattering crowds, busy bartering, ignore the threatening gestures as though the rolling monoliths don't exist. This must be a Guatemalan standoff.

With saddlebags strapped down, my bike is three and half feet wide, yet I somehow manage to weave and honk my way through the maze of babbling confusion to the first immigration outpost. There, I am greeted once again by a barrage of ranting money changers, slobbering beggars and gold-toothed hustlers. While I reach for my wallet with its vital documents, the pestering crowd falls silent as a hundred eyes focus upon it — they all want to see what's inside. Although I repeat, I'm not interested in their offers they follow in droves, hammering away at why it's essential to do business with them.

After I wait in line for a half hour in the sweltering heat, an overweight cigar-smoking immigration official in a uniform much too small for him claims that before he can stamp my passport, it's necessary to pay a five-dollar fee. No problem, just give me a receipt please. Sorry that is not possible, we are out of them and so says the next six officials. And everyone has a fee for something.

Bringing a vehicle across international lines is a complicated procedure throughout Latin America: buy a form at one window, then take it to another window and pay to have it stamped. Then pay fifteen dollars to have another thief hunt-and-peck type a special form on a fifty-year-old typewriter that must be signed by somebody else. This is the last straw. So far it's cost twenty-five bucks instead of the official one-dollar import fee.

I know the Fifteen Dollar guy is in a building off to the side cutting up his fee with a half dozen other officials in the main office, and I know they must have a fixed price for graft so at the end of the day they can keep track of who owes what. While getting more document stamps, I casually mention to a couple of other officials that somebody typing forms had just charged thirty bucks for that service. They appear startled and ask if I am sure it was not fifteen dollars. "No I'm positive it was thirty." They huddle with raised voices and angrily march off to deal with the dishonest typist.

This comedy of bureaucratic shakedowns consumes three hours. Meanwhile the unknown sickness returns while my stomach is dancing the Central American cha-cha. But even if able to get by the stench of the bathrooms they are too filthy to even wash in. Finally my last form is stamped, the wooden barrier arm is raised, and the race is on for the first gas station. South of Mexico, gas stations are no longer owned by the government, so here I see familiar signs, Shell, Texaco, and so forth. Most are new, with reasonably sanitary facilities, and fortunately I find one just before bursting.

It's a one-hour ride to Santa Ana, the first border town inside El Salvador. Upon arriving, I'm so desperate to lie down I accept the first safe hotel that appears. Courtyard hotels are the best because they lock down at night behind tall iron gates, which they refuse to open until daylight. The snotty desk clerk assures me this is a secure hotel, and advises not to go out after sundown. Once in the room, I notice that the door is solid steel with three half-inch-thick sliding dead bolts. Tonight I will sleep in a vault.

There are clean sheets, a color TV, and no hot water. I don't have enough cash to pay for the hotel but the receptionist said he could wait until I visited the ATM. Great, because I'm ready to drop. An hour later there's a pounding on the door — this time it is not friendly staff checking to see if I'm okay. It is the manager wanting his money — now. Time to turn plastic into paper.

I soon discover that most locals don't know what an ATM is because they have never used one, so I just ask where is a bank. After locating the closest one, I learn that there is no ATM and the tellers inside don't know where to find one. A man waiting in line says in broken English that he knows where there are several and will lead the way.

Off we ride, me following his racing battered mini-pickup for several miles of crooked turns and dirt alleys. I try to keep track of the return route because I forgot the name of my hotel. If I'm lost, how will I find my way back? We finally arrive at an upscale, glittering shopping mall surrounded by tall block walls flanked with a dozen armed guards sporting automatic weapons. Sour looking men lurk behind stacks of sandbags every hundred feet cradling machine guns, ready for action. It's a citadel of fast-food marts and designer stores protected by a small army. So far in Central America, security appears a major issue and boutiques selling expensive items have had at least one armed guard out front, but this is the heaviest yet.

Since El Salvador uses U.S. currency, the ATM spits out dollars. At least it won't be necessary to make mental conversions. Just as the sun disappears I make it back to the hotel, and in perfect sequence, steel doors slam shut along the narrow cobblestone street. Moments later, the entire city is closed and deserted, as though prepared for assault. Still feeling queasy, I ask the security guard where a pharmacy is and he says, "About three blocks away, but it would be better to wait until morning." Yet my fever is heating up again and I think maybe just by moving around I'll feel better and decide to walk. A few minutes later my senses go on alert, and I opt not to wait for a carload of shadowing thugs, a chance for a third pass, and stagger like a drunk back to the hotel as quickly as possible.

Without relief, the fever burns on, pinning me to the bed. My arms and legs refuse to obey commands and I ache too much to open my eyes. Boiling bowels demand sprints to the bathroom. Since I might need them later for malaria, I've avoided using antibiotics for fear of lowering my resistance. Trying to determine the cause of my illness I rule out bad food because it began with a headache — maybe it's dengue? I remember numerous posted dengue fever warnings and recall relentless mosquito attacks along the southern Mexican coast last week.

Looks like time for the big guns. After listening to Spanish TV reports on the anthrax scare in the U.S. and how victims were being treated with Ciprol, I recall packing some of that in my medical kit. I've already lost count of the Motrin and Imodium pills consumed in the last few days. The Ciprol instructions say to take two a day, so

I gulp those two immediately and it's off to sleep with three one-liter bottles of water next to the bed. Even after consuming those, I wake up thirsty.

But you never have to worry about oversleeping in Latin America. Every morning at daybreak you can rely upon early risers incessantly beeping their car horns, pounding nails, or yelling at volume ten. If it's not one of those, it's a strolling whistler practicing his skills because he likes the acoustics of echoing cement hallways and tile floors. If you want your eight hours, you have to be in zeeland using earplugs by nine-thirty.

This morning I require an hour to muster the energy to move and immediately smell the need for a long shower. Yogis teach that bathing is healthy because it alters the body's magnetic field, and that's why you feel better after a shower. Hopping around in ice-cold water with a fever, however, sounds like a bad idea and I seek other ways to demagnetize myself.

By noon I'm ready to eat and after finding the closest restaurant, I peek inside the kitchen first for a sanitation check. It appears safe enough so I order what's generally fast and easy on the stomach. Minutes later, holding down my *huevos fritos con frijoles* without incident, I'm ready to ride and head off for the capital city of San Salvador.

What should have been a smooth ride on a beautiful tree-lined highway entering the city turned into five miles of gridlock. At a police roadblock redirecting traffic over a long complicated alternate route, I meet a local biker who apparently knows a short cut and signals to follow. *Vámonos!* (Let's go!)

The first ten miles is like a crowded parking lot of pavement deteriorated enough to make me feel like I'm riding a two-wheeled jackhammer. After weaving to the front of the line, we turn off of the detour and abruptly the chaos evolves into paradise—a biker's dream of fresh laid asphalt. Recently painted white lines are barely dry and the perfectly banked curves seem engineered for racing. My new friend turns around smiling, shouts something in Spanish, and we're off into biker euphoria for the next thirty thrilling kilometers.

While leaning through the turns, I'm tempted to speed up to wear the sides of my tires but resist, recalling a pledge to slow down.

At last with only an hour of daylight left, I find the first cheap hotel, unpack my gear, and jump into the anticipated relief of a warm shower. As usual, the receptionist lied about having hot water but I'm too busy altering my magnetic field to worry about it. The headache and fever subside but with my stomach still rotating in different directions, I opt for skipping dinner and doze early.

San Salvador is a typical capital city, crowded and impersonal, a place to escape from as soon as possible. Other than the friendly local people, there's not much to explore. While in Guatemala I told another traveler that I was heading for San Salvador; his only reply was, "Why?" Looks like time to return to the countryside.

At 10:00 a.m. I am back on the road with the goal of reaching the Honduran border by 2:00 p.m. Since it's Sunday, traffic should be nonexistent. Like clockwork, I arrive at the frontier with only a few cows and donkeys ahead of me in line and no wait for immigration or customs. But an annoying civilian "helper" appears, insisting that he can guide me through the difficult temporary importation process. As firmly as possible, I tell him to go away as he reeks of alcohol and smells like he's been a month without bathing. He follows me anyway just to watch me flounder. Yet after several hours of bureaucratic mumbo jumbo exiting El Salvador, I am finally granted permission to leave.

By now it's 6:00 p.m., pitch black outside, and I have yet to begin the Honduran process across the river via a concrete bridge dividing the two countries. Both borders close at 7:00 p.m., and since I officially exited El Salvador, I wouldn't be allowed to return until morning. This means I've got sixty minutes left to clear Honduras or be trapped in no-man's-land between the two countries for the night.

The frontier is deserted because it's so late and everyone else has more sense than to attempt crossing for fear of getting stuck — so there's a shot. On the Honduran side, there's a gruff, uncooperative customs official who keeps checking his watch like if it wasn't for me, he could go home. I try a new tactic, explaining to him that I'm a travel writer working for a big time famous motorcycle magazine and would he be willing to pose for a picture to go on the cover that would be circulated throughout the world? (I was desperate.) "Why *señor*, it would be my pleasure." Immediately, he barks into his duct-taped walkie-talkie, issuing orders to all personnel to speed up my paperwork and not keep his important friend waiting. Twenty minutes later, I rode past dozens of stumbling, drunken truck drivers and passed the final military checkpoint, only to be instantly swallowed by the solid darkness of the Honduran countryside.

According to my guidebook, once in the open spaces outside of cities, there's no one else out this late except the *banditos*. There is no sign of life, nowhere to stop and an hour ride to the first hotel over a road lined with frame-busting chuckholes I can barely see. The only light is an occasional flash of a half-moon poking through the silky clouds above. It's a magnificent night to enjoy in other circumstances but I fear any humans out at this hour will be predators up to no good. Since departing California, this is my third taste of loneliness and first uneasy moments.

Recent rains have filled chuckholes with water, making them difficult to spot and their depth impossible to gauge. Most are a suspension-busting ten inches deep and if I'm unlucky enough to drop into one, they could cover the axles and snatch my front wheel. Complicating matters, my feeble headlight evaporates into stark, empty blackness, creating thirty feet of narrow visibility and only split seconds to evaluate potholes and maneuver around them. The intensity of the moment drains me of concentration. Just when I'm wondering how much more of this my nerves can stand, in the smudged mirrors I've been closely monitoring, I see headlights closing in from behind.

My imagination runs wild. This late, an approaching vehicle can only mean one thing, vultures out to run me off the road or spray me with bullets. There is no chance to outrun them. They know this road better. I must stand and fight.

In a near panic I slide to a stop, pull into a clearing aiming my lights directly into the approaching vehicle while noticing my kickstand sinking into mud, almost dumping the bike. I frantically pat the damp grass around me searching for rocks, a log, a tree branch, anything to attack with. I am a cornered animal with the instincts of my ancestors in control. With thundering heart and flared nostrils, I prepare for battle.

An eternity of seconds passes until I hear the sweet sound of high-pitched voices in rhythm as an old *campesino* with a swaying truckload of singing children putters by. He was probably wondering about the fiery-eyed *gringo* by the roadside.

HONDURAS

THE CENTER OF CENTRAL AMERICA
Monday, October 22, 2001
Jicaro Galan, Honduras
• • • • • • • • • • • • •

Since the next available hotel was another hour further, I settled for a decent but incredibly expensive hotel ninety kilometers inside the Honduran border. Given that the previous night's ride should have taken only one hour, but instead took three, there was no choice. I was mentally spent, physically exhausted and unable to ride another hundred feet.

After studying my map over breakfast, it's apparent that if I continue on the Pan American Highway south, the distance is so short I'll reach Nicaragua in three hours and not see much of Honduras. To make sure I don't miss anything, I opt for a 1,200-kilometer round-trip detour over the mountains and down to the Eastern Caribbean Coast. There's only one main road west to east across the country, so this will result in the boredom of backtracking later toward the main road to Nicaragua.

It's pointless checking weather reports anymore — it rains every afternoon. The only question is, how much? If it's a squall, I don't bother with a rain suit; a warm wind will soon dry my drenched clothing. Even with an early start today there won't be enough time to reach a coastal city by sundown, so I decide to overnight in San Pedro, about three hours shy of the Caribbean seaside town of La Ceiba. The countryside is sparse; patches of tropical foliage mix with barren hillsides but nothing as intense as southern Mexico or

Guatemala. For unknown reasons, people lack the friendliness of other Latin American countries. When I stop and ask directions, they either ignore me or walk away.

Compared to other countries so far, goods and services here are expensive and the only decent food available is in one of the greasy fast food outlets that line the roads of small *pueblos* along the way. My stomach is still in a questionable state so I continue to exist on eggs, roasted chicken, French fries, and Diet Coke.

Unfortunately, I've been spoiled by the fascinating culture and warmth of Mexico and Guatemala and thus expect the rest of Latin America to be similar. But the atmosphere is so uncomfortable here that if capable of retreat, I would do so today and head straight for Nicaragua. But I intend to give Honduras a chance, so it's off to climb the pine-forested mountain roads and back down to the sea. Reaching San Pedro, I find the only twenty-dollar-a-night hotels are on skid row, where it's likely my motorcycle will be an immediate target, whether I'm still on it or not. The next cheapest, in a decent area with security guards out front, is fifty bucks a night. These prices are budget busters when trying to live on the road for eight months.

THE CARIBBEAN
Tuesday, October 23, 2001
● ● ● ● ● ● ● ● ● ● ● ● ● ●

I finally reach the touristy seaside city of La Ceiba, check into a recommended hotel, and set out exploring the still-water shoreline along the Gulf of Honduras. The city appears to have recovered from the devastation of Hurricane Mitch a few years back but is still plagued with sleazy hustlers and toothless black hookers who scream at me as I ride by. At dinnertime, I locate a newly constructed restaurant along the tranquil bay just as the moon is rising on the horizon. A perfect place to enjoy a delicious fried seafood dinner while watching pelicans dine on fresh fish to the tune of hushing waves on the Caribbean Sea.

La Ceiba has a large expatriate community, consisting mostly of single males from Western nations, here to screw the run-down single moms who sell themselves on street corners and in grimy bars. Unless you're on a scuba diving package tour with one of the big hotels, there's not much else to do.

HEADING OUT
Wednesday, October 24, 2002
Santa Cruz, Honduras
● ● ● ● ● ● ● ● ● ● ● ●

After an early morning cold shower, I'm motivated by an increased longing for South America. La Ceiba is clearly a one-night town and I decide to depart as soon as possible to enter and exit Nicaragua by Sunday. There's a presidential election next weekend and if things don't turn out right, I could be delayed in a political situation. At least Nicaraguan officials realize politics and booze don't mix and prohibit the sale of alcoholic beverages for two days before and one day after an election.

I had wanted to overnight on the return through San Pedro but I have had such a smooth pace going, I continue toward the border. It's light traffic on a four-lane highway and I barely notice the last hour turn dark. After locating a roadside courtyard hotel-restaurant, I eat half of a dried up pizza, break out the maps, and prepare for one more evening in Honduras before crossing into Nicaragua. I will have only Friday and Saturday to see the country and commit myself to make up for it on the way home.

EXITING HONDURAS
Thursday, October 25, 2001
● ● ● ● ● ● ● ● ● ● ● ● ● ●

Bored with Honduras, I roll out of the hotel before dawn with the intent of skipping the last scheduled overnight and straight-shooting a few hundred extra miles to reach the interior of Nicaragua before dark. It's a twelve-hour ride, but worth it to avoid another night in Honduras.

The highway back to the coast is engulfed in a long cloud of black soot spewing out of trucks and buses converging from all directions. This continues until the last thirty miles through the mountains to the border of Nicaragua, when the scenery turns into rolling, emerald-green hills peppered with wandering livestock and broken-down *rancheros*. Border officials require six separate stamps for two dollars each on a form that costs five dollars, and that's just to exit Honduras. It's a relief to finally escape and the Nicaraguan side is hassle-free, with a total of seventeen dollars in import fees and immigration taxes to smiling officials. But bad weather intensifies as dark, threatening skies return, and again I set off into the pouring rain of an approaching nightfall. The first few miles are barely passable due to the deep, slick mud of new construction on the Pan American Highway, a gift from the Danish government. As I'm sliding out of control on the turns on a dual sport motorcycle, I wonder how a car without four-wheel drive would have been able to manage. Still, it feels good to enter Nicaragua.

NICARAGUA

NICAS
Friday, October 26, 2001
Managua, Nicaragua
● ● ● ● ● ● ● ● ● ● ● ●

In the relief of arrival, I spend my first night in Esteli, the closest border city with hotels and restaurants. There are no banks or ATMs and I have only twenty dollars in local currency to last until reaching Managua sometime tomorrow. Beat from the ride, I book a credit-card-friendly hotel that has the only vacancy in town. Other hotels are filled with international election monitors here to observe the voting on Sunday. Judging from the red banners hanging everywhere, this region is politically active on the far left. Daniel Ortega posters splash across buildings, wrap telephone poles, and even hang from power lines. This is Sandinista territory and, because of the Reagan administration's gift of sixty million bucks to their blood enemies the Contras, staunchly anti-American. What the heck, I'll go out to see the town anyway.

Turns out, the locals are amiable and anxious to talk. When I ask a question in broken Spanish, they take the time to try and figure out what I'm attempting to say. Thousands of miles from home speaking a strange language, it's heartwarming when people are kind to you. So far, I encounter zero animosity over politics, only curious people wanting to know what I'm doing.

When it's time to eat, *Nicas* understand how to feed a man. Typically, meals south of the U.S. are shy on protein, but not here. The best restaurant in town serves a pile of flavorful roasted chicken for four bucks; it's almost too much for one person.

Heading back to the hotel, I hear gunshots down a side street and catch muzzle flashes in the corner of my eye. As I parallel the action proceeding down the boulevard, I spot silhouettes on adjacent streets crouched behind cars. Intrigued with this pre-election campaigning, I consider stopping to observe, but pondering hot metal fragments piercing my flesh deters me. I retire to the relative safety of my hotel room to watch Spanish-language CNN covering other world crises.

In the morning, the lakeside capital city of Managua is easy enough to navigate; however, due to the radical extremes in wealth and poverty, for a change, I opt to stay in the better side of town. My first concern is motorcycle protection, and courtyard hotels with security gates are worth the few extra bucks. There's always a man with a shotgun ten feet away from my little 650 while I'm snoozing upstairs.

Everywhere, curious locals greet me with whistles and shouts to return and answer questions. It's a chance to hang out and experience city life while drinking beer on street corners. Workingmen want to know typical male stuff: How fast is my bike? What did it cost? How far I've traveled and, of course, about women.

So far, wherever I have traveled, it's funny to hear men speculate about reported dangers and where the most beautiful and wild women exist — it's always in the adjacent country. Although they've never been there, they've heard tales, which makes them authorities. Mexicans spin wide-eyed fables of promiscuous Guatemalan girls and their immediate availability. Hondurans described willing Nicaraguans and so forth. They all have reliable sources for their yarns of conquest but no direct experience. It's comical to watch the reaction when the subject of sex surfaces. Like teenage boys, grown men whistle like parrots and tap their elbows while punching the air upward with the other hand.

We have a good time, but their evenings begin after my bedtime, so it's off to zee-land for me by midnight. I prefer to be rolling at sunrise after a good night's sleep, beating the traffic out of town.

I've been stopped by crooked cops several times a day since El Salvador but so far managed to sidestep donating to the neighborhood police fund. These predators lurk at roadblocks, selecting traffic violators according to the make and model of vehicle, which affects the amount of fine to charge. The comment I overhear most is, "How crazy the *gringo* is to ride alone," but I explain that traveling solo is the best way to get to know the people of each country. This always prompts a smile.

Since learning long ago to never speak the language of the man holding a gun until certain of his intentions, I've kept greedy cops at bay. When signaled to stop, I immediately address them in the most rapid-fire, slurred English possible. When they claim I've broken their law, I offer only a puzzled smile, repeatedly inquiring where Kansas is on my tank map. They laugh, shaking their heads in friendly disappointment, concluding it's a waste of time, and wave me on.

Time passes quickly and I'm sad to think there's only one more night in Nicaragua before entering Costa Rica. Then in a few days onto to Panama for air transport to Bogotá. From all reports, the civil war situation in Colombia is touch and go. As always, I will reevaluate my plans at the last minute.

SAN JUAN DEL SUR
Saturday, October 27, 2001
San Juan del Sur, Nicaragua
● ● ● ● ● ● ● ● ● ● ● ● ● ● ● ● ●

The newly constructed Pan American Highway southbound through Nicaragua improves once past the mud at the border. This famous international roadway varies between two and four lanes and at times narrows briefly to rutted dirt and mud. Surrounding yellow-green agricultural fields shape the vista into scattered patchworks and wide-open countryside with rolling tree-topped hills forming the horizon. Perfect visibility and straight highways invite high-speed cruising but I stick to a meandering fifty-five. There are few vehicles to be concerned with, as Nicaragua is the second poorest country in the region and most people can't afford them. Half the population lives on a dollar a day, meaning many can't even buy a bus ticket, let alone their own car. Outside of the city, the only drivers are foreign businessmen, aid workers, and wealthy Nicaraguans driving Mercedes and expensive SUVs.

Tonight I visit the rustic seaside *pueblo* of San Juan del Sur near the Costa Rican border. I'm hoping for an early start in the morning and since Sunday crossings mean double customs fees, there shouldn't be any long lines. After unloading my gear at the first hotel, I head out to cruise the neighborhoods in search of a restaurant. If ordering meat waiters ask, "The dollar-fifty plate or two-dollar plate?" If requesting the latter, one should be ready to eat a rather tough yet substantial slab of stringy beef. Everything is cooked on open fires with fresh-baked, extra-thick corn tortillas, a meal in themselves.

As dusk settles in, I wander through the dusty *barrio* alleyways, talking to families indulging in the Nicaraguan national nightly pastime — hanging out on doorsteps and debating politics with neighbors over coffee after dinner. The main event for locals tonight is questioning the big crazy *gringo* who's riding a motorcycle to South America. By now I'm ready to print up question-and-answer sheets, but at least it's a good opportunity to practice Spanish.

But dialects and accents varied significantly from region to region within Mexico and only become more difficult to understand farther south. It requires patience to communicate but when everybody tries, we get by. While in Honduras, the accent was so heavy and people were so uncooperative, I might as well have been speaking Chinese.

Shortly before midnight I follow the sound of live, thumping Latin music down zigzagging stone corridors to an outdoor dance party. Booming tunes lure me closer, but since there are several fistfights in progress I instead opt for a peaceful stroll to the beach. Lightning flashes from a summer squall over the Pacific provides daylight glimpses of gently rocking fishing boats moored in a sleepy harbor. The glowing moon fades behind a veil of silvery-gray clouds in a passive gesture of surrender. Light mist turns to steady drizzle and knowing a fire hose blast is moments away, I cut the night short and head for a hotel.

My nine-dollar room is ten feet by eight with child-size bunk beds crammed beneath a six-foot ceiling. A communal bathroom and restaurant are down a rickety flight of stairs. Being well used to cold showers by now, I'm content as long as the sheets are clean. However, sinister looking bugs the size of my thumb climb the walls, providing something to twitch about while fading off to sleep.

COSTA RICA

COSTA RICA
Monday, October, 29, 2001
Santa Cruz, Costa Rica
● ● ● ● ● ● ● ● ● ● ● ● ●

San Juan del Sur is so peaceful and quiet, I long to stay. However, tantalizing South America shimmers within my grasp and there's no holding back. If I continue this pace, it's possible to reach Panama City in time to make final preparations for air-freighting to Colombia by Thursday — and maybe fly out over the weekend. The excitement of reaching the real jump-off point has me sleepless.

Weather is a consideration: it's best to reach Bogotá in early November after the seasonal mountain rains subside. I hope to spend a few weeks roaming Colombia before riding south to Ecuador. Air-freighting could take several days as it involves crating the motorcycle and substantial paperwork. There are differing reports on the customs procedure, ranging from lengthy delays to outright rejection. After contacting the Colombian Embassy in the U.S. they advised me to question their staff in Panama when arriving because they could better deal with such a peculiar request. A foreigner flying into Bogotá lugging a motorcycle is unusual. But to authorities everywhere, this entire journey is surprising.

Nicaraguan cops score points for creativity though. They managed to pull me over once more before exiting, this time for driving with a headlight on during the day. Two blue-shirted, weaponless policemen eye me carefully as though trying to determine the worth of their prize. One begins lecturing on how my headlight could blind an oncoming driver and cause an accident. I speak only English back, while they keep pointing somberly to my headlight and shake their heads. I innocently flip the key on and off to demonstrate how the lights come on when the ignition is turned on. As they persist, I keep smiling, repeating rapid-fire explanations in English until they laugh and wave me on.

It takes twenty bucks and waiting in eight different lines just to depart Nicaragua, but Costa Rica only required a twelve-dollar insurance card. Not only is the Costa Rican border crossing easy, it is completed in fifteen minutes without the help of any paid "helpers." So far none of the so-called threats about this adventure have materialized. This is encouraging — maybe Colombia won't be so bad after all.

Since events are going so smoothly, I opt to take the longer route west down the Nicoya Peninsula and then catch a ferry at Puntarenas and back to the mainland. My final night in Costa Rica will be in San Jose with a good Internet connection and a chance to dry out my sodden gear, damp from the steady afternoon rains that leave everything a little wetter each day.

It's a spirit-tickling ride through the jungle with the sun flashing through overhead tree branches like a flickering strobe. Towering tropical hardwoods and plush green jungle are held at bay by a narrow strip of asphalt that slices a clear path ahead. The air is heavy and sweet with the moist smell of blossoming orchids — yet this sugary scent also indicates impending rain. The normally brief afternoon squalls are growing more persistent, each lasting longer and dumping more water. Today looks like more rain suit weather.

The speed limit is sixty kilometers per hour (thirty-six mph) but when passing through small towns drops to thirty kilometers per hour (eighteen mph). Since traffic laws are seldom enforced, it's never certain what you can get away with. I usually just mimic other drivers, figuring if they can get away with something, so can I. Road rules are unimportant unless a lazy cop needs rent money.

Today, for the first time in dozens of police stops, it is justified. My speed was faster than eighteen in an area where a few shacks were set back off the roadway — the cop had me cold on radar. I opt to wait and see before making offers. Halfway through his spiel on driving safety, I say, "I don't speak any Spanish."

He knows this trick. In his notebook he writes down two numbers, ten and five. Pointing to the ten he says, "ticket," then pointing to the five says, "no ticket." This is a bargain, though I don't feel right about bribing a police officer. I offer him only a fake sincere look and begin reciting the Gettysburg Address as fast as possible, slurring the words just in case he knows a little English.

He returns a puzzled expression, and says he also can't understand a word. Encouraged, I babble faster, inventing lines that would have made Lincoln cringe. Exasperated, he smiles in meek surrender and grasps my hand repeating several times, *buen viaje*, then walks away shaking his head. Welcome to Costa Rica. I like the place already.

Having spent most of the twenty bucks I arrived with on gas, I now must hunt down an ATM for a local currency infusion. There are three downtown but because it's late Sunday, all are empty, and I'm broke and hungry.

My search for a late night, credit card-accepting restaurant leads to a nearly empty Chinese diner. As I'm the last customer of the evening, the family staff is already crowded around a corner table enthusiastically gorging on plates of chow mein while watching television — what else but Chinese kung fu movies dubbed in Spanish.

Yet industrious Chinese are never too busy to sell food and don't allow the enjoyment of their own meal to interfere with business. A wrinkled, hunched-back old woman scurries over to my table while chomping her noodles, then blabbers the menu in singsong Spanish. With my stomach growling, I ask what's the quickest food to prepare? Before answering she pauses for a belch that would make any high school football player proud. Longer than it was loud, it was still intense enough that I check for debris on the table. It's hard to not laugh out loud. Without skipping a beat she scrapes a remnant from between her teeth, then continues reciting the late night menu. I love this woman.

STORMING IN THE TROPICS
Monday, October 30, 2001
Puntarenas, Costa Rica
• • • • • • • • • • • • •

Since entering Costa Rica, the rain has intensified into a horrendous nonstop downpour, the likes of which I've never seen. No more thick drizzle or heavy squalls, but pounding, fire hose blasting, driving rain, lasting all last night and up through my delayed afternoon departure. I tried waiting it out, convinced the storm must eventually subside, but so far, it's only getting worse. Who would have guessed that clouds could hold so much water? It's bad enough getting caught in a downpour but beginning a day's ride suited up in rain gear and rolling off into a torrential assault is discouraging. I'd planned on taking the ferry back to the mainland and reaching the capital city of San Jose tonight. However, ten miles down the road in a relentless tropical storm, it's apparent this isn't going to happen.

When manufacturers call their rain suits waterproof, they lie. There is no rain suit made that repels water indefinitely. As any geologist will attest, water will ultimately have its way and travel where it wants. In this case, water wants to be inside my rain suit and make my situation miserable. Water has its way.

The initial phase begins with headwinds forcing chilling trickles around my rain suit collar and down my neck to the front of my chest, causing waves of muscle-tensing shivers. Next, persistent cross breezes push little streams around my wrists, past the cuffs and up my arms. Drop by drop water seeps through the plastic zippers and soon, splashing through deep puddles in the road fills my boots to the brim with chocolate colored muck.

Fortunately, this whole process requires a few hours, during which time I stay fairly comfortable. I started at three in the afternoon and it is now six in the evening and pitch black. I'm not only well soaked under the rain suit, but also visually impaired by darkness and freezing cold. Traffic is heavier than normal and the rain is only getting worse. The drenching is so strong that the only time it stops crashing straight down is when it blasts diagonally head-on. Combined with the wind, it feels like a crush of water pushing me backwards as though swimming upstream against a powerful current.

What little sunlight that existed earlier above the clouds has long since fled to the other side of the planet and it's a struggle to see anything ahead designating a lane. My face shield has a dark tint and droplets of rain diffuse the lights from oncoming traffic into streaking, blinding blurs. I strain to imagine where the actual road might be. My headlight reflects off puddles in the blackened roadway, providing somewhat of an idea where to point my front wheel. While traveling only thirty mph, I am riding totally out of control.

Speeding oncoming trucks and buses have little regard for motorcycles, refusing to dim their bright lights. As they approach out of blackness, their piercing beams create a shimmering reflection on my watery face shield, which turns into an opaque sheet of white. I am dead-ass blind and all over the road. To keep from driving off the highway, all that's possible is to aim for their lights and try to veer away at the last moment. When they pass, I'm back in rock solid darkness, disoriented and swerving over both lanes. In an attempt to restore my equilibrium, I flip open my face shield just as a fist of water slugs me in the face, leaving me gasping for air and unable to open my eyes.

Costa Ricans maintain their roads well and faithfully fill most potholes or I would have crashed hours ago. It's hard to tell which side is up, let alone what's in the road. The highway is good but the storm has ripped branches from trees and tossed them into my path as though intent on impeding my way. The only time I see one is when my front tire stumbles over it, as it takes a second or two for my brain to register what just transpired. All I need is to run over one with a three-inch diameter that will send me into a ditch somewhere with the dogs and donkeys.

Reaching San Jose tonight is impossible and the next closest city is Puntarenas. The last road sign indicated sixty miles, which at this speed means another two hours. I glance down at my gauges in a vain attempt to mark an odometer reading — all that's visible is a faint blur and sprays of water. It's one close call after another. Half the time I'm straddling the centerline fighting to control my balance and the other half skirting the edge of the pavement on what should be a shoulder. There's no place to pull over, no gas stations or restaurants, and the only lights are the dreaded approaching painful high beams that send me reeling into vertigo.

Life is a statistical risk and the odds of making it to safety tonight are heavily out of favor. Even the years of training, the research, and high tech equipment couldn't prepare me for this. All that's left is to play the cards viciously flung at me as a question echoes in the back of my mind: "Would I trade places with any other man on earth?" And the answer is still a resounding "No."

MICHELLE
Wednesday, October 31, 2001
En route to Panama from Quepos, Costa Rica
● ●

It stormed again all night, not letting up for a moment. Once squirming into a soggy rain suit this morning, I ride off to meet the fury of Mother Nature on the rampage. And again it's about being waterlogged.

I hope to travel far enough today to find better weather after I received a tip from a local about a shortcut to reconnect to the Pan American Highway farther south, avoiding San Jose. The only problem is thirty miles of dirt road is followed by thirty more of severely gouged-up pavement. Ahead lies a total of sixty miles of hard riding in a brutal tropical storm with the only certainty being this will test all my limits. Still, it should be better than a busy highway; at least there would be no traffic to crowd me off the road. According to CNN, this treacherous weather front is currently erasing towns off the map throughout Central America. (Later, I discovered it was the initial formation of Hurricane Michelle.)

Dirt road only means dirt when dry. When raining, it's mud road, but that's okay, I'm well equipped for this with a dual-sport motorcycle and I presume there will be few if any cars or commercial vehicles. Most of the road is slick mud or washboard gravel, and the frequent two-foot-deep flooded gullies require careful navigation. As I cross dozens of tiny bridges, I avoid staring down at the churning muddy rivers. Excessive rain has swollen watersheds far over their banks, stranding panicked cattle.

The single-lane rickety bridges are narrow, lack guardrails, and are made of scrap pieces of rusted steel with cross members separated by gaps of several inches. If I stop to examine the structural integrity of any bridge, I will surely lose my nerve and never attempt to cross. I can't think about it, I just ride on and hold my breath. Wet steel and rubber are tantamount to riding on ice and I certainly don't want to go over the side wearing all this gear.

It seems like every mile, landslides block the road with tumbling boulders while I skirt the opposite shoulders. Once-gentle roadside waterfalls spew with such force that they bore gaping holes in the roadway. I'm sprayed with muck and debris even while dodging the bulk of it on the far side of the road. The only other human in sight is an occasional farmer out trying to rescue a bawling stranded calf. Today it's only me against an escalating tropical storm, each of us with equal determination.

Internet weather reports indicate this is merely a preview of Bolivia next month where only five percent of the roads are paved. With the anticipated late rainy season at 15,000 feet in the Andes, most of South America won't just be wet, it will be freezing wet. Yet if I back off now, there's no point in attempting those mountains later; my spirit will be too weak. I must accept the obvious — that the majority of this ride will be in some kind of rain. My options are limited: adapt or go home.

PANAMA

GOT CASH?
Thursday, November 1, 2001
South into Panama
● ● ● ● ● ● ● ● ● ● ●

After ten hours of battling the elements, I finally reach the border, exit Costa Rica, and easily enter Panama. For the first time so far, my bags are inspected by a customs agent. On the back of my bike for extra storage space, I installed a rectangular aluminum toolbox, cable-locked down with two padlocks sealing the lid. Apparently, criminals smuggle money into Panama for purposes of laundering ill-gotten gain in one of the capital's many crooked banks established for this purpose. A million dollars in cash cleaned up, no questions asked, for a twenty-percent commission.

Once my passport is stamped, a narrow-eyed, customs official in a sweat-stained uniform stares longingly at my gleaming metal tool-box, envisioning treasure within. If there's cash inside, he'll demand his cut to allow safe passage. "*Señor*, how much money are you carrying in that box?"

"Sorry *amigo*, it's only electronic gear and medical supplies." He clearly doesn't want to believe this and the disappointment spreads across his face when I open the lid, confirming my claim. He drops his head, grimacing as though he was one number off on the lottery, and waves me on.

By now, it's too dark to ride farther, so I check into the first available hotel and take another cold shower. Because tomorrow I have a long ride into Panama City I bed down early, concerned about

71

needing two full workdays to make arrangements for air-freighting into Colombia. As it stands, I have only one day before the weekend and could get stuck waiting for government offices to open on Monday.

The Pan American Highway extends from Alaska to Chile, briefly interrupted just below the Panama Canal where the road temporarily ends in a two-hundred-mile-long swamp known as the Darien Gap. A few have hiked it and a Norwegian motorcyclist named Helge Pedersen once winched his way across it to prove a point. Either way, it could take weeks to cross and reach the Colombian border. I don't like the idea of not riding through it but there's no solid ground to ride on.

After the last month of pure Latin culture, Panama provides a sense of familiarity with its modern infrastructure, concrete roads and U.S. business franchises — combined with the tropical atmosphere it's almost like Florida. There's no hassle with mental calculations before spending money, as the U.S. dollar is the local currency. For the last three days the storm had not shown signs of relenting, until in one miraculous moment, stubborn overhead dark clouds begin to part, barely enough for the late afternoon sun to peek through — the first encouraging gesture in days. Crossing the bridge over the Panama Canal marks a major milestone. All that's left is to look forward to a new continent—South America, a distant dream about to become a reality, only with even stronger challenges ahead. CNN weather forecasts indicate it's also raining in Bogotá, only at 9,000 feet, and twenty degrees colder. They also report a lull in the Colombian conflict, likely a result of the upcoming annual Christmas truce. I can hardly wait and doze off, visualizing crossing the line into forbidden territory.

COLOMBIA

Saturday, November 3, 2001
Bogotá, Colombia

• • • • • • • • • •

In Panama City, Girag Airlines tells me over the phone there are flights daily during the week but if I am at their hanger ready for processing and crating by 2:00 that afternoon, we can fly out that night. This is a no-brainer, ship out now or delay until Monday and maybe catch a passenger flight on Tuesday. But this also requires a major hustle as my gear is still waterlogged and that means repacking everything wet. After remaining soggy in the tropics for weeks with no opportunity to dry out, I notice what appears to be lint covering my leather jacket, then realize it's actually a fuzzy fungus — my clothing is now alive!

Sliding into the Girag airfreight terminal after a banzai run across Panama City, I barely made it in time. To my surprise officials only ask for a copy of the motorcycle title and 250 dollars. "That's it?"

"*Si señor*, you may pick up your bike tomorrow in Colombia."

All that's left is a taxi ride to the main airport to catch an evening flight to Bogotá. Still, I'm suspicious because the process has gone too smoothly; Latin America doesn't operate like this. At the airport, the ticket agent says, "No seats available for three more days, except one in business class on the flight leaving in two hours." This is a gamble because confirmation that the bike arrived in Bogotá first is essential in case there's a problem, but that isn't going to happen. So much for the chance to watch ships pass through the Panama Canal;

I'll return next spring for that. In order to spend more time meandering through South America I've been in a hurry but soon I'll be able to slow down as planned.

Strolling through a glittering international airport after straddling a motorcycle through six developing countries in the last month, mostly in the rain, is a peculiar feeling. And I too must be a strange sight. Puddles of water gather where I sit as chunks of mud crumble off my boots. I left my saddlebags on my bike and the aluminum box with my irreplaceable gear is cable-locked on the back. My Sony digital camera, GPS, and word processor ride along as carry-on luggage packed in the tank bag slung over my shoulder.

During a turbulent takeoff, the storm continues to rage with lightning bolts streaking through the clouds. Hopefully, I have seen the last of Hurricane Michelle. But CNN satellite photos show the long arms of swirling storm clouds stretched all the way to the upper regions of South America, even though the eye is bearing down on Cuba. The forecast for Colombia is another week of intense rain.

Customs processing in Bogotá is a slam dunk; I'm neither searched nor questioned. Concerns regarding smuggling must only go the other way. The last snag is an immigration official who insists on knowing what hotel I will be staying at and isn't satisfied until I invent one.

This is my eagerly anticipated official embarkation point for the rest of the continent, yet my guts warn me the odds have just shifted. From the glaring lights of the arrival lounge, I am about to walk out into a crowd of barking cab drivers with no idea of where I should go or how to find a hotel. Accustomed to my own transportation and suddenly at the mercy of strangers, I'm a fish out of water and momentarily unsure how to proceed. I have serious doubts about the arrival of my bike, I don't know a soul, and it's midnight in a country with as many travel advisories as Afghanistan. Just down the road are all of the places I've planned to visit; some of them might be inhabited by people capable of making trouble for a wandering *gringo*, or they could greet me with open arms. This is why we call it adventure travel, right? For only the fourth time since California, I feel alone and empty. I stare enviously through giant glass windows separating arriving passengers from throngs of waiting loved ones eager to hug and head off to a cozy house with a home cooked meal. Still, I'm glad to finally be in Colombia.

They say we make our own luck; tonight there's no choice but to rely on fate as I climb into the first taxi in line outside the terminal. Glancing into his rearview mirror, the driver asks where I want to go; at first all I manage is a deep breath. Then, as I suddenly flash back to friends left behind, it's hard not to answer, "Home."

Instead I ask him to pick a cheap hotel near the airport, because I must return in the morning for my bike. He asks what I can spend. I tell him twenty bucks. No problem, we're off. The taxi ride from hell takes us on a half hour road race of daredevil stunt driving through the hand-laid brick boulevards of Bogotá. Finally we arrive at a ten-story, fancier-than-my-budget hotel and although I'm relieved the ride is over, I'm steaming mad. Cab drivers are known to steer tourists to businesses where they later pick up a commission. I suspect a hustle and start to berate him but he replies, *"No, no señor, es barato."* (No, no sir, it's cheap.)

I agree to check it out anyway. Sure enough, after a minute of haggling, we settle on thirty-two bucks a night in this mighty palace. This still exceeds my budget, but it's hard to turn down a bargain. Such luxury is a generous leap upward from the cement rooms of the last month. There's a piano player in the richly marbled lobby, massive brass and glass staircases, big soft leather couches, and elaborate chandeliers dangling from fifty-foot ceilings. Instead of having to lug my bags up five flights of cement stairs as usual, there are three elevators to choose from, and smartly dressed young men anxious to assist.

My oversize hotel room contains handmade, brightly polished wood furniture, a color TV, king-size bed, granite bathtub, and real paintings on the walls. The curtains open to fourteen-foot windows overlooking sparkling Bogotá. Yeah, I could get used to this.

Normally, my bedtime is accompanied by the search and destruction of insects before going to sleep, knowing I will be the main course later. Here, it's like a hospital ward without a trace of cobwebs.

Daybreak goes unnoticed in dead silence; no roosters crowing, no children screaming in the hallways, no pots and pans banging, and no cheap music blaring. This is South America — there have to be horns blasting somewhere below, but I can't hear them in this acoustically dead pocket of inner space.

For breakfast in the elegant dining hall, eggs Benedict is served with freshly baked pastry, sliced fruit and hot chocolate — all for four bucks. Five weeks of pounding out 5,000 miles on some of the harshest roads in the hemisphere merits a stay in one place to recuperate. Down ten pounds after my bout with dengue fever, it's time to gorge like a pig while allowing the time needed to dehydrate my gear. With temperatures outside in the drizzling rain hovering in the low fifties, there couldn't be a better place or reason to hole up for a while.

One day later, Girag officials call to politely announce that my bike is ready to be picked up as soon as customs clears the paperwork. In my Internet searches, I found varying accounts of bribes, delays, and outright entry denials when entering Latin American countries. So far, most of them turned out to be wrong. The *aduana* (customs) officials are especially helpful and stop their other work to help me fill out papers. Within an hour and a half, I am back on the road, this time 9,000 feet up in the mountains of a new continent.

Because of numerous daily assassinations carried out in Colombia on motorcycles by two-man hit teams wearing full-faced helmets to prevent identification, legislators have created special laws. When riding a motorcycle here, everyone must wear a bright orange vest with license plate numerals written in big fluorescent numbers on the back and front. If caught not wearing this vest, you'll be treated as a potential assassin. This is deadly serious in Colombia, with warnings of certain arrest if even attempting to ride back from the airport to the hotel without a vest. There's no place nearby to buy one, so using a sheet of white paper, I write my plate number with a black marker on it and tape it to my back, hoping this will suffice until I find a shop to have a proper vest made. It works; none of the lurking motorcycle cops on street corners looks twice.

I'M HERE
Sunday, November 4, 2001
Bogotá, Colombia
• • • • • • • • • • •

It's still cold and drizzly as I wander the spacious, tree-lined boulevards and relatively safe sections of north Bogotá, visiting museums
and quizzing people in sidewalk cafés about the security situation
and safety of overland travel. It's reported that an agreement has
been signed between FARC rebels (the major guerrilla group) and
the government to temporarily halt kidnapping for ransom, the
question being — will all the factions respect it? Most university students I spoke with commented that motorcyclists are not bothered
because they are considered too poor to waste their time with. This
is good news for a change. I'll settle for a decent chance of making
it across the country; luck will carry the rest of the day.

At the first break in the weather, I'll ride northwest to Medellín
for a test run to get the feel of the situation. If all is smooth, from
there, Cali is next for a short stay and then to the border of Ecuador.
There will be a lot of fate blowing in the breeze the next few days.

THE ODD COUPLE
Monday, November 5, 2001
Bogotá, Colombia
• • • • • • • • • • •

It's a toss-up which is a nicer city to visit: Bogotá, Colombia or
Guadalajara, Mexico. They both overwhelm visitors with elegant
old-world charm and amiable atmosphere. Wide, tree-canopied
avenues crisscross beneath modern skyscrapers in an architecturally
pleasing blend of the new Latin America and old Spanish plazas.

It's easy connecting with locals. I just wish I was more proficient in
Spanish, but most people speak some English and are anxious to communicate. The university students I meet at downtown restaurants

continually question me, and they provide valuable insight into the real situation here. Because of the recent terror attacks of 9/11, international politics are on everyone's mind, but such topics always lead to discussions regarding U.S. government foreign policy. While I want to quiz them on local issues, they have questions about my journey. There's friendly rivalry — I try to practice Spanish while they try to practice English; eventually we communicate.

Because of violent street crime, I stick to upper class areas of *el centro*, a relatively peaceful sector that proves to be ideal for R and R. Downtown traffic is too aggressive and I am still drying my riding clothes so a convenient twenty-minute taxi ride costing three bucks takes me where I need to go.

And for a city of such reputed violence, everyone is abnormally polite to each other on the streets. It's difficult to comprehend the history of bloody civil wars that have sporadically raged here for centuries. Conservative and liberal Colombians have politically polarized their society, expending enormous effort killing one another for reasons that seldom appear significant to outsiders.

Most street police are armed only with billy clubs, strange considering the violent robbery statistics. Downtown cops are mainly young men wearing fashionable, pea-green wool uniforms and they don't do much more than direct traffic or give directions.

At night, big-city streets throughout Latin America belong to two-legged predators and people adjust their lifestyle accordingly. Citizens fear them like vampires, rulers of the night that prey upon the innocent with impunity once the sun goes down. In every city so far, the locals warned me not to go out after dark, especially alone. Fear of this sort is alien to me and it takes a few close calls with street thugs to become a believer. At dusk, sidewalk shops and hotels lock down behind barricaded doorways as humans evaporate from sight.

Bogotá also has its share of other crooks. This afternoon I observe a couple of unusual pickpockets at work at a downtown flea market. It's a peculiar two-man team, with both sharp-eyed men dressed in suits and ties, well skilled in their trade and well into their seventies. Since there is no retirement plan for thieves, they'll likely keep stealing until they are too sloppy to continue or wind up in jail.

Yet this aging odd couple's pickpocket scam is amusing to watch. One spunky grandfather type does the bump and snatch, immediately handing his booty off to the other, who passes in the opposite direction in case the first man is caught. They later regroup in the park, methodically splitting the loot, and are soon off to find another mark.

In any high concentration of people there are always professional larcenists set up to steal from the unsuspecting. They are experts at watching for unwary travelers and their common mistakes: flashing wads of cash, wallets in the back pocket, cameras dangling or exposing expensive jewelry. Often, just not paying attention, with that common wondering look of a tourist, is enough. No one is immune. A backpacker is as likely to have his rucksack smoothly slashed open with valuables removed unnoticed, as a businessman is to be stealthily pickpocketed. Then there is the pretty girl offering candy or a soft drink spiked with tasteless knockout drops. You wake up with empty pockets while she and her boyfriend happily spend your traveling money.

Wherever you venture as a foreigner in a major city, you should assume a professional criminal is watching, studying, and reading your every action. When dedicated master crooks are at work, their moves are executed with scientific precision, and they're sophisticated enough to fool the most seasoned traveler. Sometimes when stopping to read the street, I note the purposeful and the wanderers — it's comical how easy it is to spot targets. We are busy looking at maps and bumping into things. Sometimes a simple lame facial expression gives us away. We all have bull's-eyes on our backs.

DETOUR AT GUNPOINT

"Courage is the art of being the only one who knows you're scared to death."
— *Harold Wilson*

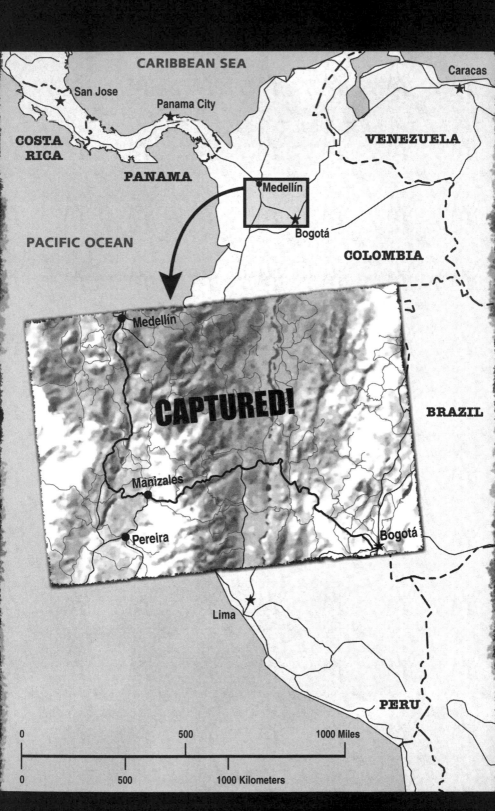

COLOMBIA

● ● ● ● ● ● ● ● ● ● ●

What was amazing this morning was how everything began so normally. Departing Bogotá was like riding out of any major Latin American metropolitan area. There were smooth intersecting multilane freeways, modern restaurants and toll plazas with armed guards crouched behind sandbag bunkers. Even though I have received assurances the road ahead is safe, I am still uneasy over the upcoming ride to Medellín. Under the friendly surface, Colombia is still locked in a culture of violence.

Once on the road, my anxiety lessens as I observe military convoys of dull green eight-wheeler trucks packed with grim-faced, machine gun bearing young soldiers dutifully eyeing traffic crisscrossing around them. This is a relief. I feel safe. Without the military presence, this would be almost like cruising California, only with jungle terrain and much steeper mountains in the distance.

Although it's only 200 miles to Medellín, because of the steep winding road, driving time is eight hours if you keep moving, which I intend to. Following the advice of the locals, I don't want to get caught out in the no-man's-land countryside after dark. It's been confirmed numerous times that a Christmas truce has been signed between the government and the dreaded FARC rebels, declaring a temporary end to hostilities. Authorities in Bogotá declared the road northwest to Medellín is now patrolled by the army. Although still apprehensive, I convince myself that the rumored threat, along with others so far, is overrated.

The highway south, leading to Ecuador via Cali, is my eventual route out of Colombia. But this is directly through territory ceded by the government to the rebels a few years ago in an effort to jump-start peace negotiations. The rebels' tactic of taking hostages for ransom has supposedly ended but I want to wait a few weeks and ride around the secure zones to build my confidence before attempting that route. I don't want to become part of a terrorist fund-raising drive, but I also don't know how valid the danger claim really is. After all, there have been warnings about every country since leaving California.

After four pleasant and uneventful hours into one of the most spectacular jungle rides yet, my self-confidence grows and I wonder "What's all the fuss about anyway?" Soon the curvy two-lane road narrows as long stretches of pavement disappear, and there are now fewer structures or signs of normal activity. After riding over several breathtaking 7,000- to 8,000-foot-high mountain passes, a few small broken-down one-room houses called *casitas* pop into view with enterprising locals selling fuel from fifty-gallon barrels.

Running dry isn't a worry because I topped off my six-gallon tank thirty miles outside of Bogotá, providing a comfortable 220-mile fuel range. Yet locals selling gas roadside indicates there are probably no stations ahead. This means there will be fewer people around, a concern that is soon verified by an empty, crumbling roadway. Suddenly I notice that there are no other vehicles traveling in either direction. The environment abruptly slips into the stillness of a graveyard. Before long, it's alarmingly obvious I am alone.

For the first time since leaving Bogotá, I sense that something is about to go wrong. With a fluttering stomach, I consider turning around in a frantic flight to the safety of a city. However, I keep going, slowing only to navigate the precipitous climbs and ever-sharper turns. The vibrant green jungle turns eerie while a lifeless landscape pumps shivers up my spine like a fluttering electrical current. Considering my background, I don't scare easily, but I am now in the grip of powerful, unmistakable fear. Death is in the air.

After clearing the last hairpin curve, I come upon a two-ton truck with a canvas-covered bed being waved on after apparently being stopped and searched by armed men in dark clothing. What happens next, on a warm, sunny afternoon, in the spooky silence of a towering encroaching jungle, will forever alter the course of my life. I am 5,000 miles from the safety of my home, on a desolate stretch of a Colombian roadway, two hours from the security of Medellín, when I'm stopped at the military-style roadblock by about thirty heavily armed young men.

They're clean-shaven, shorthaired, dressed in black sweatpants and black long-sleeved T-shirts with nylon ammunition vests. They bear AK-47 assault rifles. Several of the men step out from behind the truck, while others line the road in front and behind. They wave me over with their rifles in firing position, aimed directly at me.

This is my first encounter with rebel forces. I had imagined guerrillas would be attired in camouflaged uniforms with some type of military appearance. Still, I'm uncertain who they are. It's possible they're only bandits. My mind races to a pulsating red alert and for a moment, I consider making a run for it. The jungle on either side is an impenetrable wall of tangled green, shooting straight up the mountain on the right, and dropping off perilously on the left. There are only two choices, forward or backward on the road. I deliberate revving my motor and running on through until I notice the tall shiny antennas glinting in the air, connected to radios in hand. I assume they're talking to lookouts in both directions.

It's unlikely I can safely elude a barrage of machine gun fire from so many troops. Even if I do, more gunmen up the road are certain to have better luck. Before I can collect my thoughts, the men shout commands in an unfamiliar *campesino* slang that doesn't register in my mental dictionary of second semester college Mexican Spanish. Gesturing by jerking their guns to one side and ordering me off the bike, several of the men jam gun barrels in my ribs as I dismount. I scan the scene, trying to stay calm as the reality sinks in. A moment I had feared has arrived with no escape. Then it hits me — I may die here today.

As I step away from my bike, in a wild frenzy, several of the men rip the electronic equipment off the handlebars while others feverishly ransack the contents of my saddlebags, tossing clothing into the road. They are shouting, *"Ropa, ropa."* (Clothes, clothes.) I'm not sure what they want, and still don't know who they are. I hope maybe, because they are stuffing my clothes in a sack, I'm just being robbed. Then an older, light-skinned man in his mid-thirties, apparently the leader, yells, *"Vámonos!"* (Let's go!) Thinking he means for me to get on my bike and leave, I start to do so. This enrages him and it's back to the gun barrels in my ribs. What he means is, we are leaving together.

Other stern-faced men motion with their weapons for me to accompany them behind some dilapidated deserted shacks half buried in the jungle. My mind races for a way out — there is none. I have never felt heart-thundering, cotton-mouthed fear like this before. I now believe with absolute certainty that this is execution time. They want me behind those structures for fun and games before blowing my head off. Positive my life is about to end, I'm determined not to die alone in the jungle and never be found. My only option is to stonewall, and try to take it in the street where a bus had been stopped next to us. Let the terrified passengers be the witnesses to my murder. At least then my loved ones might hear what happened and get my body back. I intend to have a say in where I spend my final moments.

"No quiero ir!" (I don't want to go!) I respond, shaking my head while trying to conceal the fear in my quivering hands.

The men angrily shout back — *"Vamos!"* as the force of their rifle-jabbing increases.

"Yo no voy!" (I'm not going!), I yell. The situation is exploding out of control, with everyone shouting louder and louder in languages neither understands. Then the leader levels his machine gun at my face.

Convinced death is imminent and terrified to perish undiscovered, I provoke him to action, *"Chinga tu madre puto, hazlo aquí!"* (Fuck your mother, punk, do it here!) Gritting his teeth with a look of vicious determination he lowers his rifle and yanks a nine-millimeter pistol from a shoulder holster, chambers a round, and points it directly at my forehead from ten feet. *"Andele pues puto!"* (Get on with it, punk!), I yell. I clench my eyes and hear a deafening crack. For a few moments I am uncertain if I'm dead or alive. Nothing registers in my brain. My body freezes.

His bullet cleared my head intentionally. But as I open my eyes he takes careful aim at my upper arm. My brain re-engages. I realize they want me alive, and that I will be accompanying them, with or without a bullet in the arm. This is no bluff. I look over at the bus. Some of the people are crouching, some are crying, and some look away pretending not to see. I plead with my eyes — tell someone what you have seen here.

Several men flag the bus onward. And as it slowly chugs away in a cloud of black sooty smoke, I manage a stiff-legged walk toward the edge of the menacing jungle. There, a dozen more armed men wait with weapons pointed at me. Two other guerrillas are busy hiding my bike in the abandoned *casita* in an effort to conceal what has occurred. I become acutely aware — I'm about to fall into a nightmare from which I may never awake.

Once swallowed by the thick, gloomy countryside, the trail becomes a weather-eroded gully, steep and narrow, forming a deep V shape. It starts ten feet wide eight feet up at the top, and narrows to ten inches across at the bottom — just enough for a heel-to-toe step on the wet slippery red clay. Although this maneuver appears to be a well-coordinated ambush, there's no mistaking the excitement and shouts of bravado among the victorious marauders. We descend rapidly for fifteen minutes with twenty or thirty men strung out ahead and behind, trudging steadily downhill until they halt for a quick radio check. They converse in coded phrases but somehow I know the word was put out: the ultimate prize is in hand, an American has been captured.

I still don't know who these men are or why they have taken me prisoner. When they finish on the radio I ask, *"¿Quien son ustedes?"* (Who are you?)

The leader thrusts out his chest and responds, *"Eh Eleh Eneh!"*

I don't understand that this is the Spanish pronunciation of the abbreviation ELN at first, and give him a puzzled look.

Offended by my ignorance, he places his beard-stubbled face close to mine and screams through stinking, rotting teeth, *"Erjecito de Liberacion Nacional!"* (The National Liberation Army!) They are Fidel Castro's favorite Marxist thugs, who have financed a forty-year leftist rebellion against the Colombian government by kidnapping civilians for ransom and assassinating those who fail to support them. These rebels have a brutal track record of murdering civilians and holding and torturing hostages for years while ransom fees are negotiated with tormented families. Along with several other groups, including the right wing *Paramilitare*, they have recently made U.S. Secretary of State Colin Powell's list of most aggressive world terrorist organizations.

I dig deeply into my mind, searching for a way out, an escape plan, words of advice from my long-dead father — something in my martial arts background or years of meditation training. I come up empty, drawing one blank after another. Until now, I had always believed there was a solution to every problem if I searched hard enough. Today is different. The hostile expressions on the faces of these terrorists tell me they are anxious for me to try something stupid, for the honor of slaying a *gringo*, a Yankee *imperialista* — an enemy of the people. For the first time in my life, I feel I have no chance.

One final hope emerges — dangling from my neck is a phony plastic-coated press card made on a computer back home indicating I'm a correspondent for *Cycle World* magazine. This bogus ID had worked previously with bullying soldiers in Central America and saved me from having to pay bribes to officials. It's a long shot and I'm under no illusions; the challenge for now is to stay alive. I test the waters using my only proven strategy:

"Soy un escritor y he estado buscando para ustedes" (I am a writer and I have been looking for you), I lie. *"Quiero escribir en sus vidas."* (I want to write about your lives.)

I feel like an idiot, as they clearly don't buy it and chuckle back at me, *"Que bueno, nosotros tenemos mucho tiempo para usted, muchos años.*" (Good, we have much time for you, many years.) With that and a wave of machine guns I'm ordered back on the trail.

We are at 6,000 feet in the foothills of the Andes. The temperature is dropping faster than the sun while we scale hurriedly up and down the unforgiving, near vertical slopes of the sub-tropical wilderness. I'm exhausted after the first thirty minutes, with cramping leg muscles on fire, gasping for air trying to keep up with sturdy mountain *campesino* guerrillas half my age. There is no stopping to rest. They plainly fear military pursuit, which everyone else in Colombia knows will never be considered by the complacent government. At times I collapse and lie panting before being prodded back up by gun barrels.

They state several times that soon there will be a mule to ride, but so far nothing — only more relentless staggering into the far-off darkening clouds. I can hear the fading rumble of semitrucks backfiring down the steep grades of the roadway far below. And my pathetic hopes dissipate like the headlights in the distance, vaporizing one by one.

A few hours later, an early evening thundershower bursts down upon us as we reach a small hillside clearing and connect with another group of rebels. Apparently members of the same front, this new group is holding three Colombian hostages who have frightened and confused expressions on their faces. I don't trust them enough to talk much. They explain they had also been grabbed off a bus earlier today at the same blockade. I stick with my tale that I'm a journalist who came all this way looking for the ELN to write their story. They stare at me hoping for some good news. The only good news is that a dozen scrawny old mules are finally gathered for us to ride. We mount up, setting off under heavy guard, heading deeper into the damp chilly mountains that resemble an endless forbidding pathway into the dark purple sky.

The saddle on the mule is made of crude burlap and leather with aluminum stirrups designed for the smaller feet of mountain *campesinos*, not size thirteen steel-toed motorcycle boots. My legs swing wild while trying to stabilize by squeezing my knees together.

The trails are at such acute angles of incline and decline that it's hard to keep from sliding off. When descending, I hold onto the leather back strap and let my legs straighten out while leaning backward as far as possible. When ascending, I stretch all the way forward and hang onto the horn.

On such a steep grade, it isn't any easier for the mule to keep its footing. On one slippery, narrow uphill section of the trail we both lose our balance simultaneously. As I hold onto the saddle horn trying to stay upright, I pull the mule straight up and onto his back, nearly landing him on top of me. The sharp V-shape of the gully lodges the thrashing legs and rump of the mule directly overhead, keeping it from crushing me beneath. The impact renders me unconscious and I awake to the stench of mule dung and cursing rebels dragging me feet-first back up the trail. I throw up several times, then hustle forth again on foot, a rifle in my back. There is not a second to waste. I'm a prize possession. Americans make for the world's best bargaining chips or symbols for revenge and they want me well hidden.

Nearly ten hours after my capture, we finally stumble upon a deserted straw-roof shack adjoining a broken-down barn. We are handed a small plate of cold rice and a cup of *panela*, a sweet drink of brown sugar-water boiled from dehydrated blocks of cane juice. A few minutes later the rebel leader points his gun toward a rickety makeshift wooden ladder leading to a barn loft used for drying coffee beans. He orders us up. Rain has been continuously falling since late afternoon, leaving us soaking wet and, now that we've stopped marching, freezing cold. There is barely room to crawl around in the loft but I manage to strip off my wet clothes. In the cold mountain air my muscles instantly cramp and lock my entire naked body into a massive charley horse. Unable to sleep bent forward, I remain upright for the night. As I sit shivering in the cold, a rebel shouts up that the perimeter area is mined and if anyone tries to get down from the loft, they will be shot.

November 7, 2001
• • • • • • • • • • •

The sun rises to the tinny sound of cheap transistor radios blaring out the accordion tunes of Colombian folk songs, while young guerrillas tear down tents and meticulously clean their weapons. The camp has an air of smug victory. The enemy has been snared.

One of the older terrorists singles me out in the loft. *"El Comandante quiere hablar con usted."* (The commander wants to speak with you.) I have been summoned to interrogation. He marches me to a small tent with a solar-powered radio communications setup. Two thinly bearded white men in their late thirties with steely blue eyes order me to sit. The men, who remind me of actors from a sixties biker movie, bind my hands behind my back with nylon cord. I soon learn this is the *Comandante* and the *Mondo*, his assistant. Both are better equipped than the others, each wielding newer, stainless-steel versions of the AK-47 machine gun, with hand grenades clipped to their ammo vests.

The *Comandante* with the pockmarked face stares at me intently while setting his radio aside. *"¿Como se llama usted?"* (What is your name?) *"Me llamo Glen Heggstad y soy escritor y estoy buscando para ELN."* (My name is Glen Heggstad and I am a writer looking for the ELN.) I try to explain as sincerely as possible that I wish to interview the commander of the ELN and write his story. This buys only laughter and a shaking of their heads as though a child has been caught lying.

"¿Tiene una esposa?" (Do you have a wife?)

"No, yo no tengo una esposa." The probing continues. What is my job? How much money do I make? Do I have children? Do I have friends in Colombia? What am I doing here? I repeat claims that I've come here looking for them to write about their lives and that I have prostate cancer, which needs treatment.

Before leaving California, I had established a contingency plan with my trusted friend Joe Gallagher in case I encountered unfriendly forces of any kind. We concocted a story (with phony ID to back it up) that I was a writer and I'd come looking for them to write about their lives. This is somewhat correct, since I did hope the trip would give me an opportunity to write about the people of Latin America. But not exactly true either, since I had hoped to avoid violent terrorist rebels.

I would also claim that I had terminal prostate cancer that required special medicine to manage. Dead *gringos* have no value I figure, so if they believe I'm dying, maybe they'll decide I'm not worth their time. I keep insisting I need medication. They ask the name, so they can have it brought out from the city. I explain that it can only be bought in the U.S., but my supply is in the tail box on my bike back down on the highway. They have listened to unconvincing stories from captives for forty years and respond with broken-toothed, nice-try smirks.

The interrogation escalates beyond questions into accusations. Do I have a family? No. They claim to know about my family and my job. They declare that I am a rich American like all the rest and I will pay lots of money or die. I continue to insist I'm a journalist who came specifically to interview them. They only laugh. I tell them the world will be watching to see how they handle this. It's a long shot that isn't working but it's all I can think of at the moment.

One of the first things they asked for the previous evening was my social security number. I told them I forgot it but was unsure if it was listed in my passport, which they had seized earlier. Rebel groups have support from misinformed, idealistic university students who are Internet savvy, and I have dreadful visions of them running an online computer property profile to discover that I own land. According to their Marxist doctrine, landowners are oppressors of the people.

The Internet address for my web site is listed on my business card alongside information about my judo school. I've uploaded my daily journals every other day on average. By the time I reached Colombia the statistics page indicated almost 5,000 people per day logged on to read my diary. (The abrupt end to my postings was the initial indication for my team back home that something was wrong.) I have to assume the ELN's city-based political operatives would soon be evaluating my words. For now, the rebels in the mountains demand to know whom to contact in the U.S.

I am somewhat prepared for this scenario and give them a name and telephone number of my friend Joe in California. He knows the codes and signals to be used if disaster strikes and we're forced to negotiate with bandits, guerrillas, or crooked cops. If I ask for money, he is to say he has none. If I order him to sell my tractor, it means to come up with five grand. If my captors are unsatisfied, we are to heighten the intensity of our exchange with, "Well then, sell your mother's car," feigning arguments between us. If I mention the color red in the conversation, death is imminent. Don't pay anything. (There were no telephones in the mountains where I was being held and it's a good thing that we were never allowed to communicate. I later learned through the media that ransoms for Americans begin in the millions. We would have been laughed at for our antics.)

More questioning. Do I have a girlfriend?

"No."

They reply, "Every man has a girlfriend."

I need a story and explain that I had a girlfriend but she left me because prostate cancer had rendered me impotent. I keep insisting that I have no family. They ask dozens of times about children. It's better they believe there is no one close to me; I fear that they may mail body parts home in an effort to terrorize my daughter. Again I repeat the story about being a writer and ask if anyone had taken my laptop from the toolbox on my motorcycle. If so, would they give it back or provide something to write with? I have to hammer away with my only hope.

They grow annoyed by my answers and charge, "*Mentiroso.*" (Liar.) Next, the *Comandante*'s assistant delivers a swift boot from behind to the side of my head, causing an explosive ringing in my right ear. I don't want to take a beating on the ground and try to get up, which only provides a better target. Thus far I had complied with all their orders and had not given them any reason for abuse. From their political ranting it's apparent they consider me as an American, their enemy and responsible for their misery. They take great satisfaction in venting their rage, laughing while they kick and stomp my chest and back. They tire of it after a minute then drag me back to the loft, untie my hands, and order me to climb up.

A different group of teenage guerrillas is now in charge of guarding us. They don't seem as angry or aggressive as the others. While trying to scale the ladder I fall down and just sit there for a moment, asking for a chance to rest. Surprisingly, they offer water and help me back up into the loft while repeating, *"Tranquillo, tranquillo compañero."* (Relax, relax comrade.) Most of these mountain *campesino* kids turned rebels live so far away that they have never seen a city. A few have never touched asphalt. I'm certainly the first American any of them had ever encountered up close. They have no knowledge or understanding of the outside world, just the stark realization that the poor people of the mountains are starving. They have been told that it's the fault of the United States government. My presence represents everything they had been indoctrinated to despise.

They must be uncertain about my story. A few hours later after sitting in the loft nursing my lumps and bruises, the *Comandante* climbs up and hands me a small notebook of lined paper and a pen to write with, along with ELN literature to study. My spoken Spanish is poor; I'm able to read better than speak. I understand most of the propaganda from their newsletter called *"Venceremos"* and a biography of their founder, Manuel Perez. This information might come in handy later, verifying my story about coming to write about them. It's critical to be careful what I write. I must assume they will eventually translate my words to see what I have written. No one has yet indicated they can speak or understand English. They could be playing dumb.

Still, I need a secret diary, one that they can't access. I carefully tear out a dozen pages from the inside of the notebook to record separately what is actually transpiring. From now on there are two diaries — one out in the open, containing ridiculous entries describing how misunderstood the ELN is. The other, concealed in a plastic bag, stashed inside a sock with the end ripped off, worn high up on my leg as an inner pocket, contains the truth. In the event that I'm murdered and dumped in a ditch somewhere along a mountain trail, this will be a final accounting of my thoughts, something for my daughter to read one day if my body is ever found.

This afternoon when I need to defecate, a younger rebel hands me a stick to dig with and points toward the trail, motioning for me to head off alone. He didn't follow. This, I realize, is a means to gain privacy and an opportunity to fill my secret diary. Although they speak no English, if they find and translate it, I will surely be made to pay a horrible price.

By the end of the day, my clothes, soaked from last night's rain, are nearly dry. Maybe it won't be so cold tonight. I'm given another small cup of rice and again instructed to remain in the loft or be shot.

MIDNIGHT VISITOR
November 8, 2001
• • • • • • • • • • •

Standard-issue military equipment for the average, five-foot-five-inch-tall rebel is a one-size-fits-all black uniform, consisting of a long-sleeved cotton T-shirt, black sweatpants, knee-high black rubber boots, two spare banana shaped ammunition clips, a hand-sewn green Naugahyde backpack, black nylon utility vest, hammock, Mag flashlight, shoulder harnessed machete, a small Sony transistor radio, and an AK-47 machine gun. Every morning and every evening from seven to eight, the anti-American hour is broadcast throughout the mountains on an AM radio frequency. This is when the rebels stop what they are doing and tune their personal radios to listen while a Cuban commentator expounds a hateful diatribe about the terrible things America is doing to Colombia. He claims Yankee *imperialistas* are directly responsible for the misery of the Third World by supporting multinational corporations that exploit the poor. These are tense moments for me, as I am forced to sit in their circle and listen as vile accusations are spewed about my government. All the while, armed, angry men glare at me and debate amongst themselves the merits of making an example of this *gringo* — with a bullet.

Each platoon has its own political officer in charge of indoctrinating younger rebels on the ideals of Marxism. But these are teenagers who grew up in remote regions and know only the simple life of mere survival and nothing of politics. They sit listening obediently, yet appear bored, staring off into space or fiddling with their weapons, which they spend hours cleaning every day. It's apparent they understand little while being lectured about a man called Carlos Marxo. At heart, they are good *campesino* kids, born innocently into extreme poverty, caught up in a struggle of oppression and corruption.

This morning, after a small teacup of cold rice, several guerrillas approach one of the two other Colombian hostages who claimed to be a traveling shoe salesman. They grab and pull him to his feet while the rest watch me warily. He is told that he is being released because members of the ELN city faction have inspected his living conditions at his home and surmised that neither he nor his family have money to pay. I never trusted him anyway, suspecting he was a guerrilla plant trying to trick me. He had asked some of the same questions my interrogators had asked previously. I'm glad to see him go. Even if another hostage is not an actual member of the ELN, he could share information about me to gain favor with our captors. I trust no one.

Soon thereafter, the other prisoner and I are marched up a rocky trail by a new group of twenty guerrillas. We are ordered to haul our share of the heavy rice sacks over our shoulders into the jungle for an eight-hour trek to build a new camp. When we stop, they have a brief conference among themselves to decide where to set up for the night. Within minutes, the rebels use machetes they'd grown up wielding as farming tools to masterfully hack out a clearing on a tangled jungle ridge. Next they build elevated platforms out of bamboo lashed with reeds to tree limbs to sleep on. In the early evening, after the daily late afternoon thunderstorms end, the other hostage and I are left on our own to sleep under guard in the bug-infested mud. We are allowed to gather leaves to lie on but they afford no protection from the rain or waves of attack by numerous species of nocturnal insects.

This evening around midnight, I'm startled from a dreary semi-sleep by a thunderous pounding enveloping the surrounding terrain. The humus-covered jungle floor shakes as trembling bamboo stalks are bent over from an overpowering hurricane-force wind roaring down from above. An enormous booming mechanical beast lingers a hundred feet overhead like a winged monster about to strike. It's so alarmingly close we smell the foul exhaust fumes violating the sweet, pungent jungle air. We are caught within a tornado, with the bellowing bass of giant engines shaking our bones.

I know, as do the rebels, that this distinctive earsplitting throb is the sound of a military helicopter and notice two guerrillas slide over toward me on their stomachs, taking careful aim with rifles at my head. In the midst of this mysterious intrusion all seem puzzled by why it's happening; however there is no doubt who will be the first to die if this is a rescue attempt or attack.

Venturing into guerrilla territory by air is a rare occurrence. The Colombian army is acutely aware of the Chinese-made fifty-caliber machine guns set up around camp perimeters, well able to pepper them out of the sky if they fly too low. We also know that this chopper, inexplicably hovering above, has sophisticated electronics on board capable of reading our heat signatures. It also mounts weapons that can shred the surrounding trees into toothpicks and us into splattered hamburger in mere seconds.

The camp is now on full alert, while troops scramble on their knees and elbows, chambering weapons in ready positions. The rebels are a heartbeat from opening fire when suddenly, as mystifyingly as it appeared, the chopper slowly creeps away along the ridge top, fading to a grumbling murmur across the night sky. For the rest of the evening I try to calm myself and consider the irony — I could have died by hardware supplied by my government and bought with my tax dollars.

In the morning, *Mondo* Leo asks if I liked the feeling I got from the helicopter incursion the night before, as we were all equally terrified. I replied that I did not.

"It was a gift from your government to the Colombian government to kill *los pobredores*" (the poor people).

I said, "It was provided to the Colombian government to assist in the fight to curtail the cocaine flow that was poisoning our cities in America."

That's when the conversation turns argumentative. "Only *los ricos* (the rich people) in America use cocaine and they deserve to suffer as we suffer," he growls. I want to continue, but this is not a discussion, it's a lecture, and further disputing his views will likely result in another beating.

BLACK LACE UNDERWEAR
November 9, 2001
● ● ● ● ● ● ● ● ● ● ●

The last Colombian hostage, still dressed in loafers and a sport coat, was released this morning because his family evidently paid the standard fifteen-million peso ($7,500) ransom established for locals. We were forbidden to speak as he was being escorted out, but he handed me his toothbrush and toothpaste — a welcome gift. He bounded down the trail to freedom, happily relieved at his change of fortune. Now I have become the last prisoner, with little to do except ponder my fate in the hands of American-hating terrorists.

As I sit in the mud brushing off insects, one of the younger guerrillas asks if I wish to bathe. *¿Quiere bañar?*

Relieved by the gesture, I reply, *"Si, como no."* (Sure, why not.) He leads me down a muddy jungle path to a large creek that has been dammed with rocks and clay to form a shallow pool. There, a dozen other rebels are finishing bathing and getting dressed. Among them are two teenaged, machine-gun-wielding female rebels. They are clad in black brassieres and panties, drying their freshly hand-washed clothes in the afternoon sun on boulders along the water. Everyone bathes in their underwear, rinsing their soapy bodies with metal bowls of cold creek water and then changing into fresh clothes underneath towels. Amazed at the ritual, I try to humor myself. If I'm ever relating this story, who would believe I was being guarded by armed young women in black lace underwear?

No one provides me a towel so I strip naked, noticing while I struggle to maintain balance on sharp slippery rocks with bloody, aching feet, how they keep curiously glancing at the bruised and battered anatomy of a man a full foot taller than they. Annoyed, I stare back until they turn away embarrassed. While pouring icy mountain water over my goose-pimpled skin I shiver but it's pleasant relief from the burning welts left by insect bites.

One of the girls complains of a swollen bug bite on her breast and pops her bra off to show Leo, who administers some type of cream with his hand. Momentarily forgetting my situation, I also steal glances, and think, even facing death and danger, men will still sneak a peek. Later I ask Leo if she is his girlfriend, as I've noticed them sleeping together at night, yet never heard any sexual activity. "No," Leo tells me in Spanish. "Why, do you like her?" He rocks his hips forward and backward with his hands pulling toward him in simulated sexual intercourse, asking if I want her.

I shake my head.

"*¿Está bonita, no?*" (She is beautiful, no?) he asks, smiling. Then he says he can arrange sex with her if I want. Suspecting a trick, I tell him that I would very much like to have sex with her, but remind him that, because of prostate cancer, I am impotent. This is likely a test regarding my story of why I live alone and have no family.

INTERROGATION
November 10, 2001
• • • • • • • • • •

At sunrise, a garbled radio message crackles in over walkie-talkies and abruptly the lounging rebels are on their feet. *Vamos!* They are a totally mobile fighting force, always ready to move throughout the mountains on a moment's notice. The entire camp is broken down and packed up in less than a minute. We're off again for a long march back to the loft where I spent the first night.

When we arrive, I'm again taken before the *Comandante* who first questioned me. Same interrogation, same questions, same answers, and same boots. As a grand finale one of the rebels approaches with a wooden club but is stopped by the *Comandante* who steps in front of him, uttering something I could not understand. Uncertain if this is the "good guy, bad guy" routine, I am shaken and relieved it isn't going any further at the moment. There seems to be a lack of consensus on what to do and how to treat me. The older combatants are filled with hatred for Americans and would beat me to death if given their way. The younger teenagers like me and because the word is out I teach martial arts, they ask me to show them moves. Even Colombian mountain *campesinos* have heard of legendary hero super-fighters like Chuck Norris and continually ask if I know him.

The *Comandante* and his gang of older thugs don't approve of this friendliness but tolerate occasional moments. They eventually direct the youngsters to go about their various duties of maintaining the camp and standing guard at the perimeter. I return the cordiality as best as possible, hoping for information from them later about what's in store for me — maybe future assistance in an escape. The rebels are uneducated but well trained enough to quote the standard frustrating response to any question by a prisoner, "*¿Quien sabe?*" (Who knows?)

We march again for a few more hours to another confinement area where I am locked in an old abandoned wooden shed with nothing inside except a filthy cement floor surrounded by wasp hives and insect nests in the ceiling and walls. These are the most hideous bugs yet, and they proceed to devour me without delay. The heat is unbearable. Sealed inside the well-guarded perimeter and left to do battle with aggressive critters, I'm unable to brush them off fast enough before reinforcements join in.

Guards deny permission to relieve myself as before; instead, they hand me an empty jug and order me to remain inside. There's nothing to do but stand and wait. If I sit, the bugs attack twice as fast and it's a constant battle swatting them off. This deteriorating shack appears to have been vacant for years. I can peer out through gaping cracks in the wooden walls to watch mule teams hauling supplies being led by guerrillas down a trail at the end of the clearing. Most are loaded with elongated wooden crates, which likely contain weapons or ammunition. The rest appear to be smooth rice sacks or bags of canned goods.

At nightfall, I'm taken from the day cell and marched down the same trail that after a few hours leads to a larger rotting wooden house with an electrical tower behind it. Suspecting this may be some type of headquarters or rendezvous point, I try to remember as much detail as possible. There is fresh-turned earth and I imagine this is a site where they buried whatever was being hauled in by the mule teams.

Before observing too much, I'm again ordered inside before a new *Comandante* for more questioning. This time it's my turn for tricks so I prompt interest in my handheld GPS that they had seized from me earlier when taken prisoner. They had never seen one before and were curious. I give them a short explanation on how it displays an electronic map pinpointing the user's precise location on the planet and how it's utilized while traveling to keep track of positioning. They want to know more. I show them how to turn it on and the second the screen lights up, I hit the waypoints button and memorize the coordinates that blink on indicating our position. Later, during a private moment, I record this data in my own code so in the event of escape I might have a bargaining chip with the military. I can offer an exchange — information where a munitions dump exists for help retrieving my motorcycle.

The interrogation begins again; this time they demand an explanation as to why I have a credit card. They've heard only *los ricos* (the rich) are able to have credit cards, therefore I'm rich and an exploiter of the people. More questions about my family, my personal income, and the cost of everything from my motorcycle, camera, and watch, to the boots I'm wearing. I try to pick an amount they might accept as reasonable and tell them I earn 1,000 dollars a month. The *Comandante* knows this converts into two million Colombian pesos, which is a fortune to him, and after relating that to his troops they gawk at me like I'm Donald Trump. I try explaining how expensive it is to live in America compared to Colombia, but they've suckled on the Marxist doctrine so long they don't care and are angry that I should be so rich while they are so poor.

It's time for some fast talking. Knowing they also hate banks, I claim that my passport contains falsified information in order to obtain bogus credit cards to steal from banks. I hate banks too. I must cover myself in case they find out about my ranch. It's a simple explanation: I've stolen another man's identification and it's he who is on the passport, not me. I also must convince them I have no value to the U.S. government and if the American Embassy finds out about me they will arrest me and put me jail. I point to my tattoos explaining that the American authorities don't like men like me and would be happy if the rebels killed me.

Initially they seem to accept my explanations. However, after a conference amongst themselves, they change their minds and I wind up tied to a tree getting kicked until they tire and find something else to do. It's difficult to forget the hollow sound and feel of rubber boots thumping on my ribs as I try to keep my chin down, awkwardly curling up in a ball with my hands bound behind me attempting to protect my face. I think, though, that it could be worse. If they were bigger, like most Europeans, and had more weight behind them, they could do more damage. So far, they've not hurt me that bad; at least they've not broken bones. I interpret this as an indication they still want me fairly intact and optimistically assume it's so I will be able to march. If this is true, they want me to live for a while longer.

FALSE ALARM
November 11, 2001

Before dawn I am again awakened by the *Mondo*'s gruff voice and *vamos* command, but I am too stiff to move. A new recruit, a teenage mulatto boy standing behind him, looks at my face and winces. Moments later as I struggle to rise, he brings a cup of cold rice and freshly boiled *panela*. He is so new to the ELN they have yet to issue him a machine gun or uniform; he still wears the worn-out clothing of a local mountain *campesino*. He carries only an old broken .38-caliber revolver in his waistband that I doubt would even fire. Most rebels are recruited at an early age and fed stories that they are Robin Hood–type fighters, righting societal wrongs by robbing the rich, who are all exploiting the poor. In spite of the hostage taking and the murder of civilians who resist, they are naively convinced that the ELN only kills in self-defense. Although I have not been physically abused in front of the younger guerrillas, it is obvious that someone is beating the hell out of me. He is surprised when he sees how I'm being treated. I consider how to develop this to turn him at another time. I could use an ally.

My jaw aches too much from last night's beating to bite down or chew the rice they bring, so I merely pour a cup of hot sweet *panela* down my throat and wad up the rice to stuff in my pocket for later. I suspect there are more covert activities today because once again they order me back up the trail to be locked in the same shed full of bugs as yesterday and left to wait and sweat. I'm certain there's something happening that they don't want me to see back at the *ranchita*. This is a good sign because it means I may be freed someday and they don't want me to tell about whatever they are hiding. Nothing they say or do makes any sense. I constantly attempt to analyze each situation for some insight as to whether I will be shot or freed. Unless I escape, I'll likely be held for years.

I try to think positive and busy my mind with planning how to continue my ride to Tierra del Fuego if I'm ever liberated from these mountains. Surely I have seen the last of my equipment. And depending on what month or year I get released or escape, the seasonal weather patterns may have shifted. I may need to reverse the route and ride down the east coast of South America and return up the west. I must believe that it's possible to finish the ride if I can stay alive.

This afternoon, a fresh team of guerrillas who I've never seen before arrives and marches me back to the first night's camp. A new *Mondo*, a short, blond-haired, bushy-bearded white man of about thirty named Jimmy takes command. He informs me that we have a long, difficult trek ahead that will take several days. This is the first time anyone has been truthful with me about what's happening. Yet it's news I hoped wasn't true as my stamina is rapidly dwindling, intensified by the growing malnutrition. I explain to him that I'm not able to march that long. I'm too beat up and need to rest and gather my strength. He offers no reply as he walks away to organize his men and equipment. Anyway, I'm grateful for some straight information.

After Jimmy leaves to gather supplies, the camp takes on an uneasy feel and I can sense a few older guerrillas who had shown a blatant hatred for me earlier are plotting something. They keep looking over in my direction while speaking low enough for me not to hear. My guts shout to get ready. No one has kicked my ass in front of the younger rebels yet but I notice they have all been sent away. I'm thrashed so bad I can't imagine that they want to pound on me anymore if they want me to be able to march. I'm growing more and more frustrated at my predicament and inability to affect this situation. There's no choice but to submit for fear of being shot. As long as I'm alive, there is hope for escape or someday a release. It's necessary to focus on events moment-to moment until I can develop a plan.

The scheming rebels walk closer and surround me but I comply with their order to place my hands behind my back to be bound. I sense a new kind of hell awaits. They lead me off into the jungle at gunpoint while repeating, *"Tranquilo, tranquilo"* (Relax, relax). I feel if Jimmy were here to see whatever is about to happen he would put a stop to it and hope he returns in time. I attempt to bury my anxiety by calm, deep breathing, which is difficult to do as my mind swirls with ugly possibilities.

I have studied and trained hard in the martial arts for twenty-three years. I thought I was not afraid to die or I would not have undertaken the risk of this journey. Before leaving California, I considered potential disasters that could occur. During my studies, I often reflected on the famous sixteenth century Japanese swordsman Musashi's belief that once a man overcomes the fear of death he becomes invincible. Today I consider this philosophy once again, and suspect I'm about to be tested.

I'm no stranger to violence. In my youth I worked as a bodyguard and even rode with an outlaw motorcycle club. I've learned the consequences of danger from my share of street brawls, motorcycle wrecks, and a short stint in jail. I thought I had done it all and considered myself stable in the face of adversity when the adrenaline was pumping. Today, I'm starting from zero.

A dozen rebels march me outside the camp to where a fresh man-sized pit has been dug. They order me to stand at the edge with my back to them. I want to run but am too terrified to move. My rubbery legs won't respond. I hear the bolt of an AK-47 machine gun clacking back and releasing into position with a bullet silkily sliding into a well-oiled breach. I hold my breath for what seems like an hour but is more likely thirty seconds. Then a vulgar explosion socks my eardrums and sends me collapsing to my knees. I am stunned into oblivion, my senses smacked numb. I struggle to regain composure and what remains of my dignity. In my moment of truth, a chuckling band of terrorists is savoring this *Americano*'s humiliation.

A minute later, as I lie straining to collect my thoughts, these same men casually pull me to my feet as though nothing had happened and lead me back to camp for a feeding of cold rice and *panela*. It's as if this is all part of some terrorist right of passage — no harm intended. "*Vamos a comer*" (Let's go eat), they say while untying my hands. I wondered if Jimmy knew what they had just done.

Thus far, I have been fed only a small teacup of rice twice a day with several cups of *panela*, yet expended tremendous amounts of energy from the long hours of hiking up and down steep trails. Between the bloody blisters on my feet and lack of nutrition, I'm doubtful about moving on. There is no choice — we head off into the jungle once again at sunset, in a single-file line.

After a long, exhausting climb up to a knife-edged mountain summit, we pause for a brief radio check. The commanders keep careful track of me; they take no chances with the only American they have ever seen or captured. No one has yet answered any question I've asked and no one except Jimmy has volunteered any information. He now points across the valley below to a second mountaintop and says that is where we are headed. A *las casitas* (to the little houses) — a small strip of about twenty tiny, crudely constructed one-room wooden shacks.

Some appear to be lit. "*¿Hay electricidad?*" (Is there electricity?) I ask.

"*Si, hay electricidad y television.*"

"*¿Muy lejos?*" (Very far?) I ask, hoping he would deny the obvious.

"*Si, es muy lejos, son como veinte kilometers*" (Yes, it's very far, like twenty kilometers), he explains while waving his hand in an up and down motion. "*Mas arriba y mas abajo.*" (More higher and more lower.) Meaning more relentless, exhausting climbing up and down mountains in the numbing misery of captivity.

Still, my hopes are boosted over the thought of being near electricity again and perhaps a road to freedom. Yet opportunity for escape is doused by doubts of surviving a trek of this duration with my energy depleted and strength so rapidly diminishing. The guerrillas have been delivering this same treatment to others long before me and must be aware of the consequence of my weakening condition. I now realize this is their way of controlling me, to keep me disoriented while starving me to a point where I'm too weak to attempt escape, even if there's a chance.

JIMMY
November 12, 2001

• • • • • • • • • • •

We rise with the sun and as always, I'm wet and cold from the previous night's rain. It's another day of trekking up and down broken trails toward a muddy river far below. The nearly vertical descent requires tedious and careful sidestepping to avoid the disaster of sliding into a fall that would not end until hitting the rocks on the distant riverbank. My captors appear relaxed and confident. I can only focus on the risk.

Foot trails are the main transportation arteries for local mountain *campesinos* and are maintained by them using machetes to chop away the overgrowth of bamboo that sprouts along the way. Their cuts are made with downward angular slashes. This leaves inch-thick, knee-high, needle-sharp bamboo stalks lining the trail. If someone slides on the slick wet clay and falls, they could become impaled on one of them. Each step is taken with caution. A bad slip or stumble, at the very least, will result in a sprained ankle, at the worst, a bamboo spear through my back. In an effort to find my bearings, I try to keep track of the surrounding terrain but it requires such intense focus just to hike without injury that I seldom take my eyes off the trail directly ahead.

While walking along a ridge top, Jimmy calls a halt in the march when we come upon an empty cement slab on an overgrown clearing.

He develops a momentary faraway gaze then mutters something about blowing up a school here a few years before. I ask him why the ELN would commit such an atrocity and he replies, *"Un accidente."* He then explains that while he and his best friend were securing a load of dynamite, it was inadvertently detonated, leveling the government-built schoolhouse and blowing his partner to pieces. The ELN claims to be religion-free atheists, yet they're also reared with deep Catholic beliefs. I watch Jimmy make the sign of the cross before turning misty eyed with a comment about his *mejor amigo* (best friend). Relating this to a what-if-it-were-me situation with my best friend back home, I share his grief as we sit resting in the warm noontime sun.

Later, my feet have swollen tight inside my soggy boots and ache so fiercely I think it impossible to continue. I remove them to discover bloody socks with two clumps of raw meat inside resembling feet. The stench of rotting blood and fungus growing in damp leather turns my head and I wince at the piercing odor. This deep in the jungle, infection becomes a new concern and I consider what will happen if I can no longer walk. It's doubtful the ELN leave prisoners behind alive.

Jimmy notices this situation just as we encounter a young

campesino boy riding a mule along the trail. After a brief conversation, he orders him to surrender his mount. Without hesitation the teenager complies and continues on foot, apparently not angered by this demand. Jimmy then offers me the mule to ride, assuring it would be eventually returned to the owner.

So far, it appears the young people of the mountains look up to the guerrillas while the older generation plainly disapproves of them. This is obvious when we pass through rows of shacks scattered along mountain ridge tops. Older *campesinos*, in a distinctive gesture of resentment, turn their backs and refuse to acknowledge any greetings from the rebels. The guerrillas explain that they obtain supplies from the inhabitants of the mountains with or without cooperation and feel justified in doing so because they're fighting on their behalf. Stated differently, they rob innocent people, even their own. Anyway, we turn the mule loose an hour later to wander home because the trail has become too narrow for an animal to pass.

Even the guerrillas are tired today and we stop to overnight early at the bottom of a spectacular granite boulder-filled river gorge. This location is unusual because the rebels generally prefer mountaintops for security and radio communications. Jimmy produces a fishing line and hook claiming there will be plenty of fish tonight for all of us. He looks at me when he says this, so I assume I'm included. This leaves my mouth watering in anticipation for hours at the prospect of actual food after a week of little cups of rice. Unfortunately, we discover over the next several hours, there are no fish to be caught. This is bitterly attributed to the U.S.-supplied herbicides leeching into creeks and rivers after careless overspray on legitimate crops as well as the coca plants during government antidrug efforts.

The fast-moving river is fifty yards across; however, I'm allowed to bathe in a shallow section near a bank of sand and I ponder an escape by diving underwater and making a run for it swimming downstream. The powerful current is swift and not only are there dangerous rapids close by, but guards stand ready with guns always pointed at me. I have to assume that each opportunity for escape is my last and wonder if I will regret years later not taking the chance while it was here. Every day I grow weaker and soon I'll lack the endurance to hike back to safety even if I know what direction to head. For now, I must bide my time.

They have me turned around so bad from crossing numerous rugged mountains and doubling back that I'm worried even if I do manage an escape, where would I go? The jungle is too dense with tangled vegetation and undergrowth to consider passing through on foot. I would have to stay on an established trail, hoping it led back down to the highway. What if I manage to slip away and flee for miles in the wrong direction or run into one of the many other guerrilla patrols? I would need assistance from locals to get past the enemy but I wouldn't know which *campesinos* are supporters of the ELN or who to trust. This is what I think about every night.

The rebels never keep fires burning after sundown and seldom use flashlights for fear of being spotted by enemies. When darkness falls, everyone goes to sleep except for those on guard duty. Jimmy has shown a willingness to talk; we stay awake tonight speaking for long hours as two men should speak, almost without reservation or fear of reprisal. I ask him about his life and he says he has been with the ELN for ten of his twenty-eight years and knows no other way anymore. He claims, if he has to, he will die fighting the corrupt government in Bogotá which is responsible for the suffering and exploitation of *los pobredores* (the poor) of Colombia. The other enemy, whom the guerrillas loathe and fear more, is the right-wing Auto Defense Forces, a.k.a. *Paramilitare.* This is another army of thugs hired by wealthy landowners and cocaine warlords to protect their operations and attack rebel groups whom the government no longer has the will to resist. Although they have been declared to be a terrorist organization by the U.S. State Department, it is widely known they receive a wink and a nod from the Colombian army because they both battle a common enemy. The *Paramilitare* is blamed for most massacres carried out against the *campesinos* for cooperating with insurgents, but the *campesinos* are also murdered by rebels for failing to aid them. They are caught in the middle, damned if they do and damned if they don't.

When I raise the subject of narco-trafficking, Jimmy vehemently insists that the ELN neither uses nor traffics in cocaine but he thinks the FARC (Armed Revolutionary Forces of Colombia), another much larger rival guerrilla army, might do so. I ask if they are friendly with the FARC and he claims they all get along fine. I also want to know what would happen if we encountered a FARC patrol sometime, as their territories were bound to overlap. Would there be a confrontation? He says the procedure is for both sides to simultaneously lay down their weapons as a gesture of non-hostility. But I'm not so sure and wouldn't want to be there if it happened. He has also boasted to me that the ELN is the major dominant fighting rebel force in Colombia but the FARC is well known to be four times the size of the ELN.

I inquire if there are limits as to whom the ELN takes as hostages and he states anyone over eighteen, male or female, with no upper age restriction if an elderly person has money. Are the women ever raped or abused? He assures me that, to his knowledge, this had never happened. He also reaffirms the party line in true-believer fashion, while staring at my lumped up body, that the ELN only kills in self-defense and does not torture its prisoners.

Thus far, Jimmy has not participated in any of my mistreatment and has been kind to me while attempting to make the best of a bad situation. When the guerrillas had split open a few cans of sardines earlier, as usual there was none to share with me. In an unusual gesture of benevolence, he offered me his portion, a tasty six-inch-long chunk, and went without himself.

He has seen a city only once in his life and has many questions about America and if our government is really so evil. He's been indoctrinated with Cuban propaganda that the island is a worker's paradise, a utopian Marxist society with no corruption or poverty. After explaining to him that I had visited Cuba several times and found the people to be extremely poor and struggling to exist in an authoritarian police state, he does not seem surprised. I share my belief that governments throughout the world lie and none could be fully trusted. He agrees, adding that he feels all men are brothers, even *gringos*.

It's evident by his nodding head that this is not the first time he's heard or discussed this. Jimmy is an idealistic, brave young man willing to fight and to die for what is right for Colombia, yet experiences the frustration of knowing he has not been told the whole truth. I don't go as far as accusing the ELN of exploiting the *campesinos* as much as the government does, but I'm sure he has his suspicions. I ask if he knows what his commanders are going to do with me and he says that he does not. "*¿Tal vez me matan?*" (Maybe they will kill me?) I ask point-blank.

He looks away saying only, "*¿Quien sabe?*" (Who knows?)

Jimmy has been taught that there are guerrilla movements in the U.S. fighting the government and wants to know if I belong to one of them. I inform him, in the past we have had incidents where small groups bombed banks and blew up federal buildings but for the most part we settle our differences at the ballot box. He asks if our elections are fair, and I reflect back on the Bush/Gore showdown of 2000, replying that it is impossible to be totally fair when there is so much power at stake. Then he wants to know how many men I have killed. "I have been in fistfights over foolish things, Jimmy, but never have I killed." I am afraid to ask him the same question.

We talk about his family and he speaks sadly of his wife and two sons, ages eight and ten, who live with his parents in a remote one-room mountain *casita* a month's hike from here. He joined the rebel movement ten years ago because there was no more food and no chance to survive any other way. The ELN supplies his family with enough rice to keep from starving. It's too emotionally painful for him to communicate, so he has not spoken to them for five years. The guerrillas are always on the move from camp to camp. They have no home to return to; in a way they are also prisoners in the mountains.

I want to talk about my life too, but must be careful to stick to my story of having no friends or family and resist the urge to speak of my daughter. I want to describe the hell my loved ones are going through at this moment, unsure if I am dead or alive, but I know it won't change anything. Jimmy must follow orders, whatever they are.

The guerrillas have nylon hammocks to sleep in, with tarps that fold overhead (utilizing the same cords they use for tying me up) to form a shelter against the nightly storms. Terrorists don't provide a hostage kit for their captives. There are no goodies like tents and sleeping bags. Unless holed-up and resting on the concrete floor of an old deserted *casita*, I am left to lie in the mud on a piece of plastic, while being gnawed by insects until dawn. When I attempt sleep at night, I pull an extra set of boxer shorts over my neck and stretch the sleeves of my cotton shirt down over my hands for protection and attempt to doze off before the munching begins. Always when awakening, it's the same — ants in my nose and ears, with God knows what crawling around on my body inside my clothes. I've never seen so many insects before; my skin has turned into a solid itching purple welt from all the stings and bites. I have almost given up swatting and brushing them away, picking off only the most painful.

Tonight, Jimmy offers me his hammock, which I gratefully accept, while he in turn lies on my piece of plastic and endures the intense rain unprotected. It's as though he is an idealistic comrade and does not like these circumstances either. Yet I must remember, he knows escape is in my thoughts. Jimmy is a trusted officer who has earned his way through the ranks of a vicious terrorist organization to command position. I must assume he will not hesitate to shoot me if I flee. Our talk is still guarded on my part. We carry on until midnight and for the first time since being taken prisoner I spiral off into deep slumber without worrying about being executed in the morning.

MARCOS
November 13, 2001
● ● ● ● ● ● ● ● ● ●

Directly after my morning cup of rice, Jimmy announces he is turning back and I'm to be handed over to another ELN group across the river. As he stammers out a goodbye with clumsy apologies on the tragedies of war, I believe he is genuinely sorry for what has happened here. He also says the new *Mondo*, Marcos, is a good friend of his and that he will put in a word for me. He momentarily appears to want to shake hands with the Latin embrace reserved for *amigos*, but after glancing across the river at the other men curiously watching, changes his mind. He doesn't want to appear too friendly with the enemy *gringo*.

There is a five-by-five-foot, flat metal-framed cart hanging off a steel cable that stretches across the river gorge between car-size boulders on either side. I'm first to glide across with rusty pulleys squeaking overhead. The guerrillas push hard enough to roll the cart out to the middle, leaving me dangling thirty feet above the water. I pull myself hand over hand the rest of the way by a rope draped below the steel cable toward Marcos and his fresh troops. The pattern grows clearer. I'm a hot potato being handed off to a different group every few days, each time a few of the last troops rotate in with the new. Often, men reappear from the first days of captivity. I can't understand how they are able to catch up with us in such short periods of time. Jimmy comes across next, carrying a canvas property bag containing my camera, GPS, wallet, and my precious passport. The bag follows wherever they take me. I've noticed when other hostages have been freed they were given their personal effects back as though a goodwill gesture. Since they hand my property over to each new platoon that takes control of me, there is a possibility of being released someday and my possessions returned.

Jimmy and the new *Mondo* greet each other as long-lost friends and chat enthusiastically for a few minutes while watching me. Marcos, with his thick drooping mustache, reminds me of Juan Valdez in the coffee advertisements. He betrays no emotion when looking my way. Hopefully Jimmy will honor his promise about putting in a good word but nothing is for certain. He nods farewell once again and rolls back across the river. The new *Mondo* turns, pointing to the rocky trail disappearing almost straight up through the jungle, and orders *Vamos!*

A ROUGH TIME
November 14, 2001
● ● ● ● ● ● ● ● ● ●

The first overnight with my new captors is without conversation, just a cup of cold rice and hot *pancla*. We are back on the trail at first light after again waking up soaked. No one has yet spoken to me besides basic commands; I have not engaged them either. They laugh and joke amongst themselves more than any other rebels so far and I'm waiting to see how they will treat me. I damned sure don't want to be questioned again and piss them off with wrong answers. Even if Jimmy passed along a good word to his friends, it means little — the last guys who thumped me were also his friends.

After a few hours march, we pause while Marcos retrieves a hidden stash of buried dynamite and blasting caps from a jungle cache. He is cursing and yelling, *puta* this and *puta* that because animals had chewed the plastic covering off his explosives and fuses, rendering them useless. These men are my enemies and I enjoy their misfortune but conceal my amusement.

Later we stop at a small overgrown deserted *ranchita* while Marcos climbs a tangerine tree gone wild and tosses fruit to his troops. He looks at me, sitting alone, says something about the *gringo* which makes everyone laugh and then rolls a tangerine toward me. I'm not sure if there's a trick involved and don't move until he asks, "*¿No quiere?*" (You don't want?)

I nod, *Sí, quiero* and reach for the fruit, which after more than a week of only two tiny cups of rice a day, is like a feast. I'm hoping this is a sign of good things to come, like real food.

The trail eventually widens into a washed-out dirt road bearing recent tire tracks. My spirits soar with thoughts of escape, a bolt for freedom on a road that must eventually lead to the main highway. However, after a time we stop at a cement-block shed with a rusty roof where the guerrillas are served Colombian soft drinks supplied by friendly *campesinos*. I try to memorize the terrain and road position for future reference but know that within hours, they will again work to disorient me.

There's an old battered blue pickup truck pulling up letting off passengers and I think, "If I could only escape long enough to get to the truck, I could commandeer it and flee to the highway." I'm confident about taking a gun away from one of them and shooting the rest but would that buy me enough time? Another question: What's up ahead? The entire region is a guerrilla stronghold with supply routes crisscrossing in front of and behind us. Then there's the sickening possibility of fleeing directly into the hands of another faction.

A furious late-afternoon rainstorm erupts and we take shelter in an empty three-sided brick hut with another platoon of older rebels in their late thirties, apparently my new escorts. By their age and rough looks, I can tell they are hardened combatants. These men clearly don't like me and I fear I'm in for problems. None of them speak to me, only give me suspicious stares and I cringe with a familiar uneasy feeling there's trouble ahead. Although Marcos and his troops had not conversed with me, I never got the notion they were doing anything other than following orders to deliver a prisoner to a new team higher up in the mountains.

We wait for a break in the storm inside the shelter until dark before trekking back down another trail leading away from the dirt road and away from hopes of escape. I try to remember which path we took in case there's opportunity to backtrack later but I am soon lost as they crisscross the same trails in a successful attempt to confuse me. The system is obvious — starve me, exhaust me, and disorient me. I stop asking questions because they get such a charge out of answering with annoying smiles, "*¿Quien sabe?*" (Who knows?)

Steady rains have rendered the hardened clay trail slick as ice and I spend most of the time sliding downhill over rocks on my butt. They occasionally jerk me to my feet with the all too familiar command, *Vamos!* They are in a hurry and don't permit resting.

Far into a state of dazed exhaustion, I count my stumbling steps in hypnotic fashion, telling myself, "Just another hundred before collapsing again." Much to the terrorists' amusement, I've become a mumbling fool, but in reality I am reverting to my deepest roots of determination, my martial arts inner strength. Earlier in life, during difficult marathon training regimens preparing for competition, I learned to focus my energy and blank out everything else around me. Now, I spin off into a robotic trance with an empty stare, chanting out loud as a mantra, "I will survive, I will survive."

As we approach another rain-swollen creek, my count is reduced to fifty steps between collapses. When I fall, I crawl on my hands and knees, fumbling in the darkness trying to feel my way along. Suddenly, and without warning, a rubber boot crashes up between my legs smashing my testicles. I hear malicious laughter as I land face forward into a stream. I struggle to rise but strong hands push on the back of my head holding my face underwater for what seems like an eternal trip echoing through a tunnel of cold blackness. I wonder if this is now the end. Am I about to be finished off for entertainment by strange men in a faraway land who know nothing of my life or those who would be devastated if I die?

In a near powerless panic I struggle to twist my head up to suck in air. I am too weak to fight and wind up inhaling the black water instead. There's nothing left but gagging for oxygen and coughing up fluid while harassing guerrillas yell insults at me about *los ricos*, and *gringo* this and that.

They permit me a few minutes to throw up and gather what's left of my strength before prodding me back on the trail in the pouring rain. I'm down to stumbling only a dozen steps before collapsing, disoriented and delirious. I keep insisting to myself I can get through this. I will my mind to another place, in another setting back when training in an old east Los Angeles judo school called Tenri. Soon all I hear anymore is my old coach Tony Mojica, yelling to pick up the pace. I smile, relieved to hear a familiar voice and drift into another world, functioning only on spirit and will.

In a few more minutes we reach a shoddy deserted *ranchita* with a wooden pole fence around it. I try to hold myself up clinging to a post — there is nothing left inside and I fall back down into the mud, unable to move. Four guerrillas hoist me up and over the top rail, dumping me into the muck on the other side. Another bunch drags me into a crumbling thatched-roof adobe hut.

Like a sack of human garbage, I'm heaved into a corner of a wet clay-floored room with two other hostages. One of the prisoners is wearing an army uniform and looks over at me in despair uttering, "*Soy militare.*" For once, I think there is someone here more hated than me. Burning with fever, I mumble senselessly like a wild-eyed madman. The two other Colombianos only stare, appalled by what they see. I've not been able to view myself in a mirror since being captured but expressions of pitiful shock on their faces reveal all I need to know. My chanting turns to ranting — "I will survive, I will survive."

A fiercer storm is raging outside, and as the wind pummels and tears at the straw thatched roof, rainwater splashes down upon us from the broken ceiling, forming puddles where we lay shivering. Flashes of lightning illuminate the jungle with snapshots of daylight punctuating the violent, booming thunder, exploding like cannon fire rolling across the South American sky. With a final moan of relief, I dismally spiral off into unconsciousness.

THE JUNGLE NEAR THE PUEBLO, SAN FRANCISCO
November 15, 2001
• • • • • • • • • •

At daybreak, a pimply faced, fair-skinned young woman twenty years old bearing cups of fresh boiled *panela* enters the dank, waterlogged chamber where three of us are being held. As I finish gulping down the first, she brings another that she swaps with the empty I set aside. Later, without speaking she kneels down to wash the blood and mud off my face with a wet dirty rag. She doesn't stay in the room long enough to talk, although I waited for the chance. There is only opportunity for "*¿Como se llama?*" (What do they call you?)

Her only reply is a soft-spoken, "Anna," as she drops her head, hastening out of the room.

Soon, male thugs return. I'm tied up again and taken to the new *Comandante* for questioning. My feet ache so badly with every step

I wish they had left me shivering in the mud. Up until now, the younger guerillas had been nice to me, some actually in awe of my role as a martial arts teacher. This morning however there's one punk kid in need of an ass-kicking. He's not in charge of anything, yet somehow works his way into the interrogation team. During the questioning, he keeps spitting in my face and yelling, "Geo Butte and Bewoo Gintin!" It took me several days to figure out this fool was referring to Presidents George Bush and Bill Clinton and must have read their names in the ELN newspaper, "*Venceremos.*" He is intent on impressing the older men by how miserable he can make me. It's surprising what a jerk he is for being so young.

Since first captured, it has been a struggle to remain emotionally in check, knowing the consequences of losing control. My only tool has been to compare each ELN experience to something that I've experienced before in life and repeating "this isn't so bad." Judo is one of the roughest of the martial arts and I've suffered losses in the ring where I was sometimes severely injured. I am familiar with pain and distress.

Earlier in life, I have twice trekked the Himalayas for weeks at a time, once nearly dying of altitude sickness. I survived two major bike wrecks that the doctors were surprised I lived through. There were a few occasions when riding with a biker crowd in my youth, when we had guns pointed at us by aggressive police. I even convinced myself that it was healthy going without food because it was a cleansing process. Heck, I even thought there might be people who would pay money to hike through scenic mountains like these. I also try to control my animosity toward my captors by mentally referring to each *Comandante* as "Mr. C" and the teenage rebels as "the kids" and often speak to them as I would my students. But this youngster today stretches my patience. Along with the others, he issues his share of body shots when his turn comes, but that's not what makes me want to attack him. It's when he asks, "*¿Quiere ser mi novia?*" (Do you want to be my girlfriend?) This is beyond what the others had done. I consider it a personal insult on my manhood and worth breaking his legs, even though it would result in another beating or maybe worse.

While lying on the ground with him standing above and running his mouth, I consider a judo leg technique called a scissor where free hands are not necessary. It's possible to reach up with my legs, scissor his, and using hip force, break his knee against the joint. Before there's a chance, he spits on me once more and stomps off laughing, leaving me bound on the floor screaming at him in English about what I did to his mother.

He knows that he is being insulted but isn't sure of the meaning. Realizing that it's necessary to decide if temporary satisfaction is worth getting shot over, I reconsider. If I die, he wins. I shut up, but put him on my to-kill list, if the opportunity arises.

The incident earns me another mock execution and I'm marched off outside camp. This time is different though. I'm too numb to care and merely stare off into the jungle while they go through familiar paces. These rebels probably don't realize what has happened previously at the hands of other platoons and seem surprised that I'm unfazed by their cowardly attempt to unnerve me. They've threatened me once too often. My attitude has changed from fear of what's going to happen next, to: "If you are going to do something here, then shut up and do it." By now, I've figured out they obey orders from their political wing and a decision to execute me will come from higher up, and there would be little I can do to alter that. It would be nice to be able to detect some change in the behavior or attitude of a friendly captor like Jimmy that might signal my demise is near. At that point, I will abandon hopes about riding this out, disarm one of them, which would be relatively easy, and then kill as many as possible while escaping. Or maybe take a *Comandante* hostage and barter for my freedom. This is not my favorite option, but it may be my only option and one I must be prepared for every second.

AN ALLY?
November 16, 2001
● ● ● ● ● ● ● ● ● ●

The rebels have a rule requiring a light to be shone in the face of prisoners every fifteen minutes during the night in order to make positive identification. Real sleep is nearly impossible. This treatment, along with the stress of pondering my fate, is taking a heavy toll on my nerves and decision-making process. I try to neutralize concerns of dying and attempt to deal with everything one moment at a time, focusing on staying alive. What the future holds is something too distant to worry about. This morning after climbing out from a state of semi-slumber and almost too sore to breathe, I find a young guerrilla is sitting patiently nearby with a cup of water and some aspirin. I ask him where he got the aspirin and he replies pointing north, *"Dos horas."* (Two hours.) Like Himalayan Sherpas, the mountain *campesinos* measure distance by the time it takes to walk somewhere. This means that he hiked a total of four hours to get the hated *gringo* some medicine, a move that showed kindness typical of *campesinos*. This act could also cause him problems with his superiors for appearing to be too sympathetic with the enemy. He has taken a risk for me because of his kind and helpful nature.

Even with the aspirin and a full day's rest yesterday, my body is not ready to travel. I am covered in welts from insect bites and bruises from the slipping and sliding along the trail. There's been no protein to rebuild damaged tissues for the last ten days and, by look and feel, a weight loss of ten to fifteen pounds of muscle. As an athlete accustomed to constantly fine-tuning my physique and metabolism, I am acutely aware of the slow starvation. Yet there is no choice — they will kill me if I refuse to continue. Today, we are being handed off to another unfriendly group again and I sense they want me to refuse to march so they can have an excuse to abuse me.

The rebels grew up in this remote region and are masters with their machetes. When we come to rain-swollen streams too swift and deep to walk across, they build makeshift bridges out of tall tree limbs lashed together with reeds. In minutes they can hack away with razor-edged blades and construct walkways stretching as much as twenty feet. These are flimsy structures that flex with every step. Yet they hold together well as we cross, carefully balancing one at a time. It wouldn't make much difference falling into the water; I'm always wet from marching in the rain anyway.

Fortunately it's a short trek to the new confinement area, the first lived-in structure yet. It's a two-room masonry house still in the process of being sloppily built with bricks that do not line up and crooked doorways. After being fed a cup of rice, myself and another prisoner are locked in an eight-by eight room with a tin roof and cement floor. The temperature inside soars well above a hundred in the afternoon and drops into the fifties at night. Streams of sinister looking giant ants crisscross the walls and ceilings in long lines searching for something to gnaw on, which is me the second I doze off.

At least there is company. Although I'm not yet sure if he is trustworthy, I'm locked in with Sgt. Gonzales, the Colombian military prisoner, a potential ally and information source. He says that he has been in the army for twenty years and only worked as an office clerk. I think what the heck else would he want the ELN to believe, that he is a field soldier who had killed their comrades? Just in case, I reconfirm my story about coming to write about the rebels and how I have prostate cancer and am getting sicker.

Sealed in the brick room and allowed out only to bathe or urinate leaves me with little to relieve the frustrating monotony and strangling heat except to speculate about my fate and the terrible thoughts of what my loved ones back home are enduring. With no way to pass or receive messages, I can only assume they don't know what's happened. While out on the trail we occasionally encounter other hostages being led off into the mountains. They are all unfortunate Colombians either kidnapped while driving or snatched from their homes. We are not permitted direct communication so I can't be sure. The bewildering terror in their eyes confirms they are recent captives who have not yet adapted to our circumstance. Some are still dressed in torn business suits and expensive loafers caked in red clay that give them away as *los ricos*. Their fancy shoes won't last long on the ragged muddy trails and I feel lucky to have been wearing boots when taken prisoner.

Unlike foreigners who are held for years with unrealistic demands, locals are generally released within a few days after paying the standard fifteen-million peso ($7,500) ransom. Their misery is only temporary. Assuming that these other hostages are soon to be freed, I try to use them to get a message out. So as not to alert my captors, I make jokes about how American martial arts teachers riding motorcycles spend vacations in Colombia. I hoped they would relay this information to authorities when ultimately released. They wouldn't know a name; however, that description should be enough to identify me to whomever might debrief them. I pretend to be in good spirits so no one back home will know how horrible this is. It would only increase their suffering.

It's now just myself and Sgt. Gonzales, a hostage for only three days, locked down together, trying to pick each other's brains without giving up much truthful information about ourselves. He knows a few words in English and I manage some Spanish; we get our thoughts across. The *campesino* accent spoken by our captors is hard for him to understand but he fills me in on what could be in store for us. It might take years to get released, if we live that long. We are more than simple hostages. We symbolize the enemy to the ELN and it's certain that we are destined for special treatment. Worry about my fate, incessant hunger pangs, and lack of sleep have frazzled my nerves beyond anything I could imagine. I wonder if my mind is deliberately being stretched to a point from which there is no recovery.

In the last twenty years of practicing meditation, I've learned that intentional fasting for extended periods of time results in enhanced states of awareness. Before a meal, food will look, smell, and taste better. As a blind person's hearing is more acute, a hungry person has all five senses expanded.

Accustomed to daily meditation before my capture, I continue this exercise while a prisoner when locked down and starving with nothing to do. There are long periods of hunger available in which to drift deeper than ever. Whenever hitting low points in life, I look for silver linings. In this case, it would have to be self-discovery and how although my body is held in captivity, my mind is free. Meditation becomes an escape from relentless torment. My fellow prisoner must think I've gone mad. He watches me warming up in yoga postures that culminate in a sitting cross-legged-lotus position with my eyes closed for an hour at a time, bouncing around the void.

The terrorists are demanding not only cash from the military man's family but also five army radios, a request everyone knows is impossible to fulfill. An ultimatum is given: come up with money and radios or fifty uniforms or Gonzales will be shot this coming Saturday. We feel they are making impractical demands for an excuse to kill him. Up until now, it was hard to be certain if any of the other hostages were real or plants to get information about me, but the way he weeps and prays at night makes me believe in him. Because of our status representing sworn blood enemies of the ELN, we know our treatment will be different, and we both are taunted continuously with threats of execution. It's something we are facing and accepting while we both silently plan an escape.

It's a difficult hand to play, constantly weighing the odds of being released someday versus those of surviving an escape attempt or being murdered by our captors. I have been studying their every move, from timing their rotation schedules to counting the bullets they replace after cleaning their weapons. I speculate who will be the least and most capable of shooting at us in an effort to determine the first targets once controlling a weapon. Some of the AK-47s they carry are so old and banged up, it's questionable if they will fire; others lack full magazines.

It would be unfortunate to wind up with a gun lacking enough bullets to finish what we start, or one that may jam. When there is an opportunity to get close to their weapons while they clean them, I look for serial numbers to record, only to discover that they have all been ground off. Manufacturing dates of 1963 and 1965 remain, indicating Vietnam-era guns, likely used in subsequent leftist insurrections in other countries. The leaders carry modern stainless steel versions along with hand grenades clipped to their vests and, although they will be the toughest to disarm, I'll need to go for one of them first. Gonzales will know what to do if things get rolling, but up until that point, I must keep any plans to myself. As a soldier, he must be thinking the same.

I decide to trust him with an idea to relay a message if either of us gets released or escapes separately. Next to freedom, my first priority is to get word to my loved ones that I'm still alive. In case we are searched, I scribble down some numbers on a scrap of paper that appear to be mathematical equations. If the zeros are eliminated it becomes a telephone number for either of us to call with information about the other. Our physical location changes too often for it to do any good providing that — this is only to let people know we are alive.

Yet I'm still too unsure of him to talk about my secret diary and the information I recorded describing geographic coordinates of rebel supply and ammunition dumps. I only write when I am alone. To test his knowledge, I bring up the subject of satellite navigation and, as a military man, he understands the technology. I tell him about my GPS that the rebels are holding and suggest that we could steal it back to compute our position and then make our escape. Because of his background, he should be able to hold his own if it comes down to a blood and guts bolt for freedom. I've only seen scenarios like this in movies and realize this is going to involve people dying, and in order to keep that from being me, it will be necessary to kill. Gonzales has the drop as a trained soldier programmed for situations like this. Me, I will be functioning with the focused determination that accompanies dazed desperation and will take lives out of panic and likely make serious mistakes. What's most disturbing about this is I may end up shooting one of the kids who has befriended me.

Gonzales explains we don't need the GPS. He knows exactly where we are, but we will have to pass through the nearby guerrilla-held *pueblo* of San Francisco on the way back to the main highway. There are homemade ELN flags flying on makeshift poles near scattered remote *campesino* houses throughout this region, indicating they are rebel supporters or at least intimidated into it. Some flags are flown out of fear for the rebels, others, out of loyalty; we can't be sure which is which. We'll just have to take our chances.

Today, Sgt. Gonzales is marched up a high mountain peak by the *Comandante* to a place where it's possible to receive a clear cellular telephone signal. He is ordered to plead with his wife over the phone to coerce his army buddies into stealing the military equipment the rebels demanded. Later during the conversation, the *Comandante* repeats death threats to her to ensure that she is sufficiently terrified. Convinced he has only days to live, Gonzales weeps and prays throughout the night, making peace with his God. Even the young guerrillas take pity on him and bring cups of *panela*.

CASA DE MANUEL
November 17, 2001
● ● ● ● ● ● ● ● ● ●

This tiny *casita* we are holed up in atop the mountain ridge belongs to Manuel, a twenty-two-year-old *campesino* boy. He lives here with his undernourished eighteen-month-old son and scrawny, hunched-over, seventy-year-old toothless father. To barely survive, they grow corn and sugar cane. Manuel's wife deserted him for another man shortly after their child was born; now he, his father, and his son struggle to stay alive. There are no food supplies when we arrive, only two ragged hammocks and a few oily blankets. These are the people Jimmy spoke of, the mountain *campesinos* who have nothing to live on and exist without hope. They will ultimately migrate to a major city to beg for food and sleep in garbage dumps. Late at night I hear Manuel's child cry. It's not the normal 3:00 a.m. wailing for milk or attention. These are open-eyed, bloodcurdling, gasping shrieks of horror — as though this innocent wisp of life is peeking into the impossible future and can see what lies ahead.

Manuel and his father permit the rebels to use their one-acre plot of land in exchange for rice and pork, the only food they've seen in days. The rebels and their weapons frighten the father. Manuel accepts them and the toddler wobbles shoeless among the armed troops with muffled laughter and empty eyes. Forty men are bivouacked here, rotating in and out of the nearby hills. There's no toilet, only a brick tub in the front yard that everyone uses for bathing. The vile stench of semi-buried feces and stale urine burns our nostrils.

The days are long and boring; I begin writing a dictionary of Spanish words using the back pages of the bogus journal about the ELN. Manuel has given me his Catholic missionary schoolbook to read and it contains basic information about science, health, and agriculture. Combined with pictures, I can determine what new words mean. Confirming the information with Sgt. Gonzales by pantomiming and gesturing, I record them with their meanings. The younger guerrillas are constantly thumbing through my journal, often asking what I have written about them. They like the idea that I'm trying to learn more about their ways and their language. Most are illiterate but enjoy helping me with new words in exchange for "secret" judo moves.

The older guerrillas see the friendliness building and order us apart when we are caught talking too long. A student-teacher relationship is a powerful tool that I'm accustomed to developing in my profession as a judo instructor where I frequently interact with teenagers. These young people who are supposed to be guarding me are showing signs of split loyalty. Given enough time with one group, I'm certain someone would help me escape. I must also consider that they would be severely punished or executed. These developing loyalties are not one-sided.

ANNA
November 18, 2001
● ● ● ● ● ● ● ● ● ●

When allowed outside to relieve myself, I take advantage of the opportunity to try and speak with Anna, the pudgy short-haired female rebel who had been kind to me previously. She permits only a few minutes of conversation before walking away in mid-sentence so as not to look bad for being friendly with the enemy. She's a homely, dejected-looking city girl from Medellín, one of the few guerrillas not born in the stark poverty of the surrounding countryside. Her fair-skinned appearance is in distinct contrast to the jet-black-headed young women with olive complexions I've encountered so far in the ELN. And although everyone is supposed to be equal, they have a special name for people of her color: *"Güedo."* (Whitey.) I ask her why she joined the ELN. She explains that unlike the other guerrillas, who grew up in despair and starvation, she came from a middle-class family and was a university student when she decided she wanted to revolt against the corrupt government in Colombia. Her family does not know where she is, or what she is doing. She just disappeared two months ago and joined the fight using connections from her school to rendezvous with the rebels in the mountains.

I ask her if she would kill with the gun she is holding and she tells me that she would not. I ask her if she would shoot me if I attempted to flee. And again she says that she would not. "Why then, Anna, do you carry that gun?"

It is only for self-defense, she rationalizes, but it is obvious she doesn't fully believe this. I tell her that if she carries a gun, sooner or later, for one reason or another, she will have to kill another human being. She seems disturbed by this notion. It's as I suspected — these kids are recruited and hoodwinked by professionals with fairy tales of Robin Hood struggles against evil oppressors and are therefore justified in their murder, robbery, and kidnapping. Teenage recruits begin their tour of duty guarding hostages who have been captured by older, more experienced, and violent combatants. They are not ordered to kill anyone and they actually believe what their manifesto states: the ELN kills only in self-defense. Few captives have ever escaped and even fewer resist when taken prisoner because it is certain death to do so. Anna listens to me and I think there is a shot at turning her. She is my best hope yet for escape but I must be careful; she may be just chumming for information. Later, she fails my first test. I ask if she knows how much longer we will stay in this location and she replies with the dreaded, "*¿Quien sabe?*"

PORK
November 19, 2001
● ● ● ● ● ● ● ● ● ●

The troops have been congregating from the nearby mountains for an upcoming special event that calls for the slaughtering of a pig. Catching and wrestling a 300-pound sow to the ground involves a dozen rebels and is a tiring and lengthy process. A handful of men pull the screaming pig onto its side with ropes around its neck while three others ram two-foot-long, sharp pointed rods into its heart. It takes an hour before the bloodcurdling howls and spasms of thrashing hoofs finally subside into murmurs of gurgling fluid. Considering my circumstances, this gruesome spectacle is more than I can stomach, making me wonder if a similar fate awaits me.

Later, I can smell the sizzling pork cooking at night and rotting in the stifling heat of the day, covered with salt and flies. It doesn't matter. I will gladly eat the raw decaying flesh of any animal or insect at this point. Hunger burns continually. My bones have begun poking through my clothing, a periodic notification of slow starvation. It's painful to lie on bare concrete at night with no flesh to cushion me. The question looms, "How far are they going to let this go?" I keep trying to convince myself they need me alive and as long as I'm still breathing I have value. The more radical older rebels don't care; they clearly have other desires.

At night, as our captors feast, Gonzales and I are each given a one-inch chunk of fat to chew with skin and coarse hair still attached. Next day, we receive a bone with the meat boiled off to gnaw on. Because the pig must be divided forty ways for several meals, the rebels' portions are small but contain meat. My slightly overweight companion has only been a prisoner for a week; soon he too will begin to see signs of starvation. I keep hoping one of the youngsters might defy orders and smuggle food to us — so far, no one seems ready to risk it.

The *Comandante* feels generous this afternoon and offers me a chance to bathe in the brick water tank in the front yard. After I finish splashing the soapsuds off, I dry myself with a pair of boxer shorts while the guards seem to momentarily lose track of me. Everyone is occupied doing camp chores or cleaning their weapons and I am in no hurry to return to the oven heat of the insect factory. The afternoon sun feels good, much better when accompanied by a refreshing mountain breeze on the pointed top of this mountain ridge. Before someone comes to order me inside, I meander back on my own, absorbing the stunning views of jungle terrain. The other door to the two-room shack is ajar. Out of foolish curiosity, I nudge it farther for a peek inside.

I am shocked and scared over what I see. The *Comandante* and a female rebel are busy counting a half-roomful of 20,000-peso notes stacked two feet high across the cement floor. It must have taken two mules just to haul this much cash, a sum totaling over a million U.S. dollars. My fear is that I have witnessed something I should not have and now, no matter their prior intent, they will need to silence me. This much currency has to be drug money, maybe a payoff.

I turn immediately and withdraw from the room, pretending I had not seen anything. The door slams immediately as the *Comandante* barks out orders to lock me back up. Afraid to even think about what just happened, I don't mention any of this to Sgt. Gonzales and spend the rest of the night fearing I will be shot in the morning.

WITCHES AND PUPPIES
November 20, 2001
• • • • • • • • • •

Cooking, cleaning, and camp maintenance duties are divided equally between both sexes. Older male rebels oversee security while younger ones guard prisoners. I've been watching three mean, ugly female guerrillas in their mid-twenties stealing food when no one is looking. They know I see their pilfering acts and have decided to have fun tormenting me. As I wait to be locked up in the shed after being allowed out to urinate, the three piglets huddle together where no one except me can spot them eating fried pork and noodles from a clay bowl. I can smell the steaming, succulent food from twenty feet — with primal cravings taking control, I am thinking like an animal. They are busy gabbing and using their hands to pack as much meat into their gaping, rotten-toothed mouths as possible while glancing over at me spitefully. They complain of being too stuffed for another bite and rub their bulging stomachs in mock satisfaction, then snicker while showing me that there are still remnants left in the bowl. Manuel's emaciated puppy, ribs protruding, sits next to me with similar cravings for the leftover scraps — both of us now begging with our eyes and drooling.

Cackling like a witch, the most hideous of the foul-breathed witches tosses the contents of the bowl on the ground between the dog and me as a game to see which of us dives for it first. I flinch for a moment; then think better. For at least another day, I am still a man.

Although most of the youngsters are compassionate, the compassion ends when it comes to animals. Throughout Latin America there's a propensity for needless cruelty toward livestock. This evening, in a display of teenage machismo, one of the male youngsters attempts to demonstrate his bravado by antagonizing Manuel's sunken-eyed puppy, already little more than skin and bones and tied to a tree. He pokes and jabs at his snarling victim with his AK-47 while shouting and spitting on him. The others egg him on with malicious laughter while the enraged pup furiously snaps and bites at the hardened end of the cold metal barrel. Manuel's father reluctantly responds to my pleading for a halt to this cruel entertainment and brings the puppy in with Sgt. Gonzales and me.

Once safely inside with us, I try to coax him over. But with his matted scrawny tail tucked up between his legs, he only growls with curled lips, baring chipped little fangs as he cowers, shaking in the corner. For Sgt. Gonzales, this is another baffling *gringo* action. After an hour of cooing and cajoling, the battered pup curls up at my feet, enjoying probably the first scratches behind the ear he has ever experienced.

DEPARTING LA CASA DE MANUEL
November 21, 2001
● ● ● ● ● ● ● ● ● ●

Sgt. Gonzales and I are unexpectedly rousted early and hustled outside to be led away at gunpoint, each in separate directions. We are forbidden to speak but manage a goodbye glance. We both notice a fresh hole dug on the hillside and each wonder who will occupy that grave.

Today is one of the steepest climbs yet. The rebels have backpacks to balance their heavy loads — I have a ragged forty-pound rice sack to awkwardly sling over my shoulder. The heat and stifling humidity bring insects by the hundreds to munch on my unprotected wrists and neck as I sidestep up and down a rocky trail. This trek is exhausting enough that even the guerrillas need to stop for rest every twenty minutes, each time passing around a water jug to everyone except Anna and me.

She is in serious trouble because of our conversations. This morning, she has announced a desire to resign from the guerrilla force, declining to carry a weapon any longer. Yet angry rebels refuse her request. The *Comandante* singles her out with ridicule and mockery, calling her a traitor. As punishment, she is given a double pack to carry on a full day's march. At mid-morning my legs are already shaking and she is carrying twice my load. I fear for her safety as she continually collapses, delirious, her face purple. I relate to her condition and ask for permission to carry one of her packs. The other rebels scream out vicious insults at her while ordering me to keep moving. Although they did not shoot her today, I suspect they will soon.

Late in the afternoon, we arrive at an old, abandoned, three-roomed adobe bricked *ranchita* and I am told to use an inside corner to sleep in. After setting my sack down and spreading out my plastic sheet, I notice thousands of small holes pockmarked in the ancient adobe walls, each with tiny sets of insect eyes peering out like an audience of hungry spectators. Later, as the insects emerge to feast on human flesh, I decide that tonight, the tables will turn. I shall now feast on them! Without sufficient nutrition I am deteriorating so rapidly that I fear that it is only a matter of days before I'm no longer able to walk — with or without guns pointed at me. My body and human dignity are both rapidly wasting away. I no longer have much to lose except life itself and bugs contain the protein I need to survive.

The guerrillas normally cook one five-gallon pot of rice each day that lasts for several meals; one feeding is warm and the other cold. I get what they don't eat, most often a small teacup — sometimes less. Tonight the rice is warm, and after pinching the creeping critters one at a time, I stir them in and gulp the disgusting concoction down in lumps. It's okay as long as I don't chew but I have visions of wiggling insects in my stomach.

THANKSGIVING DAY
November 22, 2001
I am thankful to still be alive
● ● ● ● ● ● ● ● ● ● ● ● ● ● ● ●

While waiting to be locked down after bathing, I lean against one of the wooden support posts holding up an outside wall of the *ranchita* when an unexpected explosion booms through the air. The noise is so loud I feel the concussion against my skin. Stinging debris sprays across the front of my body accompanied by the irritating acrid smoke of discharged gunpowder. My first thought is that someone had detonated a cherry bomb as the echo under the porch painfully resonates like a slap against my ears.

It takes a few moments to realize the pole I'd been resting against had disintegrated into wooden fragments and splinters across the front of my shirt and face. I'm baffled by what's happened until noticing one of the younger rebels, who had been carelessly cleaning his gun, sheepishly looking up at me with a "woops" expression. Even stranger is my lack of reaction — I'm so numb over what has occurred in the past several weeks, I'm unfazed and merely shuffle back inside and fall asleep. Life has evolved onto a new level: I now exist within a psychological vacuum, without emotion, mentally withdrawing at every opportunity from this world of misery, my captors' and mine. They too, along with the local *campesinos*, live within a prison of despair.

All that's left is to think only of more exhausting hiking and imagined food, dreaming of the next teacup of rice and dreading the next day's march. There are no more recollections of freedom. False hopes must not be allowed. Because I have been missing so long, I know that my friend Joe is out there somewhere on the edge of the jungle determined to find me and, one way or another, he will bring me home; that's all that I have left to believe in anymore.

THE SUPPORT TEAM
November 22, 2001
Bogotá, Colombia
● ● ● ● ● ● ● ● ● ● ●

The last six nights have been gut burning and sleepless for Joe Gallagher, my support team member chosen to handle life-and-death emergencies when I travel. Without belief in him, I may have collapsed under the psychological strain of terrorist captivity.

Joe is well versed in watching my back, having performed a similar role in the eighties when I rode throughout southeast Asia. The Internet didn't exist then, so to keep everyone at home apprised of what part of the world I would be wandering, I faxed my routes and timetables back to him in California. I checked in every few weeks or whenever there was phone service and although there was never a mishap, he was always ready. It would take a bullet to stop him from coming to my aid or me his — we've had this mutual arrangement for twenty-eight years.

The night before being taken prisoner, I sent him an email expressing satisfaction with the trip so far and emphasized my desire to see things through no matter what. My final words to Joe before the fateful ride to Medellín were, "Win, lose, or draw, brother, this is what my heart craves and I would not have had it any other way." Hopefully he understood.

Joe Gallagher is the kind of guy nobody likes — everyone who knows him uses the term "love." When his name comes up in conversation, people invariably say, "Don't you just love Joe?" He is a New York guy who migrated to Palm Springs, where I met him in 1975. He still uses phrases like, "Geet outta heah," and, "Are yous fahkin crazy?" He owns the two biggest nightclubs in town, and wherever he goes, he is greeted respectfully by people who have been treated well at his businesses. Joe would not only die by my side, he just might die in my place.

Thirteen years ago, while on a solo cross-country motorcycle ride, during a moment of pleasant introspection, I found myself thinking about the friends who had stuck by me for more than a decade of tumultuous activities through all kinds of crises, mine and theirs, and how we had all grown together as a result. It was then that I realized that the true measure of wealth was the quality of friendships, and the importance of making them last. I was alarmed that my closest friends might not know the sincere regard and appreciation I have for them. Upon returning home, I designed, and had made, seven identical rings, one for each of the guys who went back with me for over a decade. Each gold band contained a single carat Thai ruby with two baguette diamonds on each side. These rings are more than souvenirs of time spent hanging out together; they symbolize a lifetime bond between us.

I wrote a personal letter to accompany the rings describing the effect of their friendship on my life. Five of the recipients are successful businessmen and one is a California State Superior Court judge. The letters said that I would not have succeeded in my chosen endeavors and would likely not even be alive without their guidance and example. Men seldom reveal such thoughts to each other, but I wanted a permanent record. The first to receive his ring was a tearful Joe Gallagher.

There is a code that some people live by, to stick together no matter the odds and whatever the consequence. Although many claim to abide by this, few are ever tested to the point of life or death. I've heard it said that you'll learn who your friends are when you're in the hospital or jail — and captivity by a terrorist organization is a form of jail. The term "when the chips are down" was coined for events like this. From the moment of being captured, I never had a second of speculation — I knew my team was in place doing all they could and I knew that someone would have to kill Joe to stop him from searching for me. If someone managed that, then they must deal with Brad, who would be following close behind. That belief is what kept me from giving up.

As I was being led off at gunpoint by terrorist rebels, Joe was leaving a Palm Springs, California hospital after undergoing surgery for a torn bicep muscle and was under strict doctor's care. Between the post-surgical pain of a fresh wound and two days of silence from me, he was on edge. By day three, he and the rest of the team discussed the next preplanned step: to contact local hospitals, wrecking yards, and police stations between Bogotá and Medellín. After striking out with those, they concluded with certainty: if I am still alive, I've been taken prisoner.

For nearly a month, the ELN, in typical terrorist fashion, released no information about my capture — their sadistic way of building suspense and terrorizing families. Joe contacted the U.S. State Department, which reported it had no direct information, but if I was missing, I'd most likely been taken hostage by one of several leftist guerrilla groups. The question being, which one? Their advice: keep silent, wait for contact, and hope the press doesn't get wind of the situation. Worldwide publicity would only make the guerrillas consider me an important person and thus hold out for an unreasonable ransom.

This is not good enough for the team and, according to plan, six days after my disappearance, my close friend and judo student Brad Neste is busy setting up a command center in Palm Springs to accumulate every type of information of value to coordinate with Joe who is already en route to Colombia. Nine hours later, Joe touches down in Bogotá, somberly determined to bring me out of the jungle, dead or alive. Already angered by Uncle Sam's lack of concern, he will personally search for me and is not about to take "no" for an answer — from anyone.

A Colombian national, Katrina Mendez, accompanies Joe on his flight to Bogotá. She works in the U.S. in the computer field and is a friend of a friend, who heard of my plight and offered to join Joe on his dubious mission. You have to know Colombians to realize how commonplace it is to jump in and help a stranger, even in the face of obvious danger. She instructs Joe that it will be necessary for him to blend in with the local populace and has him dye his hair black and dress like a *Colombiano*. She warns him against speaking in public lest someone discover he is an American and become suspicious of their activities.

As a means for Joe to keep track of my whereabouts while traveling, the plan was for me to use a Merrill-Lynch Visa card at least once a day. I have an old friend at the company who can instantly pull up on his computer the location wherever the card had last been used. The last known location was a gas station restaurant outside Bogotá at 10:00 a.m., November 6, 2001, and that is where Joe and Katrina head to begin their search.

In a rented car, they begin tracking the route I traveled only nine days before, questioning people along the way. "Has anybody seen a greenish-multicolored motorcycle with a big tall *Americano* wearing a fluorescent orange helmet?" A man of my size with such a description would have been hard to miss had I stopped anywhere else. Unfortunately, I had been in a hurry to reach Medellín before dark and kept moving. No one recalls anything. It's an hour to nightfall and now, fearing a similar fate, Katrina persuades Joe to return to the relative safety of Bogotá for a night's rest and an early start in the morning.

Kidnapping for ransom is such a lucrative enterprise in Colombia that the government has made it a federal crime to negotiate with or pay off rebel groups. Anguished families receive prison sentences if caught attempting to retrieve loved ones from terrorist organizations, or the certain death of a relative if they don't comply with demands. Such is the tragedy of Colombia — living between rocks and hard places. Having aroused too many suspicions, my rescuers must also dodge the Secret Police (DAS) who are now aware of why they are in Colombia.

Joe rents a cell phone to develop and maintain a growing list of local contacts. Trying to sort out the bogus leads and police informants from people with valuable information is a risky chore. Everyone wants money. Katrina is from another region of Colombia but has friends of friends who might help out with leads and advice necessary to conduct the investigation. They must trust somebody, yet each time they do, it's a gamble, as betrayal spells certain disaster for them also. Their own lives and freedom are at stake.

They assume their phone calls are being intercepted by police and use Yahoo! email accounts to communicate with Brad back in Palm Springs. Meanwhile, Brad is busy on another research front — a crash course in left-wing rebel groups. Within days, he becomes an expert on the behavior, history and policies of the FARC and ELN as well as their sworn enemies, the right-wing vigilante death squads of the *Paramilitare*.

The news is not encouraging. Even a representative of Amnesty International tells him, "If your friend is still alive it will be years before you'll see him and then you won't recognize what's left." The most uncomfortable part of Brad's job becomes controlling the flow of information to the media and those at home. He cannot risk so much as a whisper concerning their mission lest the FBI intervene and stop them. Even worse, if the press obtains details, it will become headline news and my captors will be convinced I am an important man worth a high ransom. On the other hand, maybe international exposure would get faster results but that would only be if the U.S.

government saw a value in assisting. My team gambles on silence.

Joe and Katrina are on the road early and by 11:00 a.m. have passed yesterday's turnaround point, with several more hours of daylight to conduct their search. They're straying farther from the city and encountering the same desolate stretches of roadway, with the same spooky feeling I experienced. They know whatever had been my fate, if they continue, could likely be theirs. Joe offers Katrina the chance to turn back — she refuses. He speaks no Spanish and there are other dangers besides guerrilla groups. This is also bandit country with no legitimate law enforcement authority in control.

By noon they reach the sparsely populated *pueblito* of San Luis, a place with only a gas station and a restaurant that specializes in roasted chicken. In a moment of excitement Joe calls out, "Hey Katrina, that sign back there that said *pollo asado* — doesn't that mean roasted chicken in Spanish?"

"Yes, why?"

"Turn the car around, Glen would have stopped there, I know from his journals he has been eating *pollo asado* every day."

A friendly young couple is working the counter. They have good memories and offer details in Spanish. "*Si*, there was a big *Americano* in here a week and a half ago. Here is his card he left for us to look him up on the Internet but we don't know what that is. He was very friendly and told us about his trip and that he was anxious to reach Medellín before dark. Why, is he in trouble?"

"We don't know but if you hear of anything, please call us at this number. We will pay for information." Joe and Katrina now have a marker. They know I made it that far but once again, it's getting late and time to head back to Bogotá. Reluctant to return and wanting to give it one more shot, Joe says, "Let's ask that bus driver over there a few questions before we leave."

At first the driver is nervous and afraid to speak, but as he looks around and sees no one near, he opens up. "*Si señor*, I have seen your friend. I watched him being taken by guerrillas nine days ago in the roadway a few miles out of town. I recognized the uniforms, it was the ELN." They don't ask why he failed to report this to the authorities. They know that he fears retaliation against him or his family. No one is safe from terrorists in Colombia. If terrorists want you, they will come for you and if they can't catch you, they will settle for a family member.

Joe and Katrina return to Bogotá, elated by their growing confidence that I'm still alive. It should be only a matter of time before a demand is made and arrangements for my release will lead to freedom. That night in a coded email message to Brad, they relay what they had learned. Brad is relieved but, ever sensitive to security, still does not risk sharing details with anyone, even my daughter, Skye.

This is tough duty for Brad. He's a backwoods boy from Dawson Creek, a friendly town in northern Canada. And he can't comprehend a deadly game involving international terrorism and the murderous brutality of a senseless civil war. He had always been a willing and able bar-brawler while growing up but the only time he ever looked down a gun barrel was when cleaning his hunting rifle. He has spent the last decade diligently training in my judo school and through hard core competitive fighting, rose to the position of senior black belt. He is more than my brother and road dog — he is my other half. If men have male soul mates, Brad is mine. We study life together and are each other's heroes as well as mentors. I know how he suffers at my disappearance.

I know his every thought and agonize with him. We are cohorts from different backgrounds, with him winding up for the last thirty years married to Wanda, a stunningly beautiful mountain climber. Together they founded a tri-state corporation consisting of a chain of Gold's Gyms. Me the wanderer and he the businessman, yet we still attack and perceive life with a shared passion. Brad is beyond frustration. He desperately wants to be with Joe in Colombia, searching for me. However, Joe and I already had a disaster plan in advance that requires Brad to stay put and coordinate. This is the hardest part for Brad to deal with.

The Colombian Secret Police (DAS) as well as the FBI are now fully involved. The problem is that they are spending more time trying to keep track of my rescue team than doing anything for me. My team doesn't want or need their help and they sure as hell don't need their threats. They are finally flat out ordered to cease and desist any further attempts at locating me as they are now interfering with a federal investigation. The Feds assure everyone they are on top of the situation and have it all under control.

"Okay," Brad says to them, "I guess you know Glen was grabbed by the ELN around the town of San Luis?"

"What? How did you know that?"

"How come you didn't? I thought you had it all under control and knew what was going on?"

"Uh, well, er, um, we do, but just in case, tell us everything you have found out."

"No deal guys; you give us information and we'll give you information. Quid pro quo."

The problem is, the Feds have no information because they have done nothing except spy on my team and investigate them. They have all of our life histories yet nothing on the issues at hand, like who is holding me and what they want before they will release me.

I love my country but fear my government. I respect the FBI, but question their methods. How would they want matters handled if a member of their family was captured and possibly about to be murdered at any moment? Would they prefer everyone to sit around and wait? How would they feel if officials told them to just sit tight, they were working on it, when it was obvious they weren't? Could they merely relax and trust that someone else was "on it"?

The cat-and-mouse game continues for two more weeks. Joe and Katrina are not only able to find the exact spot where I was taken prisoner, but they also trace down the thieves who stole my bike, which had sat in the deserted *casita* for three weeks before being snatched. Acting on a tip from a local in San Luis, they located my bike but, while returning to get help from the military to retrieve it, it disappears again. Because of so much double-crossing, Joe believes this is a trap to snare them, too.

Another member of the team, a close friend for whom I'd previously worked as a bodyguard, Dennis Hof, was also experiencing the aggravation of being unable to get anything done. He operates the

Moonlight Bunny Ranch in Nevada and is used to getting what he needs with a few phone calls to the right places. Nothing is impossible to him and he loves the challenge of achieving what other men cannot. Dennis is a natural-born problem-solver, he lives for it, but this is not the type of crisis he is accustomed to solving. Finally out of patience, he contacts ex-U.S. Army Ranger acquaintances living in Colombia to set up a helicopter rescue attempt. The situation turns cloak-and-dagger quickly as the word gets out that Dennis will pay whomever, whatever is necessary to go in and get me. This information is passed on, most likely through the CIA, to the FBI, which in turn contacts all parties with a new set of threats — stay out of the way or face arrest.

Dennis must sit and pace in his Carson City headquarters and fight the urge to call Brad every hour for news. This is a new game for him, having to do battle with his hands tied behind his back. In earlier years we traveled to Cuba together and had also forged our friendship through motorcycling and having our backs against the wall together on numerous occasions. When life caves in on me, whether from a soured love affair or a financial crisis, it is he that I call for advice. All who know Dennis trust him unconditionally. Up until now, he has always had an answer for everything. For the next few weeks he gets less sleep than I do. All he can do at the moment is to play back our good times and sweat it out. For my friends back home, life has come to a frightening standstill and their personal lives are on hold indefinitely until they have me back.

Ultimately, the efforts of Joe and Katrina earn them a deportation order from the Colombian government, no doubt instigated by the FBI. The charge was that they had filled out an immigration entry document incorrectly by stating that their visit was for tourism, not a hostage situation, which would have fallen under the heading "humanitarian reason." Joe and Katrina are forced out of Colombia by the secret police at the most critical moment on a technicality.

ANITA
November 23, 2001

● ● ● ● ● ● ● ● ● ●

I've been curious to discover why, among the rebels, the women are overweight and the men are skinny. Adhering to Marxist doctrine, they eat the same food and do the same amount of work. They carry similar loads, have the same diet of canned sardines, dehydrated vegetable protein, and rice, and chew on sugar cane stalks during treks. Still, there is a vast discrepancy in their body fat.

Anita is a chubby, pretty fifteen-year-old with dark sparkling eyes filled with the typical curiosity of teenagers anywhere else in the world. She's been with the rebels for three months since being recruited by an older man from her village. Today when the mule team arrives carrying supplies, she is given a personal package containing a special present, a laminated photograph. It's an eight-by-ten color portrait of her crouching, holding an AK-47 machine gun at ready position across her chest, with a poster perfect look of serious conviction. The pose and print are professional quality, with the obvious purpose to glorify her role as a noble freedom fighter in a struggle against oppression. She has no idea that she is a mere pawn in a game of international terrorism for profit.

My mind toggles back and forth between sadness and wonderment, from the picture to the youthful girl before me. This is but a child, someone's little sister, someone's hope for the future. She's the age of a friend's daughter back home in her first year of high school who at this moment is likely yakking on her cell phone with her best friend about the guy she has a crush on. We take it for granted that teenagers should be allowed to be teenagers regardless where they live in the world. But not so in the midst of civil war in Colombia.

Anita fiddles with the lethal automatic weapon that she may not have yet fired. She tells me how she misses her family, murdered last year in a massacre by the *Paramilitare*. There is nowhere for her to return to. In a few years, the ELN will transform her from a heartbroken confused teenager into a full-fledged combatant. If she stays with them long enough, she too will directly participate in cold-blooded executions in the name of a free Colombia.

A few minutes later, as I sit watching her clean her gun, as rebels do as often as twice daily, I witness the ritual of her clearing out her ammunition vest afterward. Whenever I have the opportunity, I count the bullets they put back in their clips as they reassemble their weapons. I note that not all the rebels are given enough bullets to fill them.

The older, more experienced guerrillas not only have full clips but also carry full backups in specially designed pockets on their ammo vests.

The double pockets on each side of the ammo vests are formed and stitched to conveniently house the distinctively banana-shaped clip which attaches to an AK-47 machine gun. A person wearing this black nylon vest could safely be assumed to be carrying four spare clips. Anita's clip pockets bulge like everyone else's; however, as she empties the contents I'm surprised to see only personal effects. This makes sense, though. If her superiors did not give her enough bullets to fill her gun, her ammo pockets or at least her spare clips must also be empty.

If she were a typical fifteen-year-old girl from California, her purse might contain a comb, a brush, gum, candy, lipstick, scribbled notes from a friend, a small wallet with pictures, spare change, and maybe her cell phone. Except for the cell phone and money, Anita's stash is the same. Instead of packing the ammunition needed in the event of a military confrontation, she possesses teenage female things.

As she folds her extra change of clothes in her backpack I notice among her personal effects a soft-cover workbook with assorted weapons and slogans written on the outside. Just as with all ELN propaganda, Che Guevara's motto is printed across the top, *Libertad o Muerte* (Freedom or Death). I ask her if I may read it and she innocently shrugs her shoulders, *"Si como no."*

I immediately recognize it to be a military field training manual with mostly hand-drawn sketches of different types of firearms and diagrams of troop positioning during firefights. It's like a game book by a football coach calling for plan A, B, C, and so forth regarding where the individual combatants are to stand, kneel, or lie according to a certain command code. I know someone of higher authority is going to walk up and snatch this away from me so I flip through as many pages as possible, scanning them for any type of relevant information.

Hoping to gain insight on the curious and contradictory behavior of my captors, I stop at the section on prisoners of war. I quickly scan as far as the directions that state not to provide information to prisoners, answer all questions with short uninformative answers, and leave the interrogation to the *Comandante*. And then suddenly the *Comandante* himself is standing in front of me. With a look of rage in his eyes, he angrily rips away the manual and reprimands Anita for allowing the *gringo* access to it. From what I quickly read, there's nothing so secret in the book, but it's clearly a breach of security by the girl. I'm sure the others will be advised to guard against the *gringo*'s trickery in the future.

HECTOR
November 25, 2001
● ● ● ● ● ● ● ● ● ●

This morning is another day of marching up yet another mountain. I don't bother asking questions about plans anymore. The rebels take too much pleasure in giving their canned response aimed to confuse and annoy me, *¿Quien sabe?* I try to confirm whatever I suspect by acting like somebody else already told me about what was happening. I casually remark to one of the friendlier rebels, "So, tonight will be much colder I suppose?" He responds with the dreaded phrase, *"Si, mas arriba, mas frio."* (Yes, more higher, more colder.) Higher in the mountains means a greater distance from civilization, evidencing their intention to keep me a prisoner for a long time. Every day that we hike farther, the odds shift more against the possibility of escape or being released. To further challenge my spirit, a new *Mondo* arrives, bringing with him the stern reality of this frustrating circumstance.

Hector is an ELN political officer. He holds the equivalent of a high school diploma and is therefore far more educated than the others. He is also a fanatical believer in Marxist doctrine and everything else his Cuban advisers have told him about the world. During early evenings, just after the last daily broadcast of what I call Radio "G," or the anti-America hour on the radio, he gathers the youngsters for long speeches presenting his interpretation of the commentator's ranting. Smarter, taller, and more muscular than the other rebels, he fits the profile of a born leader, but his rabid revolutionary jive is not well received. He goes so far overboard with his long boring speeches about subjects the youngsters can't remotely understand that he is a flop and comes across more like the bumbling Colonel Klink from television's *Hogan's Heroes* than a respected authority figure.

He orders me to sit and listen along with the others so he can have somebody to point his finger at while listing the dastardly deeds committed by *los ricos* and *las imperialistas*. We are all equally uncomfortable with this forced confrontation but none of us has a choice. Although most of the youngsters like me, none ever break rules on my behalf. They are polite young *campesinos*, curious regarding what is being said about me, but it is clear that Hector is revealing himself as the jerk.

Cuban advisers have convinced him that they've thrown off the yoke of American imperialism, replacing it with a utopian worker's paradise where everyone has plenty and there is neither corruption nor hunger. Sufficiently annoyed at his lopsided presentation of world events, I chime in, agreeing that Cuba has succeeded in overthrowing the corrupt government of Batista. However, I add that it has replaced it with the corrupt police state of Fidel Castro, providing nothing but misery and hunger for most Cubans.

I tell how, every Christmas for the last five years, I had been involved in a drug smuggling operation where some friends and I had gathered donated antibiotics from U.S. doctors to be given to Cuban hospitals — because they had none. Once, when we were caught at customs in Havana, officials seized the medicine as contraband. We later learned that customs officers had sold these confiscated medical supplies to the same doctors we were trying to give them to. Realizing that my revelation has angered Hector, I try to restate my comments by acknowledging that Castro began with good intentions but his program for social change has not worked out as expected. Too late.

Hector is still displeased with the challenge and I wonder how he will punish me for spouting off. At night there is no shelter to shield me from the early evening thundershowers, only a plastic sheet to lie on over the mud and a thin, cotton tablecloth for a cover. He thinks of a reason why he needs the plastic and takes it away, leaving me in the drenching rain with just a piece of flimsy fabric that almost covers my upper body if I curl up in a ball.

Occasionally, young *campesina* women who seem to know the guerrillas appear in camp. They never stay very long and I never see or hear any kind of sexual activity, but they are clearly each here for someone. The last two nights, a pregnant woman has walked into camp alone and spends her time with Hector. Her bulging belly indicates she is ready to give birth at any moment and it's hard to figure out where she could be walking from in her condition. The only explanation is that she must live in one of the remote rows of one-room shacks on a nearby ridge top.

I play the act-like-I-already-know game with one of the kids. "So, Hector wants to be with his wife when his child is born."

"Yes of course," he says, "that is why we are here. She is to give birth next week in the *pueblo*, San Francisco." This is rare information regarding our location and the future. I try to evaluate the significance — none, except we must be closer than I thought to a town. (It never occurred to me that, rather than marching deeper into the mountains these past few weeks, we were actually marching in long circles, only on different trails.) Like most of the actions committed so far by my captors, none of this makes sense and I try to let it pass.

DONATING MY STASH
November 26, 2001

• • • • • • • • • •

Although as a prisoner I am trapped in the violence of another nation's bitter civil war, the most disturbing experience is the heart-wrenching suffering of the mountain *campesinos*. While foraging an earth that no longer bears food for minimal survival, they are tormented from all sides. Surrounded by lurking *Paramilitare* death squads, left-wing guerrillas, and the Colombian military itself, they are punished for supporting or not supporting someone with a machine-gun-backed agenda. There is no relief, nowhere to turn, and nothing to eat.

After being captured, I managed to conceal a secret stash of 20,000-peso notes within the hidden pocket sewn inside my pants. When the opportunity arose, I moved those bills, amounting to 200 U.S. dollars, and two credit cards to the interior liner of my boots. And I constantly worry they will search me during a hand-off and find my stash. Not only will I lose a valuable bartering tool, there's no telling what the punishment would be. This cash is my emergency ticket out if I can manage to escape. It's bribe money for help to get back to the main highway through a bewildering maze of trails through a jungle too thick to pass. Each 20,000-peso note has the value of a ten-dollar bill, but here, in the poor wasteland of the Colombian countryside, it's a month's salary and can buy several sacks of rice that will mean a family can live a few more weeks. A small amount of money can spell life or death at the right moment and I have guarded my hidden stash fervently every moment — until I meet the old man at *la casa de Manuel*.

When finally leaving Manuel's house, the decrepit old grandfather (who, despite his own hopelessness, had prayed at my feet every morning) was there to say goodbye as I was being led away by the guerrillas to an unknown fate. When the guards weren't watching, I shook his shriveled trembling hand farewell and slid a folded 20,000-peso note into the top pocket of his frayed shirt, whispering to him what it was. Pathetic tears streamed from his milky brown eyes down the cracked crevices of his cheeks in a moment neither of us will ever forget. An instant later, I was led down the hillside with shrieks of the hungry child echoing through my thoughts and tearing at my guts. Had I not earlier decided to remove emotion from my head as a survival tool, I would have wept daily at the suffering I encountered in these mountains. Since that moment, I have secretly handed out the rest of the single notes along the trail to others I met dressed in the tattered rags of poverty, the uniform of the gasping desperate. I am fearful of the rebels' reaction if I am reported. Would my captors appreciate this gesture to a people they purport to defend or would they punish me for concealing money? Would they find my credit cards? I had a tough time explaining one credit card. If they find the other two I'm deliberately hiding, I'm in trouble with no explanation.

THE WOOD CARVER
November 27, 2001

● ● ● ● ● ● ● ● ● ●

Jorge is a thirty-year rebel who looks more like a country wood carver than a warrior. Although he packs a weapon, he seldom wields it, preferring to smoke his corncob pipe and whittle on small pieces of lumbar, reproducing wooden stocks for broken-down AK-47s. Aged beyond his years, with his shoulder-length brownish-gray hair pulled back in a ponytail, he has a thoughtful air about him, more of an artist with faraway gentle eyes — another victim of the ruthless tragedy of Colombia.

He too has left his home to fight on behalf of a guerrilla army in exchange for the monthly sack of rice provided to his starving family he'll likely never see again. The last thing he ever wants to do is take the life of another man, preferring first to creatively exercise his artisan skills. As a member of the ELN, his talent is regulated to replacing broken shoulder stocks on instruments designed to kill.

Like Jimmy, he displays no animosity toward me. He would rather talk about the wonders of the countryside while showing off his handiwork and demonstrate how he can hand-duplicate anything from the dried log of a hardwood tree. It's doubtful any of this proficiency will be much use in soldiering — he will likely die in his first firefight.

This afternoon, the *Comandante* has passed out treats to his troops, small plastic packages containing four thin cookies. In such a state of hunger, I can smell and see them being chewed from across the camp. One of the worst things about captivity, next to not knowing if death comes in the morning, is the constant desire for food, which is more pronounced at night when not distracted by a strenuous march or interrogations. It's miserable to feel an empty stomach rumbling in despondency while experiencing the frustration of my inability to affect my future. My misery is compounded by the knowledge that others could remedy this situation and instead watch with amusement as starvation takes its toll.

Jorge notices my reaction to seeing the cookies, and when no one is looking, tosses his packet to me with a wink and knowing smile. Almost too afraid to react, I shove the newly acquired stash into the rice sack containing my tablecloth. Fearful they will be confiscated, I take no chances and begin silently planning when to consume the cookies, one per day, late in the evening, like a midnight snack at home. Here, experiencing malnutrition, this will be a feast, lasting four nights, eight if I opt to break each one in half.

In case this is a trick, I move the prized stockpile twice during the day and once tonight in anticipation of how and when to consume these meager morsels of a majestic banquet. I have thought all day how to eat each candied wafer, one little crunchy bite at a time, savoring every individual grain before swallowing it.

Directly after the midnight light-in-the-face check, I reach behind a board where the coveted treasure lies hidden. Carefully separating the plastic end of the packet so as to be able to fold it back for resealing, I bite off a small corner of the sugary cookie expecting a radiant burst of sweetened delight. Instead, suddenly my face and hands burn as though caught in a fire. Even the inside of my mouth rages in acidic fury.

Holding my hands up to the moonlight for inspection, I see they are covered by hundreds of tiny ants and expect my face and mouth to look the same. The packet is also filled with the milling critters slowly devouring my dream feast.

Insect stings and bites are nothing new, candied cookies are. After wiping and brushing away most of the minuscule blistering fiends, I hold up each captured cookie, gently blowing off the rest to unknown fate, but not blowing so hard as to disturb any loosened grains of sugar. Everything counts in the jungle.

RELEASED?
November 28, 2001
● ● ● ● ● ● ● ● ● ● ●

The rebels roust me earlier than normal this morning. *Vamos!* As I begin organizing my few possessions into the rice sack, I'm told that I won't need them — they will be brought to me later. They keep telling me to hurry, skipping morning rice. I notice that the rest of the camp stays behind as four guerrillas escort me out, instead of the usual twenty or so. Is this another mind game? Am I being led to execution? I try to quiet my thoughts from the frightening possibilities.

Acting like I know what's up, I say, "So today is the big day."

"Yes, the big day for you and we must hurry or miss the Red Cross helicopter."

I try to bury my exaltation, "A helicopter for me? Why?"

"You are free, you may go now."

Sgt. Gonzales had told me earlier that the procedure for releasing foreigners is different from Colombians. They always send for a Red Cross team with helicopters because of the Geneva Convention regulations covering prisoner-of-war exchanges. It is, of course, laughable that they would suddenly abide by international protocol. Still their remarks sound encouraging.

"When and where is this chopper coming?" A foolish question.

"*¿Quien sabe?* Hurry or we will miss them."

As they run me breathlessly through the mountains, prompting me to speed up, I think about what I will do with my freedom tonight. My mind spins dangerously out of the control. I have been fighting hard to keep from building hope that they could later devastate me with, yet this seems real. I am nearly free. I think ahead to the first thing to do when I'm free. A phone call home to tell everyone that I'm still alive. Then a meal of roasted chicken, and maybe a beer. I have not dared dream of these things during the last few weeks for fear of letting my captors break me with disappointment. I struggle to remind myself: if they can get me to anticipate and then jerk away hope, they can push me over the edge.

We reach the base of a towering plateau as I collapse panting with a pounding heart on overload, my scrawny legs giving out beneath. Another step is unthinkable.

"Hurry," the rebels yell. "Hurry, or you will miss *La Cruz Roja* helicopter and they will not return for many weeks." This energizes my spirit enough for a final lung-burning sprint to the top where I imagine rescuers are waiting to fly me to freedom. I believe for certain that fate has reversed its course and this misery is moments from ending.

Once in the clearing of the plateau, I spot guerrillas we had left behind at the last *ranchita* this morning lounging around a camp that appears to have been set up hours ago. I suspect they have just sadistically run me in circles the last several hours for entertainment purposes, quietly snickering, amused by my wild-eyed stare at the sky. I strain to hear the whomp whomp whomp of the chopper.

For hours I gaze upward, desperate with hope as well as panic, while the afternoon's charcoal storm clouds roll in over the tops of distant peaks. Knowing well no aircraft will attempt to fly in this weather, I nevertheless keep thinking they might still arrive at the last second and whisk me to freedom. As darkness fills the countryside, smothering the last embers of hope, I'm still trying to believe rescuers will appear. Maybe they have lights . . .

Somewhere around midnight, during the fading hours of woeful rain, I crouch under a tree pulling my small tablecloth over my head in a futile attempt to stay dry the rest of the night. There's so much I want to know, but I still refuse to ask questions. I've learned that in captivity, hunger for information leads to an uncontrollable slide down the dangerous slippery slope of anticipation.

ANOTHER CHANCE
November 29, 2001
• • • • • • • • • •

This morning the rebels apologize and acknowledge there was confusion about where to go for the pickup yesterday but it's all straightened out now. We must hustle to another landing site before afternoon or we will miss the helicopter again. As proof of their sincerity, they offer a second cup of morning rice. This is peculiar behavior, yet so were most of their actions in the past. It must mean I'm being released and they want me to appear healthy and happy. I eagerly attempt to eat the rice but, because my stomach has shrunk so much, I cannot finish. I wad the leftovers into a ball and stuff it in my pocket for later. At noon, they give me an unheard-of midday offering of rice, which increases the certainty they intend to free me.

They also change the marching sequence, with twenty rebels strung out along the trail a hundred feet apart, ahead and behind, apparently a precaution in case of military ambush. Since the procedure changed so radically, I believe that something is finally going to happen, and this is how releases are handled when a government double-cross is a possibility. Both sides are wary of each other, that's why they use a neutral entity like the Red Cross for prisoner exchanges. Everyone trusts the Red Cross.

In early evening, after another grueling climb, we arrive at another plateau — it's the same routine, no chopper. Again I pace foolishly, searching the sky to no avail while they set up camp and cook their dinner. I try to stay calm and resist thinking about if a chopper is really coming. It's useless. I cannot take my eyes off the sky. Once more at midnight, I huddle underneath the tablecloth, sleepless with gut-churning anticipation, still straining to hear the sound of an approaching aircraft.

THE DECISION
November 30, 2001
• • • • • • • • • • •

This morning, to convince me of their remorsefulness, apologetic guerrillas offer me a fried egg. I think, "Where the hell did they get an egg in the middle of the jungle?" I suspect that it's part of the game but stuff it into my mouth before someone else has the chance to take it away. They tell me to relax, there will be another at noon if I want one. The abrupt increase in protein causes a spontaneous, piercing, painful stomach reaction. My bowels burn to be emptied as fast as I wolfed down the egg and must run to dig a hole.

After another bogus explanation regarding the Red Cross getting the landing location confused due to poor radio communications, they swear everything is confirmed. They insist with numerous apologies that I will be in Medellín within hours, enticing me to run again to another plateau for a certain rendezvous. Once more, an empty landing field and, once more, I pace with insane bewilderment through the knee-high grass of the clearing, frantically scanning the sky for some tiny speck to grow into a helicopter. My ears are aching to hear anything mechanical. There is only the incessant roar of buzzing insects pulsating in my head. I'm losing control and babble questions like a wild-eyed madman, only to receive the standard response with a familiar smirk, *¿Quien sabe?* The enemy is enjoying the show — the big *gringo* is going down.

Anna, the female rebel who previously befriended me and is now an outcast amongst her own kind, sees me starting to crack. She risks sharing information that she overheard: a decision has been made to free me. She's certain, but does not know when. Probably in a few months when I look better and my wounds heal. I suspect it might be Christmas, but that's almost a month away. I'm not sure I can make it that long.

I test her, saying, "I already know I am being freed because my friend has sold my tractor and paid the ransom."

"No," she says, "there has been no ransom paid, it was a political decision."

I argue, "I am positive a ransom was paid."

She reveals this is why the guerrillas are so angry. They are trying to crack me mentally, because they must give me back without payment. They resent this decision by the political wing but will eventually follow orders. She tells me to be careful because bad things are planned and there is great danger. And although the rebels reluctantly agreed to my release, they intend to give back their prisoner as an empty shell, a body with no mind left. There is trouble ahead.

While mentally playing back past details, it's clear that for the last month, I have been a victim of intense psychological as well as physical assault. From the starvation intended to control me, to the marching in circles to disorient me, and now the final blow, head games to destroy my sense of belief — promises of being freed that are inexplicably reversed. What is happening? I have no military background or experience of such tactics and no idea how to deal with them. There has been a game plan all along. Nothing was an accident. Everything they said and did had a purpose, the ultimate aim to weaken my resolve, to empty me to the core. This goes beyond struggles over political ideology or defending the downtrodden; this is malicious evil.

The terrorists no longer conceal their amusement. The game is out in the open as they mock and imitate the muttering, crazy-eyed *gringo*. My best hope is that they will release me in the next few months but want to push me over the edge first. I have known since the beginning of my captivity the older guerrillas wanted to kill me but were held off by their more rational superiors who realized my value alive. I knew little for certain and nothing made clear sense. Did they buy my story of being a writer who came looking for them? If so, why mistreat someone who is going to write about your cause? Did they believe my claim of personal poverty? They had to know my expenses for the trip were more than they would earn in a lifetime. I doubt my government had a hand in any of this, yet all signs still point to an impending release.

Because they offer so much food while continuing to antagonize me with tortuous mind games, I believe Anna is right. They intend to give me back in good physical shape but mentally broken. It's apparent they will comply with some type of political bargain to free the *Americano*. When and why is still unknown. Whatever it is, I'm certain they will get the best of the deal, but I will not make it easy for them. I still hold the most powerful card — my breathing body.

Tonight, I make a dead-serious decision. I will fight back with my only weapon — my life. The fun is over for them. I will starve myself to death and take away their token. Dead *gringos* have no value and I become determined to game these sons of bitches right back, even with my life if necessary. I still don't know why they want me alive, only that it is important to them that I appear well. This is the only explanation for the extra food being offered.

I have no idea what's happening in the outside world. I had heard almost no news on the way down to South America except that Uncle Sam was talking about invading Afghanistan in search of a man named Osama bin Laden. I don't know if World War Three is in progress or if I'm being used against my government for political purposes. I am now positive of one thing for certain — this particular game is over. It's time to call their bluff. I inform them, due to my worsening prostate cancer, I can't eat any more.

FIGHTING BACK
December 1, 2001
● ● ● ● ● ● ● ● ● ●

It's poker time this morning. The rebels bring another egg along with a big bowl of rice. I smile politely and tell them, "Because of my worsening medical condition, without proper medicine, I will be unable to eat." They don't believe me and say, "We'll see about that later."

At noon, they offer me food again, this time canned sardines. Again I refuse. Two decades ago as part of kung fu meditation training, I had fasted for extended periods, twice for ten days in a row. On a self-imposed fast, the first three days are the hardest. After that, the appetite diminishes and hunger pangs subside. Humans can survive without food for up to a month, depending on their original condition. However, mine is poor at the moment and I'm beginning this fast already suffering from malnutrition. Yet I am confident that I can last up to ten days by maintaining fluids.

I have insisted all along that without special medicine available only in the U.S., I would soon die from prostate cancer. There are no outward signs to persuade them of this; they have no reason to believe it. It's time to become more convincing with a more graphic display. To prove I am dying, I must figure a method to draw blood from my own body without leaving detectable marks. If they find a cut vein or open wound, my plan won't succeed. I need to show blood coming from inside my urinary tract.

Tonight, I make a second decision there will be no backing away from. I will slide a metal key up my nose into my sinuses and pound on my face to cause the blood flow necessary to implement my plan. Yet this is easier said than done. To remain undetected, I must do this between fifteen-minute light-in-the-face checks and then clean myself before they notice what actually happened.

At first I wimp out and just wiggle the key around, scraping inside my nasal passages until I sneeze so much I fear arousing suspicion from the guards. I then try tapping lightly on my nose with the key wedged up inside. None of this works and I soon realize it will be necessary to smack myself hard with a fist to get what I'm after. Whack!

As the blood dribbles from my nose, I carefully direct it down around the crotch of my pants. I will claim to be urinating blood at night because of my prostate cancer and losing blood fast. The stakes are high but my mind is made up — let me go or I will die here in this jungle and my value will evaporate. I must convince them whatever deal they made will collapse without me alive. I'm no longer afraid. My attitude has changed. Now, I'm daring them to fuck with me more.

In the morning they notice the dried blood on my crotch and ask what happened. I reply nonchalantly, "*¿Quien sabe?*"

The tables are turning. For the next several meal times when they

approach with real food, it's the same response: *"No puedo comer."*
(I cannot eat.)

SANGRE
December 2, 2001
● ● ● ● ● ● ● ● ● ●

This is the second day without food. They continue to tempt me
with eggs and canned sardines. But I've dug my heels in and have
considered if I'm really ready to die here, in this jungle. I am. There's
no question, the party is over for them and it's become their turn to
worry. I'm gambling this will hurt them worse than me. The only
way to regain control is to sabotage my own health.

Again, I ram the key up my nose at night, letting them notice
blood on my pants in the morning. I hear them mumble nervously
amongst themselves about *"sangre"* (blood) and later almost in
panic on their radios reporting, *"Sangre."*

It's now they who are concerned about my well-being. I consider
the irony. Only days ago I was struggling to stay alive and now with
the turn of events, I welcome death — the last weapon against my
captors. It's my turn to enjoy the show. Fuck them, I am ready.

SUSANNA
December 3, 2001
● ● ● ● ● ● ● ● ● ●

It's another key-up-the-nose night with plenty of convincing blood
in the morning. I must do this work after dark so they won't be able
to check my story by looking on the ground for blood mixed with
my urine. The evening storms must have washed it away. So far they
have not suspected I am causing my own bleeding, I still must be
cautious. If they discover my ruse, this whole effort will be in vain
and this situation will flip around worse than ever. I shudder to think

of what the retaliation would entail.

An ELN field doctor named Susanna was called in for an opinion and to persuade me to try and eat — I still refuse. She is not a real doctor, but probably took a college nursing course so she has some idea of what is happening to me physically. She is a compassionate person, another true believer in the rebel cause who wants to take part but without a weapon. She wants to assist by saving lives, not taking them, and I do my best to exploit that. She is kind and caring, trying to persuade me to accept the IV she has brought. I refuse.

Outside the abandoned *ranchita* we are holed up in there is an orange orchard grown wild, and upon Anna's request, younger rebels bring freshly squeezed orange juice. She mixes it with an electrolyte packet from her medical kit, pleading with me to take a sip. I'm thirsty and gulp it down but the salty liquid tastes so foul I immediately throw up. She confers with a particularly mean *Comandante* who has often gone out of his way to express his deranged hatred for *gringos*. His preference all along was to not just execute me, but to do it slowly. Now he has the duty to keep me alive. It is my turn to enjoy the show.

The asshole *Comandante* stomps over barking at me that I must comply because if I don't eat or take an IV, I will die. Looking upward from laying on the ground, I reply smiling, *"Es su problema, no es mio."* (That's your problem, not mine.) This is my first open challenge to the rebels — there is no turning back now. The gauntlet has been thrown down. Someone must back down and it isn't going to be me. He is furious, fingering the trigger on his machine gun. I know he longs to shoot me but instead stomps out yelling words I can't understand. I'm now more certain than ever that they must release me, yet still suspect that is not going to happen for a few more months. Their timing won't work for me; I made a commitment I won't back off from. Freedom will be under my terms and immediate. I've dug in my heels with no intention of allowing them to drag this out. It is now or never.

I know the hell my loved ones are going through at home, uncertain if I'm dead or alive. This is my greatest burden but also my stimulus to see things through to the end. My suffering is nothing, theirs is everything. I do this for them as well. I will bring things to a head one way or another and on my terms. I have rolled the dice. If I lose, this nightmare will be over within days but their agony of not knowing will end. I have no doubts. I am ready to die. These terrorists will have no more fun with me. Dead Americans have no value and I will take that advantage from them with a smile.

STOPPED FLUIDS
December 4, 2001
● ● ● ● ● ● ● ● ● ●

The sharp burning hunger pangs subside. The rebels can no longer tempt me with food. Everything is no longer going according to plan for them. Now, it is they who are panicked. Fretting guerrillas continually huddle to confer with Susanna about my worsening condition. Throughout captivity I have used my martial arts background to find the ability to survive in manners other than physical combat. My strategy comes down to applying the principles of judo; yielding, then passively using their energy to defeat them.

Susanna, the make-believe doctor, is increasingly worried, checking on me every half hour. We have built a trust and I am tempted to ask her to pass a message. I want my loved ones to know what has happened here in this faraway jungle in case I don't survive. At every opportunity thus far, I have scraped or scratched my name and country on every possible surface from wood to cement in hopes that someday another English-speaking hostage will read it and live to communicate to someone that I had made it that far.

I still have not seen myself in a mirror yet I know I must look bad. In contrast to my health, my thinking has never been clearer. The time I spend each day in breathing exercises and long meditation takes me deeper than ever before — it's like a drug-induced high. This morning, I have decided to accelerate the process and kick things up a notch. I begin refusing fluids. Today I passively look forward to death.

FADING
December 5, 2001
● ● ● ● ● ● ● ● ● ●

The negative effects of fasting have set in, manifesting themselves in shallow breathing and listlessness. Time is running out. I'm losing my vision and begin to hallucinate. Two new nurses are summoned from a small *pueblo* nearby and arrive on foot. They too argue with me to accept an IV. At one point they attempt to hold me down and force a needle into the back of my wrist, a needle they have already dropped several times on the urine-stained floor. I fight against this treatment, telling them I will only pull it out later. I still don't know why I suddenly have such value to the guerrillas, only that I must do the opposite of what they want. The tables are turning but this fight is far from over. There are no negative emotions remaining. I have no anger or hatred. I have no fear. I can only wait to see how the dice land.

ROBERTO
December 6, 2001
● ● ● ● ● ● ● ● ● ●

This morning I have a visitor — Roberto, a tall, slender, almost dapper young man from the ELN political wing in Medellín, a civilian commander who has been sent to interview me. With his groomed appearance, he looks as though he recently graduated from college, plainly not a killer. I note that when we shake hands, he has the soft delicate fingers of a city boy, not the hearty, muscular grip of a rugged mountain *campesino*. The black uniform he wears can't be his, as his tall, lanky frame leaves eight-inch gaps on the cuffs of his ankles and wrists. He looks out of place toting a machine gun. I doubt he has ever fired one.

He is apologetic about what has happened to me and is surprised when I relate details of the abuse. Although he stares in disbelief, I doubt he is unaware of the atrocities committed by his own team as well as his enemies. No matter the murders and robberies committed by his colleagues, he surely thinks his side is justified in doing whatever they claim is necessary. He is just another ELN true believer, one of the young idealists who are convinced that this forty-year civil war has a chance of being won.

"Look at me, Roberto, look at what your friends have done. Is this what your revolution is about? Is this how you help the poor people of Colombia? Will you change the conscience of the world by abusing an American?" My words bother him greatly when he is compelled to face me. He looks away, casting his eyes downward. Without speaking, he stands and walks out of the room. Later after a conference with the *Comandante* and others, he rides out of camp on a mule escorted by guards.

After he's gone, Susanna kneels next to me and, taking my hand, explains that a decision has been made to free me in two days. I don't believe her because she knows about the rebels' previous tricks of false releases. I insist it is only another lie to try and break me.

She touches my face telling me, "No, Glen, if Roberto said it will happen, it will happen exactly as he says, Roberto does not lie." In a precarious state of wobbling sanity, I cannot risk believing her.

Yet I think even if this is true, two days is too long. In this rapidly deteriorating state, I will be dead or at the very least, unable to walk. Susanna has grown to like me and walks out hiding her tears. I no longer stare into the face of death. I am in the embrace of it.

Tonight I pound on my face harder than ever, and the blood flows so intensely I fear it won't stop and I'll be discovered. After squirting as much as possible all over my clothes, I carefully wipe my face clean and lean my head back just when the guards arrive for the face check. I resist gagging as warm, metal-tasting fluid flows down the back of my throat. I think about this being all I had to eat or drink in nearly a week — my own blood.

A MULE RIDE
December 7, 2001
• • • • • • • • • •

This morning my pants and shirt are crusted and stained with blood. The filthy cement room is filled with buzzing flies as panicking rebels chatter on the radio, and I lay still, no longer able to move. Susanna removes my boots and strips me naked to wash my clothes. She whispers to me while scrubbing the caked blood off my body, "Today you will go to the highway — tonight, Medellín. *La Cruz Roja estan esperando.*" (The Red Cross is waiting.)

I can't reply and stare blankly into the wall. I've nothing left to say.

The furious *Comandante* storms in shouting *"Vamos!"* I refuse to acknowledge him. He only repeats the command louder, *"Vamos!"*

I manage a smug whisper, *"No puedo caminar."* (I cannot walk.) He is infuriated at my insolence and even more enraged realizing that he must now carry me out. I left California two and a half months earlier a lean, muscular 220 pounds. I have now deteriorated physically to a scrawny image of my former self and no longer have the strength to rise.

Four young guerrillas gather and forcibly stand me up to carry me outside where a mule is waiting. *"¿Y mis cosas?"* (And my things?) I ask.

"You won't need them. You are going to the highway."

I still refuse to believe anything they say.

I'm led away alone by a bitter *Comandante* who clearly hates me the most. And no one is following us. The rebels almost never moved me before without a dozen troops ahead and behind. If they are going to shoot me, they will not let the younger rebels witness it. I see none of the kids around and assume I'm off for execution. Yet I no longer care. These terrorists will get no more satisfaction from me. Whoever is in line to pull the trigger, I will spit in his face before he shoots.

But the scenario changes as hidden lookouts posted along the camp exit fall in line one by one while we tediously trek up and down the steep, rocky hillsides. Soon, a full escort team is marching ahead and behind. After a few hours on the trail, far below in the distance, I spot a dirt road next to a slow running river. Suspecting another deception, I still refuse to believe this means release.

As we approach a fork in the trail, one path leads up, *mas arriba*, and the other down, *mas abajo*, toward the road below and a likely course to freedom. After a few more steps, we veer to the left, taking the high road, higher still, moving farther away from the highway. My plan failed — damn it, that's the way it goes. No one has spoken yet and I refuse to ask questions. I just keep trudging along using what's left of my strength to cling to the laboring mule. No longer afraid, I will deal with whatever happens — one way or another, an end is coming soon.

An hour later, as we clear a bend in the trail that looks strangely familiar, I look down into a dirt clearing below and see a white four-wheel-drive wagon with a huge red cross painted on the roof and another on the door. Too afraid to believe what I see, I halt the mule and turn my back on this scene. Fighting my own heart, I stare into the eyes of my captors and plead with a cracking voice, "Don't do this to me, I know this is a trick."

Misty-eyed and trembling, I try to force the mule back up the trail from where we came — but one of the guerrillas grabs the reins and pulls us down the path toward the clearing. Suddenly, I recognize the spot; it's the same place where weeks before I had seen the rusty blue pickup unloading *campesinos*. This is the location of their supply depot that earlier I had tried to memorize.

There are a hundred armed rebels visible on the hillsides and surrounding the Red Cross vehicle. I try to dismount with dignity but fall off, collapsing squarely on my face. As I lie there for a moment, a familiar voice sharply orders troops standing nearby to help me to my feet. I look up to see *Mondo* Jimmy, with eyes as watery as mine.

Without a word, we face each other and shake hands in the shoulder clasp of the Latin embrace. Only weeks before, each of us could have been compelled to take the other's life. The unanswered question will always be, if it came down to it, would either of us have pulled the trigger? In the depths of my heart, I believe that in another setting, in another time, and without this pitiful war, we would have been brothers.

A beautiful, clear-skinned young woman wearing street clothes and wire-framed glasses, walks up holding a clipboard to her chest and introduces herself with a heavy Italian accent. "Hello Glen, my name is Anna Lisa Di Paola, I am a delegate from the International Committee of the Red Cross, and I am here to take you to Medellín, where a representative of your government is waiting to take you home." Musical words I will never forget.

She explains it will be a few minutes before we can leave because the guerrillas must give their final permission and the *Comandante* needs to sign documents relating to prisoner-of-war exchanges. As I stand in their midst, dazed and shaking, I realize that I have allowed hope to coax me beyond the point of no return. I still don't know if this is a trick. If it is, this will push me over the edge that I've been clinging to by my fingertips for much too long.

There are a dozen guerrillas between the wagon and where we stand. As they help me stagger forward, I recognize them one by one as the young teenage rebels who had befriended me at one time or another. As I pass them I hear *"Un buen Americano."* Yes, I think, clenching my jaw with determination, I am a good American.

Finally the order is given permitting us to leave. It's an hour ride on a long and rough dirt road to the paved road through the ELN-controlled countryside. And then, another eternity, an additional hour and a half to Medellín on the main highway through dreaded FARC-held territory.

I babble like a paranoid lunatic, worried we will be stopped and taken prisoner again. Anna Lisa assures me, pointing to her Red Cross identification dangling from her neck, that we are safe and that all the warring factions respect the neutrality of the Red Cross. She insists the FARC have been notified that a prisoner is being released and that commanders have granted permission for safe passage. There is still the chance that the *Paramilitare* will get wind of this procedure and take the opportunity to shoot us and blame the guerrillas. We are far from safe. I ramble incoherently, unable to drink from the water bottle the driver has passed to me. All I can think about is getting to a phone.

This morning FARC rebels blew up the bridge leading back to Bogotá in an effort to prove to the government that they have the power to control the highways. We have only one possible direction, northwest, yet it is a long road ahead. As we reach the outer mountain rim above Medellín, I still hold delusional suspicions this is a ruse. Not until we pull up to the Red Cross Center and pass through the steel-barred gates do I believe it is real. I am free.

"Mr. Heggstad, are you sure you don't want to go to a hospital?"

"No, absolutely not, but may I use your phone?"

I dial my friend Susan Aldridge at the only number I can remember, forgetting it's after-hours at her office. Her answering service responds by putting me on hold. There are several people waiting in line to use the phone. A static-shrouded voice comes on the line asking what message I have.

"My name is Glen Heggstad and this is an emergency, can you patch me through to the house?"

"What kind of emergency? Is this a medical emergency?"

"Ma'am, I am calling from Medellín, Colombia, and it's urgent I be transferred to the house immediately."

"What is your message you want conveyed?"

Before I can answer, she says, "Please hold." Click.

The line to use the phone is growing longer.

The voice returns, "Okay, now who did you want to speak with?"

"Ma'am, this is an emergency, I need to . . ."

"You'll have to speak to my supervisor, please hold."

I hang up.

I'm introduced to other Red Cross personnel and profusely thank everyone for their help. They send a volunteer out to buy fresh clothes for me and he returns with a shirt, sized medium. I entered the jungle wearing a double X yet think, "At least it's clean." I try it on. It's a perfect fit.

A Red Cross office worker enters the room and says, "Glen, there is a telephone call for you from the U.S. You can take it in there."

It's Brad Neste. With my hands trembling to hold the phone, I am elated to hear his voice and, while fighting back tears, try to joke with him about my exciting vacation. After a moment of small talk he raises the subject that is on both our minds, "In case you're wondering — don't worry brother, another bike is on its way. It will be air freighted into Quito, Ecuador, next week." Brad had a plan in mind the whole time and was just waiting to hear I was alive and free to put it in motion. He never asked whether I wanted to continue my journey or not. As my brother, he knew it for certain.

After a few more calls from California, Joe Gallagher gets through from Bogotá. He informs me that the Colombian Federal Police have ordered his deportation at the prompting of Uncle Sam. We are only hours apart, but the officials in charge will not allow us a visit together. The emotion between us is so overwhelming maybe that's a good thing.

The Red Cross personnel, disappointed I refused hospitalization, try to feed me.

"What would you like to eat, Glen?"

"Chicken! Yes, I would like some chicken, if possible, *pollo asado*."

After a half hour they bring me a whole roasted chicken, which I find impossible to eat. I cannot even drink plain water yet.

A senior Red Cross official informs me, "We do have a problem though; the DAS (Colombian Federal Secret Police) want to interview you and have requested that you be brought to their headquarters. We have informed them that you are in no condition to be moved and they said then they will come here. We are sorry Glen, but this is still Colombia and we must abide by their laws."

A four-person team of stone-faced Colombian Feds arrives carrying tape recorders, photo albums, and an antique typewriter. First, I'm fingerprinted, photographed, and handed Spanish-language documents to sign that I don't understand. Yet I am too dazed to argue.

The older Red Cross lady grows angry with them for coercing me in my weakened state into signing statements I can't read, and orders a translation. There are harsh words between them in Spanish — she stands her ground.

After these pleasantries, the Feds demand information. Between their abusive attitude and my desire to speak to a representative of my government first, I politely decline to cooperate. "Sorry guys, I can't seem to remember much. Maybe things will come back to me later." At this moment I'm having trouble telling the good guys from the bad guys.

A Colombian family that Joe had met while searching for me arrives asking if they can take me home with them for a few days to recover. Red Cross personnel again deliver bad news. "We are very sorry Glen, but according to international law, when a foreign prisoner is released to our custody, we cannot legally release that person to anyone other than official government representatives of that country."

"In other words, I am still a prisoner?"

"Well, only in theory. It is a long drive to the airport where U.S. Embassy officials have sent a plane with FBI agents to take you back to Bogotá. However, if you insist, we could slow down and allow you to flee. We must advise you though, without a passport, documents, or money, you won't get far and most likely be arrested by DAS who, at this moment, are lurking outside."

A four-man FBI release team is waiting at the Medellín airport as promised and official documents of transfer are signed. Once again, I'm in the custody of someone who carries a gun.

It's a sad farewell to the Red Cross delegates, especially Anna Lisa. I tell her that someday, somewhere she will need me and I will always drop whatever I am doing and be there for her no matter the circumstance. I give her my contact numbers and a double long good-bye hug. I will always remember her voice, her eyes, and her spirit.

It's a silent flight back to Bogotá on the embassy plane with somber federal cops declining to speak. I feel like I've been arrested. Cops find it hard to relax and be themselves around non-cops unless they're friends or family, so we stick with the cops and robber thing.

They are neither kind nor unkind and refuse to answer any of my questions. I thought I left that crap behind in the jungle.

Once the plane lands in Bogotá, we are transferred to a secure area of the airport. "Have a seat here, Glen. We're going to ask you a few questions and show you some photos and then a plane will take you back to the U.S."

"The U.S.?"

"Yes, we have arranged a flight home for you."

"Thanks guys, but that's not where I want to go."

Amused and curious they ask, "Really now, where is it you would like to go?"

With a crazed look in my eye I state, "I am going back after my fucking motorcycle and finishing my fucking ride to fucking Argentina."

"No, you will be on a flight to California in a few hours."

"No I won't. I am continuing my journey."

"That's impossible. You have no documents, passport, or money."

"I will have money wired and get a new passport issued at the Embassy."

"The Embassy won't issue you a new passport."

"Only because you won't let them."

Now they patronize me. "Just relax Glen, in a few hours a nice big airplane will be here to take you home to see some friendly doctors. You need to be in a hospital."

"Fuck you, I am tired of guys with guns telling me what to do and I'm walking out of here right fucking now. If you don't like it, shoot me in the back."

I barge past the Feds and exit the airport security area hobbling with my walking stick down the tarmac like a wild man.

"Okay, okay! Come back inside and we'll talk this over. We just thought you were a little crazy and didn't know what you want to do."

"I am fucking crazy but I still know what I want to do. I'm going to continue my ride and finish what I started out to do — period."

The best way to give the middle finger to the ELN and show the world that terrorism against Americans doesn't work is to finish my ride after they tried so hard to break my spirit and destroy me. Because UPI and Reuters are covering this story, it's being published in almost every major newspaper in the world. I feel that how I handle this situation will be the ultimate statement. I cannot give in and return home. It will destroy me as a man.

I ask them, "I am an American, you are Americans. Why the fuck aren't you helping me? Can't you see, if I give up now and run home, they win?"

They seem to agree and ask me once more, "Are you sure this is what you want to do?"

"Fucking A."

"All right Glen, we'll help you, but you must promise not to go back after your bike and you must stay in a major city until you depart Colombia. Deal?"

"Deal!"

After this, the FBI agents make phone calls rousting Embassy personnel to meet us at midnight. They pool their money and give me a temporary loan until funds can be wired down from home. The head of American Services from the Embassy also says, "When we open Monday, we will issue an expedited passport to you within hours but you must not go out on the streets of Bogotá until then. If you are stopped by the DAS, they will arrest you for not having identification. You must understand, they want you out of the country immediately, and we are pushing things with them by allowing you to stay."

For security reasons, a passport is essential to rent a hotel room anywhere in Colombia, and even the FBI can't do anything about this. I remind them that the last hotel I stayed in might still have my passport number on file and we should try that one. It works.

Once in my hotel room I cannot accept a real bed to sleep on, a television, and no threat of execution in the morning. I spend the next three nights locking myself in a closet, rolled up in a ball, beating on my own head trying to restore my senses. I know this will be a long road home.

Embassy of the United States of America

Bogotá, D.C., Colombia

December 11, 2001

To Whom It May Concern:

    This is to document the fact that American citizen Glen Paul Heggstad, born May 24, 1952, in California, the United States of America, was a kidnap victim in Colombia during the period of November 6, 2001, through December 7, 2001.

    According to information available to this Embassy, Mr. Heggstad entered Colombia on November 2, 2001, at the international airport in Bogotá, arriving from Panama on Copa Airlines flight 101. Mr. Heggstad departed Bogotá on or about November 6, on his motorcycle, en route to Medellin. Before arriving in Medellin he was stopped on the road by persons presumed to be members of the Ejercito de Liberacion Nacional, who took him captive. He was separated from his motorcycle and from all his other belongings. He was held captive in various locations until he was released in a rural location in Antioquia Department on December 7. Personnel of this Embassy brought Mr. Heggstad to Bogotá that evening. On December 10 this Embassy issued Mr. Heggstad a new U.S. passport to replace the one that was taken from him by his captors. The whereabouts of his motorcycle and other personal possessions are unknown.

    The Embassy would appreciate any courtesies extended to Mr. Heggstad by the authorities of Colombia in facilitating and permitting his departure from Colombia.

Sincerely,

Thomas G. Rogan
Consul

According to Embassy personnel, there has never been a released hostage who wanted to remain in the country of his capture. Everyone else wanted to be on the first plane out. They are not prepared to deal with me. There is no help from either government or anyone else in Colombia. I must contend with the psychological aftermath of the last five weeks alone, in a foreign country, 5,000 miles from home. I vacillate in and out of reality, constantly fearing I will wake up back in the jungle.

The press, apparently hungry for interviews, finally locates me through email. I grant two, to UPI and Reuters, with the condition that my face will not be shown on Colombian television. My statement is that I will continue the ride to the tip of South America and back to California as planned and will not back off because of a cheap terrorist game. (The next morning at breakfast, to my horror, the entire television interview was being aired locally, which would certainly enrage the ELN.)

In spite of needing to wander the streets, I stick to my promise not to venture out. From the hotel computer, I log onto Earthlink and discover thousands of letters of support from around the planet overloading the mailbox. Not only are folks from home standing behind me, the rest of the world is on board also, with lengthy essays on what my decision means to them in their personal lives. The return addresses are from as far away as the Middle East to China and Europe. I'm stunned at the outpouring; email rolls in as fast as I can read it.

A pledge to continue the journey is an easy statement to make. Now, I must re-outfit for my one-man motorcycle expedition while low on cash, thousands of miles from home, and with no help in this hemisphere. I must also consider my physical and psychological status and how to cope with the pressures ahead. In the most troubling time of my life, I am alone, with no friends around to help me return from the madness. (So physically weakened, it would take nearly a week just to be able to walk a city block without passing out, and several more just to build up the strength to balance a motorcycle.)

While sitting down to dinner in this same hotel where I slept the night before my fateful ride to Medellín, I encounter a waiter in the restaurant who speaks of Joe. "A few weeks ago there was a man here looking for you. A big man," he said in Spanish, waving his arms. "Every day he came to this restaurant and sat in that seat over there. If the seat was occupied, he waited until it was empty. He would then sit in that chair with tears in his eyes staring at the flyers in his hand with a picture of a man on a motorcycle." It was the same seat I occupied while eating breakfast November 6, 2001, just before rolling for Medellín.

PERSERVERANCE

Great powers aid those who struggle hard.

COLOMBIA

FEELIN' GOOD
December 16, 2001

● ● ● ● ● ● ● ● ● ● ●

When released from the guerrillas, half dead, to the custody of the Red Cross on December 10, 2001, I had only the clothes on my back. Everything else — motorcycle, passport, travel documents, medical supplies, tools, guidebook, maps, GPS, camera, laptop computer, and money — had been stolen. Thanks to FBI agents providing a loan, I am able to rent a room and feed myself for a few days until I can arrange for money to be wired from home. The credit cards that I kept stashed in the liner of my boot during the rebel ordeal are useless because the friction from constant hiking rubbed off both the magnetic strip across the back and raised plastic numbers.

The good news is that an agreement has been signed in Havana between the ELN and the Colombian Government for a Christmas cease-fire. My release is the gesture on behalf of the ELN; we don't know what the government gives up. Because of comments from the Red Cross, I suspect there is a deal involving the release of some ELN prisoners. It's doubtful the truce will hold much past New Year's and even if it does, there are other rebel factions harder to deal with, and separate treaties need to be reached with them.

Every day I awake in my new surroundings feeling as though I'm returning from the dead. It's still difficult to accept freedom — too painful to risk completely believing. I fear that any moment I'm about to awaken from a dream and in reality am still being held in the jungle. It's difficult to distinguish what's real, and I wonder if the current events are merely my final moments flashing before me as a bullet has been fired into my head. At times I'm uncertain if I'm even alive.

Jimmy, Brad, and Brian have been working around the clock prepping the new bike to airfreight to Ecuador. In an effort to restore me, they duplicate everything as it had been before, right down to the last detail of the homemade aluminum tail box containing my electronic gear. They insist on identical equipment as a symbolic gesture to put me back together again just as I was. They team up to accomplish in three days what took Jimmy and I sixty. The commitment and dedication of the boys back home causes such an emotional reaction in me that I cannot speak about it.

John Cockrell, president of the Guilty Clothing Corporation and faithful judo student, handles shipping arrangements for the replacement bike. My motorcycle riding and martial arts buddy, Loren Gallagher, who also helped me edit this journal, supplies the latest Sony digital camera. And my old pal Tex Earnhardt, who is indirectly responsible for some of the wild stuff I do by often egging me on, has a new laptop on the way. My senior black belt students, Daniel McCown, Anthony Montanona, and Hushang Shahidi, step up to the plate and keep the judo school running on track, probably better than when I was there. The last hurdle seems to be the complicated importation procedure in Quito. Customs there have a bad reputation and I anticipate several days of bureaucratic snafu.

OUT OF COLOMBIA
December 20, 2001
● ● ● ● ● ● ● ● ● ● ●

After a quick flight back from Bogotá to Medellín to say goodbye to the Red Cross personnel who assisted in my release nine days ago, I'm on my way out of Colombia en route to Quito, Ecuador. When reflecting on events of the last two months, I have a sorry case of the blues, not knowing what to remember and what to forget. The

Glen Heggstad

Se Busca

- 2.15 m. de altura
- 110 K. de peso
- 49 años de edad
- tatuajes en brazos

Contacto:

Luz Karime

333 - 6125

(celular)

Extraviado
desde el 6·11·01

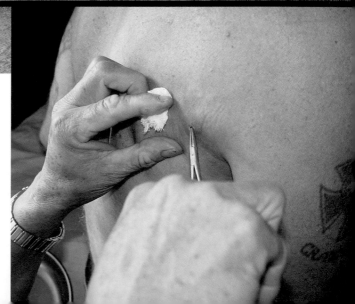

(*top*) Flier that Joe Gallagher circulated throughout Bogotá and the surrounding countryside while searching for me in Colombia.

(*right*) Ouch! A village doctor pulled this bot fly larvae (*middle*) out of my shoulder with a rusty set of tweezers and rubbing alcohol. Normally this is a minor surgical procedure but these were his only instruments.

(*above*) It wasn't easy making friends with strikers during the *campesino paro* in Peru, but they agreed to pose for this shot in hopes that it would call attention to their complaints. Only moments before, they approached me waving shovels and pitchforks after I ran their blockade.

(*opposite, top*) This television interview with Troy Roberts (CBS News's *48 Hours*) in Ecuador took place after I had been out of captivity for only three weeks. Troy was the first person from home I had a chance to spend time with.

(*opposite, middle*) This road was blocked with boulders to warn of the mysterious *paro* ahead. I kept going only to encounter angry mountain *campesinos* hurtling rocks, sticks, and other objects down at me.

(*opposite, bottom*) A thorn that my front tire picked up from when I ran the roadblock during the *campesino paro* had finally worked its way deeper into the rubber causing a flat while riding the *Camino Austral*.

(*opposite, top*) At the end of a tough day, youngsters were anxious to help unload the bike with its flat tire, after it was hauled into town by helpful truckers. This was typical behavior throughout Latin America.

(*opposite, middle*) Because I was able to weave my way past burning tires and tear gas during the student demonstration over government price hikes, I was the only guy to get out of Baños during this protesting.

(*opposite, bottom*) The dramatic scenery and high altitude on this "road less traveled" made it a breathtaking ride that corkscrewed through the Peruvian Andes.

(*above*) Even while riding at 12,000 feet, the mountains towered above me. This was on a beautiful stretch of asphalt while en route to Cusco, Peru.

(*top*) This remote Bolivian border checkpoint was only open mornings, four days a week. From there, it was a long fifty-mile downhill run into the arid heat of the Atacama Desert and smiling Chilean immigration officials.

(*bottom left*) This is my private army of helpers at the border of Peru and Bolivia vying for camera space. An inquisitive crowd formed wherever I stopped.

(*bottom middle*) The infamous Mexican *Federales* were the only federal law enforcement agency in Latin America not to jack me up for a bribe. Here I am hanging out with them.

(*bottom right*) At the traditional restaurants at the *Alacita Fair* in La Paz, Bolivia, rotund native women served things with beaks, hoofs, and eyeballs followed by sugary pastries.

(*opposite*) High in the Andes lie the skeletal remains of ancient Inca civilization at Machu Picchu, Peru.

(*top*) This is an example of a typical highway on the Bolivian *Altiplano* (High Plains of Bolivia). I was glad to see that it was at least fairly solid, as only five percent of the roads in Bolivia are paved.

(*bottom*) Competing with pack llamas for a lane on the Pan American Highway was common in South America.

(*top*) I enjoyed warm Cokes and dried llama meat with local boys in a cave while crossing the *Planar de Salar* (Salt Plains).

(*bottom*) My only guide across the solid white of the High Altitude Salt Plains was this cherry red Land Cruiser. Seconds later it sped off and disappeared into a black dot.

(*top*) I had to guess on hundreds of these unmarked forks in the Andes. If I knew the correct compass heading, I would ride for a few miles down one road until I figured out if it was the right one. If that road curved, I had to return and start over again.

(*bottom left*) If it's cold enough for llamas to wear sweaters, you know it's cold on a motorcycle.

(*bottom right*) Compacted red clay is as hard as concrete when dry, but when wet from rainstorms it becomes as slick as ice. At times, it was nearly impossible to remain upright. I went down a dozen times that day.

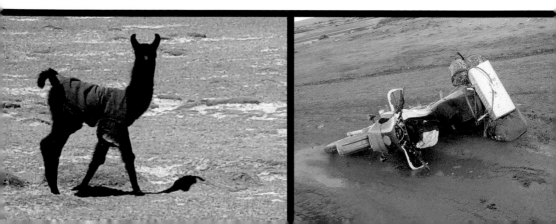

(*bottom left*) The only shade to be found above the timber line in the High Deserts of the Bolivian Andes was underneath my hot engine. At 16,000 feet, my heart beat twice as fast and the motorcycle engine responded half as quick.

(*bottom right*) In search of gasoline, I sometimes followed mere rumors of drum barrels to isolated Andean outposts only to find them deserted. None of which appeared on any maps or my GPS.

(*opposite, top*) The scenery was spectacular while heading south on the gravel *Camino Austral* in southern Chile. I often rode for hours without seeing another human.

(*opposite, left*) The approaching snowstorm, while at 17,000 feet, brought temperatures to below zero. I sought shelter in an unmapped tiny outpost, for which I had only vague directions.

(*opposite right, top*) My "Genuine American" Brazilian friend from the Hotel California proudly posed for me with his genuine American paraphernalia. I had to get his picture or no one would believe the story.

(*opposite right, middle*) It was exhilarating showering in the water thunder of Iguaza Falls on the Argentine side of the border.

(*opposite right, bottom*) Enormous crags of solid granite broke through the earth to form the majestic Horns of Payne in the wind ravaged *Torres del Paine* National Park in Patagonia.

(*above*) I had only a moment to catch my second wind at the turnaround point at Tierra del Fuego, Argentina. I had to head out quick before another storm hit. Eleven thousand miles to go.

(*opposite, top*) Mile zero of the Pan American Highway on the Chilean island of Chiloe marked the end of asphalt again for another few weeks.

(*opposite, bottom*) I highly recommend partying with the penguins on the southeast coast of Argentina.

(*above*) The boat ride plunged into a tunnel behind the falling water at the Devil's Throat at Iguazu Falls. Moments later, we were soaked in a falling river of millions of gallons of tumbling water.

(*right*) The ferry ride across the Straights of Magellan to the island of Tierra del Fuego completed my trip to the end of the world. In another hour, I would reach the least inhabited landmass on the planet.

A wind-sculpted rock at 14,000 feet on the Bolivian *Altiplano* was the only reference point to mark a new compass heading. My rest was a short one — an afternoon storm was rolling in again to greet me with more freezing rain.

doctor who attempted to take me home from the Red Cross center after I was freed received news that his cousin, also a hostage for nearly two years, was shot this morning by the ELN. His family was given directions on where to go to pick up his body by the side of a road, nothing more. Additionally, the FARC blew up a police station, killing everyone inside, and let a poor kid with cancer die before freeing his kidnapped father who could have been a donor for a bone marrow transplant. They ignored international pleas from the Pope, Red Cross, and almost every government in the world. Merry Christmas to the rebel movement.

ECUADOR

QUITO, ECUADOR
December 21, 2001
• • • • • • • • • • •

In anxious anticipation to twist a throttle, I arrive in Quito only to discover that my replacement bike is still tangled in customs in Miami. I thought Central American procedures were tough.

Towering Andes peaks to the east are so high that even at 9,000 feet we are still in the shadows of higher mountains. Yet the open road beckons, and I long to get back into the wind. My cup is half full and I still love the merry madness of Latin America.

CHRISTMAS IN QUITO
December 25, 2001
Quito, Ecuador
• • • • • • • • •

Even as a free man, I'm trapped in a hard-to-shake mental habit of waking up to the anticipation of a day's march. Only now there are no challenging jungle mountains to hike, just the steep sidewalks lining the roadways of Quito. Each morning I rise, enjoy a quick breakfast of four eggs and a glass of orange juice, then set off trekking about the city. I've grown so accustomed to covering long distances on foot these past few weeks that every morning since being freed I walk three or four miles before lunch whether it's necessary or not. Familiarized with a new method of hiking, I maintain my newly adopted mountain *campesino* trudge, a striding, loping, heel-to-toe lunge used to conquer steep, narrow trails.

Just after sunrise, off I barge into the hillside back streets of awakening barrios, wandering through colorful marketplaces of barking vendors where occasionally someone recognizes me from the CNN news broadcast. They fire questions faster than I can think and I try to answer in a heavily accented broken Spanish. *"Si señor, estuve secuestrado en Colombia."* (Yes, I was kidnapped in Colombia.) I never tire of interacting with the locals, and it's the highlight of every day to sit and shoot the breeze with them, even the Indians who invariably eye foreigners with suspicion.

I'm getting to know the layout of the city and many people greet me by name, *Hola señor Glen. ¿Como está?* Quito is a typical South American city with a skyline of modern buildings inside well-groomed commercial areas and outlying areas of filth and poverty. Worst of all, I'm getting used to it.

When I flew out of Medellín last week, I looked down at the mysterious mountainous jungle below that stretches from the Tropic of Cancer in Central Mexico to the Tropic of Capricorn in South America. For the previous two and a half months this spectacular scenery had captured my imagination, and for five weeks of that time, captured my body. I often wondered while gliding past those dense fortresses of radiating green what sort of life or adventure lurked within. Now I know. The jungle has spoken its many secrets of different lives and showed its deadly power. The jungle has become my best friend and worst nightmare.

While a prisoner, I experienced both the beauty and hazards of this breathtaking domain of tangled vines and towering trees, and was awed by the ruthlessness beneath its forbidden serenity. Time with the rebels taught me how to survive the wrath of the jungle and to realize its cruel and unforgiving justice. The danger looming within touches all, and all must yield to its compelling embrace of seduction and treachery.

South American *campesinos* have studied the ways of the mountains for centuries; they know when to yield and when to attack.

Within minutes, wielding their magical machetes, they can chop down trees to build bridges across impassable rivers, whittle out a small thatched roof shelter, or carve a new stock for an ancient AK-47. To survive, they fear the jungle as much as they marvel at its magnificence.

The future of the *campesinos* throughout Latin America is bleak as the cycle of civil war is destined to repeat itself for as long as the causes remain unaddressed. Government atrocities go unrecognized and the suffering continues. Big money buys silence and those with a conscience are left to do battle with soulless international corporate giants, drug cartels, and corrupt politicians. Enormous profits are made at the expense of human life as the little voices are drowned out by raging greed.

As a man on a mission to travel, I try hard to refrain from political commentary or judging others, because after all, this story is about adventure, not politics. However, I was unfortunately drawn into a struggle that I was able to view from several perspectives. While held prisoner in a distant land, I was compelled to examine issues that would ordinarily be of no concern to me, yet as a human being I cannot ignore. Caught in a violent conflict between polarizing ideologies, I became "collateral damage."

But whatever suffering I endured pales in comparison to what lies ahead for Colombians of all factions. After being trapped in the middle, I can see their struggle through familiar eyes. It would be simpler if one side could be blamed, but in the mountains of Colombia, everyone is a victim. It is a vicious cycle with no end in sight. Human misery has become commonplace in a land of kind and friendly people who, rich or poor, seldom fail to help a stranger in need.

HANGING IN ECUADOR
December 26, 2001
Quito, Ecuador

• • • • • • • •

After announcing on my web site that I would have a call-in day to my hotel room, I was overwhelmed at the response from friends and total strangers alike from places as far away as the Middle East and Asia. During one call after another, I talked nonstop for the entire twelve hours.

Another home team volunteer, Big Don Hinshaw, my computer genius friend from Palm Springs, has reconstructed my web site to a professional level and we are astounded at the number of new people logging on every day to read my biweekly online journals. Assuming I'm experienced enough now with the technicalities of the Internet, Don gives me a crash course by email on how to maintain the site. But learning HTML code while riding through South America is too overwhelming, so he inherits the job of coordinating and becoming my spokesman. It turns into a bigger job than either of us imagined, but he rises to the occasion and while I wander through the Andes, he keeps me in contact with the world.

Meanwhile, fellow international motorcycle traveler and head of the Ecuadorian Motorcyclists World Peace Movement Ricardo Rocco is expediting the process of clearing my incoming bike through customs. Not wanting me to be alone, he persuaded me to spend Christmas with his family although I have only known them a few days. Latin Americans know how to make a stranger feel at home; there was even a present for me to open after a traditional Ecuadorian meal. In broken Spanish I attempted to explain to the room full of festive relatives just how much it meant to me to be with such a wonderful family after just weeks ago being tormented by rebels in the mountains of Colombia.

After a short time in Quito, again a new hotel becomes comfortable and after only two days, the staff starts looking after me like family. Everywhere I have stayed in Latin America, locals have made me feel at home. Today a maid notices where I was bitten a month ago by what we presumed to be a semipoisonous insect because part of my shoulder has turned black. She insists on bringing secret home remedies to smear away effects of the venom. I prefer to wait and heal on my own but she will not take no for an answer.

While beginning to gather my physical strength and feeling confident that the new bike will arrive soon, I return to evenings of studying maps and guidebooks, plotting the next destination. The options are endless. Ride higher into the Andes or drift down toward the coastal lowlands and more jungle. Within a few hours of Quito, I can even board a ship for an excursion to the Galapagos Islands, one of the greatest biological treasures on earth. Ecuador could easily devour a month of time I no longer have available. The Colombian ordeal has cost me two months of what was intended to be meandering time.

If I visit every place I want to, I'd reach the tip of South America too late in the season, and being that close to Antarctica means sub-zero riding for several weeks. According to my map, the Pan American Highway south of Quito is a roller coaster ride up and down dramatic mountain passes, exiting the Andes into the Peruvian deserts. In travel shop windows, I've seen tantalizing photos of the intriguing scenery to come, which only makes further delay harder to endure.

HUSTLIN' IN QUITO
December 27, 2001
• • • • • • • • • • •

Unfortunately, the majority of my free time thus far in Ecuador and Colombia has been spent trying to re-equip and resupply in a shrinking time frame. With the help from weary friends back home and several cooperative suppliers, I am almost back to where I started at the beginning of this journey. And to add to the confusion, most South American countries charge outrageous duties on imported goods. It makes no difference if you're replacing lost or stolen items, everybody pays.

When an item of value is express mailed as Overnight-Next-Day-Delivery, it doesn't actually arrive for three days and then takes another three days with additional fees to clear customs. Weekends don't count, so if a package arrives on a Thursday, it won't be available until the following Tuesday.

I spend eight hours a day in front of computer screens coordinating and tracking deliveries from around the world, each uniquely difficult. Some items won't arrive here in time, so we try to forward those to countries I will reach later. I use forwarding addresses from the South American Explorers' Club home offices in various cities farther south, hoping to time the arrivals of myself and my equipment correctly. It's a challenge synchronizing dates to avoid being stuck waiting or have gear show up after I have left.

Adding to the confusion, Earthlink is losing ten percent of my incoming and outgoing email messages and sometimes delivers them days late. This is a frustrating experience and would be impossible to deal with if it weren't for my friends back home double-checking everything. We've learned to send backup messages on critical correspondence.

As I departed Colombia, officials from the U.S. Embassy in Bogotá provided a formal "To Whom It May Concern" letter typed in Spanish on official Embassy stationery outlining the unfortunate events with the ELN and requesting any assistance possible to be rendered to me. Government letters like this can open doors, cut red tape, and work miracles in Latin American countries. The more stamps any document has, the more it increases in importance. And my letter sports an impressive embassy stamp and an official raised embossed seal with an eagle. This paper becomes the magic key when dealing with uncooperative or lazy officials. When I hit brick walls, one flash of the letter brings them tumbling down.

Developing-nation bureaucracy is understandable in countries so poor they can barely feed their people. What is difficult to understand is that it's been two weeks since Brad and Jimmy dropped off the new motorcycle in L.A. to be air-freighted to Quito and there are still problems with customs in the U.S. The Los Angeles–based shipping company seems to be the culprit. They originally stated that air shipment could take as much as four days because of a procedure involving a seventy-two-hour inspection hold in Miami. That sounded reasonable. As time dragged on however, we called and emailed again and again, only to receive a different answer every time. The company finally admitted they had lost track of the shipment.

BACK TO THE COUNTRY
December 31, 2001
Santo Domingo de los Colorados, Ecuador
● ●

This afternoon I finally finished everything that could be handled on the Internet and now there is nothing left to do but wait. All parts and equipment are confirmed en route and my patience is shot. Almost all my time lately has been spent in front of a glaring computer screen in some run-down Internet café with the near-impossible task of reoutfitting. Three months into my journey, I am starting over heavily in debt, two months behind schedule and 5,000 miles away from the turnaround point in Argentina. Add to that, time with the ELN has left me weakened mentally and physically. After a brief trip to a local gym, I found myself still too weak to bench-press an empty bar. But my spirits are rising.

Every day, strangers from around the world write to share tales of disaster and how they overcame them, while others comment how my decision to carry on has inspired them to persevere in their moments of crisis. In a time of regrouping, I'm feeding on the energy of positive thinking while being reassembled by the team at home. More than anything, this ordeal has become a tale of inspiration and friendship.

After concluding the last of the Internet business in Quito, Ricardo pried me away from the computer screen for a trip to the countryside to visit his thriving no-tell-motel for some R & R, Latin American style. And today I sit relaxing in Santo Domingo, in the home of Ricardo with fellow American Lew and his dog Punky, all of us recounting tales of motorcycle travels in foreign lands.

After breakfast this morning, we received news that the crate containing my motorcycle, clothes, and equipment is still in Miami. For now, we can only wait in frustration. After more lies and misstatements than I care to remember, the air freight company has again failed to deliver my precious cargo that is now eighteen critical days late. After all the obstacles and Third World bureaucracies we overcame thus far to put our show back on the road, one U.S. shipping company broke their word and let us down. These wasted eighteen days will have to be balanced with shortcuts somewhere along the way in order to beat an early winter farther south. I must reach the tip of South America and return before freezing weather sets in.

PARTYING ON NEW YEAR'S EVE
January 2, 2002
● ● ● ● ● ● ● ● ●

The final hours of December bring major fiestas in South America, and Ecuadorians are very experienced in throwing street parties to toss out the old and bring in the new. Their New Year's celebration combines American-style Fourth-of-July fireworks, Halloween costumes, and satirical political street theater in a Mardi Gras–crowded frenzy of passion and intoxication. Sidewalks are lined with makeshift table buffets of creative indigenous cuisine.

The city's main drag, Avenida de Los Amazonas, is cordoned off for foot traffic only — tonight the boulevards belong to the revelers. Eager locals waste no time filling up the normally vehicle-congested streets with swaying bandstands, colorful floats, and shouting street vendors in a shoulder-to-shoulder sea of flowing, partying humanity. The crowd is packed so tight that if caught in one of the pulsating currents of sweating bodies pushing in either direction, it's impossible to stop. Anyone trying to resist the crushing onslaught would likely be trampled.

In the midst of this chaos, firecrackers and pyrotechnics detonate inside roaring street corner bonfires as glowing embers explode outward with the caustic stink of melting plastic permeating the cool night air. Bottles of beer, flasks of liquor, and sweet-smelling ganja openly circulate hand to hand while wary police stand by, safely behind wooden barricades. No one wants to argue with this crowd.

Elevated bandstands overflow as musicians rock the revelers senseless in a dozen captivating variations of Latin beats from salsa to merengue. Bass instruments pump hearts, jolt hips and churn buttocks of anyone swept within the throbbing sonic path. Rooftops and balconies are jammed with drunks, costumed dancers, and wriggling young children perched on their parents' shoulders echoing the merry madness below. There is simply no way to hold still.

Giant multicolored papier-mâché dummies representing things from *Año Viejo* (Old Year) are positioned center stage on brightly lit, dazzling floating platforms. Most are satirizing the U.S. government and the World Bank, sometimes in jest and sometimes not. I take offense to a few that extol terrorism and glorify Osama bin Laden. Most displays reflect an angry dissatisfaction with the status quo. The Solidarity with Cuba section has an exceptionally talented band wailing between intermissions of pro-Castro propaganda that's devoured by a cheering audience. The straw dummies burn at midnight so I allow myself a 1:00 a.m. curfew. My apprehension grows while noting few foreigners in the crowd and an abundance of the kinds of drunks who stay to the end of a party to wind up in a fight. Indeed, while walking back to my hotel, a particularly aggressive rabble-rouser, who would not let go of my shirt, went to sleep on the street head first from a straight right. He'll surely awaken with a mean headache in the morning. A gang of his grumbling friends, about to express their displeasure with this lone *gringo*, was interrupted by another pack of rowdy but well dressed locals who didn't like them circling me either. So while they hashed it out, I discreetly retreated upstairs to my hotel room.

GREAT NEWS, WEIRD NEWS, AND INTERESTING NEWS
January 4, 2002

• • • • • • • • •

The great news is, after greasing a few palms at the customs department and paying two different companies to fill out the same paperwork, my bike finally arrived this morning. The crate is easy to spot, with STRIKING VIKING spray-painted on the side in big letters — damn, I love my bros. With cameras from CBS News rolling, I fire up the replacement machine after a record-breaking three hours customs clearance. The long, miserable wait has ended. After pumping up the tires, I blast down the road for a two-hour, get-to-know-my-new-friend ride into the countryside, complete with rain in the darkness on the way back. Yet even the foul weather is a welcome relief as I'm just happy to be back in the wind under any circumstance. It's as though life flows back into me once again, while the excitement of being on the road permeates my being. Adventure is in the air.

The weird news is the lump on my shoulder we previously thought was a semi-poisonous spider bite is really the exotic bot fly completing its reproduction cycle. The bot fly lays its egg on a mosquito and the mosquito delivers it to a mammal. The egg burrows deeper into the flesh, incubates, and then eats its way to the surface. The sporadic burning inside my shoulder for the last several weeks was a fingertip-size larva eating its way out. No one knew what was happening until one day when Ricardo was helping drain the tiny hole in my back, he notices what appears to be a fat worm wiggling around inside.

We found a pharmacy in a remote rural village where the storekeeper is also the town doctor. He smoothly but rather painfully pried the reluctant critter out. The first photos taken with my new camera are in the macro setting, recording the process up close and in detail. My new concern is how many eggs do bot flies lay?

The interesting news is that a U.S. film crew organized by Peter Doyle and Troy Roberts from CBS News has flown in to document this adventure from the perspective of a motorcycle rider who has been released after captivity by Colombian rebels. Everyone is curious about why I decided to continue my ride south without first returning home. The baffling part to me is why they don't understand that a man needs to finish what he starts. Continuing the journey is a message to the rebel thugs who tried so hard to destroy me. Terrorists don't win.

EQUATORIAL ECUADOR
January 6, 2002
• • • • • • • • •

We made a short run to the center of the earth today: to the point marking the exact latitude where two hemispheres meet. While straddling a line painted on the equatorial monument's walkway, I had one foot on each side of the earth. Yee-haw, 20,000 miles to go!

The CBS News film crew has worked me from sunup to sundown the last four days until finally leaving for Colombia to interview Red Cross delegates and Embassy personnel. Although I'm wary of the media, they seem like decent people and provided an extraordinary education in television production. Peter Doyle hired Ricardo as a guide and even had him haul a cameraman sitting backwards on his bike while filming me ride through the mountains. The three of us spend evenings together and have become good friends. We all swear to meet again someday. I rode a total of 800 miles as they shot nearly twenty hours of footage for what they say will be a fourteen-minute news documentary.

I JUST CAN'T GET THIS SMILE OFF MY FACE
January 8, 2002
• • • • • • • • •

After completing last-minute errands and retrieving misplaced documents lost in the shuffle during customs clearance, the moment I've been aching for arrived. The previous month spent treading water and sorting out last-minute disasters has nearly exhausted what's left of my sense of anticipation. Cities supply access to the Internet and communications, little more. When staying in the safe part of town, I feel detached from the actual lives of the people. Yet when hanging out with locals on the outskirts, I'm devastated by the poverty and suffering. Cities reflect extremes of what's best to avoid.

With the congestion of metropolitan traffic fading behind us like a distant train whistle, Ricardo escorts me to the main road south that connects with the Pan American Highway. Following the road, the Peruvian border is two days away. We slow down enough at the toll plaza to slap hands goodbye and in this final melancholy moment of parting company, it's hard not to ask him to ride south with me. Ricardo and Peter Doyle became the psychological support I needed after the Colombian ordeal and leaving them behind means a big piece of the scaffold has been removed. I'm alone again.

Soon the countryside jungle turns to rolling hills and farmland with glimpses of the towering Andes in my mirrors as once more I merge with the open road. There's just enough light drizzle to remind me I'm still hugging the equator and there will surely be squalls ahead to justify wearing a rain suit. The Pan American Highway is deceiving. This first segment is freshly laid four-lane asphalt but at any moment it may deteriorate with potholes or turn to washboard gravel. *Quien sabe?*

Liberated from other people's time schedules, chronic delays, and bureaucratic complications, I tumble back joyously into the freedom of the road and excitement of adventure that only motorcycle travel can create. Dark moments are gone and negative images are on hold. I emerge from a foggy haze and what was so frustratingly dancing at the end of my fingertips is now in the firm grasp of my heart. Even the slow pace of traffic is welcome. Inquisitive children at gas stations, gently banked turns through the mountains, and the sweet smell of fresh-mowed meadows all remind me of why I'm here. Tantalizing exotic fruit peddled roadside next to open-air restaurants serving sizzling local meals cooked on open fires once again tease me with the urge to lay down another mile.

There has never been anything to stop me from pursuing goals, certainly not the ELN. Even though I often intentionally take the long way or know my only destination is a mere compass heading, sooner or later, I must finish what I start. Reflecting on the last three months and the extremes of experience and human emotion, what could have broken me only encouraged me, and what disappointed me only served to free me.

Ahead there's a string of monstrous semitrucks spewing black clouds of filthy fumes big enough to command my immediate attention, and the race is on to the rapidly approaching curves. I'm back into the rhythm of dueling with multi-wheeled, rolling monolithic beasts hell-bent on ignoring little motorcycles. The lumbering danger quickens my pulse, reminding me that speed and agility are all that a motorcyclist has to compete with. As anyone who has ever traveled roads like these is well aware, size does matter.

DRIFTING SOUTH
January 9, 2002
● ● ● ● ● ● ● ● ●

For the first night back on the road I target the subtropical *pueblo* of Baños. It should've been a four-hour ride had I not become sidetracked snaking through the mountains searching for the remote outpost of Quisepincha, perched high above the Pan Am Highway overlooking the sprawling municipality of Ambato. I've been shopping for a replacement leather jacket since Colombia and haven't had any luck finding my size. Locals assured me this is the place to look because most of the leather goods in Ecuador are made here.

Indeed, I probably would have found the jacket I needed if it wasn't for a three-day holiday when the stores all close and the streets are lined with locked storefronts. Behind steel gratings, leather goods are marked at a third of U.S. prices. But the locals aren't the usual friendly country folk and the restaurants are too dirty to gamble on.

Most people I encounter are scowling Indians, some dressed in street clothes and others in the traditional garb of handwoven fabrics with colorful patterns. All are on foot. I don't get much reaction when trying to greet them; they either don't speak Spanish or are obviously fed up with foreigners.

The scenic twisty roads leading down into Baños are as spectacular as the guidebooks promised, with checker-pattern farm fields resting against a backdrop of the rising Andes mountain range. Towering peaks shoot straight up into the sky, disappearing into the clouds. Brick-lined streets lie in the shadow of a formerly dormant volcano, now spewing white puffs of steam upwards in an ominous reminder of superiority. Because of sporadic eruptions over the years, the town has been evacuated several times, but nearly everyone returns for the mineral hot springs and the solitude of a tranquil valley. Baños is so charming, with its Indian markets and small town atmosphere, that I consider staying an extra day.

Except — this morning, while I'm finishing breakfast in an outdoor café, the early morning mountain air is violated by detonations in the plaza across the street. People dash in all directions from the sounds of large firecrackers exploding. But seconds later, invisible clouds of eye-stinging tear gas float eerily down alleys and into open doorways, burning the skin and eyes of anyone trapped in the silent menacing fog. A disgruntled shopkeeper says it's a student protest against the recent ten percent fuel cost hike instituted by the government. There's only one road in and out of Baños and, having heard how Ecuadorians express disapproval of government policy by blockading roadways, I figure it's time to leave while leaving is still possible.

The students, mostly high school age, merely congregate near the city's main exit, setting tires ablaze in the road in an effort to seal off traffic. Growing lines of cars and buses back up for several blocks in each direction as chubby-cheeked small-town cops converge on the mass of unruly, uniformed school kids. A few policemen have bloody faces from being smacked by rocks and bottles, but I'm impressed how they handle themselves with restraint and manage to disperse the crowd without beating anyone up.

I try to snap a few photos but by the time I ready my camera, waves of tear gas permeate the air. It is all I can do to pack up and white line it to the front of traffic to exit before anything serious happens. After weaving through the thick black smoke of burning tires, I manage to bypass the rock-throwing and slide out of town without mishap. I have had my fill of civil unrest and decide to head back to nearby Ambato for a good night's sleep and an early start for the eight-hour ride south to Cuenca, the third largest city in Ecuador.

Ambato is a grimy, loud, and impersonal town and yet there isn't much choice where to stay as nightfall sneaks up once again. The food is barely tolerable but the Internet service is fiber-optic, fast enough for catching up on email and uploading a journal. I have photos to send but this requires a computer with a USB port and so far I haven't found any equipment new enough to support this type of transfer. From here, it is a quick dash into Peru.

RIPPED OFF
January 10, 2002
• • • • • • • • • •

While packing my gear this morning, I notice my GPS is missing. To be sure, I unpack, double check everything one article at a time, and then search the tiny wooden room from inside the blankets to under the bed. This is bad news. The indignant hotel manager vehemently claims it's impossible for anyone to have entered my room while I was downstairs eating and it must have been misplaced. Yeah right, it's probably in my shoe.

I learned in Colombia there is no perfect security system when traveling. Sooner or later valuables are left unguarded. My strongbox is only a removable aluminum tool chest with double padlocks, cable locked on the back rack of the bike. It contains valuables like my camera, laptop, and vital documents too bulky for my pocket. When stashed inside hotel rooms at night, I cable-lock it to something sturdy like a bed frame, and even then I'm seldom away from it for long.

Good security also requires sometimes unexpectedly returning moments after leaving to keep thieves from figuring out my patterns. But if someone is determined to steal, they will. They can do it with machine guns, by studying habits (the most typical way), or by betraying a trust.

When it's necessary to leave a vehicle briefly unattended in poor countries, a man on the street will often point to his eye and then to your vehicle. You hire him with a nod. Sometimes this man is employed by local merchants and wears a uniform. Other times he is a jobless worker making it his occupation to provide this service. It's understood that for supplying unofficial security you will tip him some change when you return. These guardians are almost always honest.

There's no guarantee your things won't get snatched even by keeping them in line of sight. There are plenty of thieves who are experts at slash and dash. If a jacket or sleeping bag is strapped to a bike, an amateur crook can snatch these items in seconds and you'll never catch him. You can get ripped off at an intersection while stuck in traffic or get double-crossed by a paid guard. A traveler is always at risk no matter how cautious and, sooner or later, every traveler gets hit.

Last night, the hotel manager's ten-year-old son had been following me around like a curious puppy while I unpacked my gear. He was filled with the usual questions kids ask — where I came from, how fast the bike goes and so forth. While headed downstairs to eat, I gave him a buck to guard my room, a fortune for a ten-year-old in a poor country and double what you would pay a street security man. That was the only time I left my room unattended.

This morning, when certain the GPS is missing, I look at the boy, while pointing to the empty slot on my handlebar bracket. He avoids my eyes and mumbles something like it might be upstairs in the room on the nightstand, where I know I left it. I suspect this is a scam for a retrieval fee but I don't care. I offer him ten bucks if he can find it. Minutes later he returns empty-handed shrugging his shoulders. His father probably already sold it.

For now, a GPS isn't critical but downloading map information into my laptop via satellite is a convenience I've grown accustomed to and will need again when crossing the Andes off-road next week. Many of the highways in South America are unmarked and I ride off the beaten path so often, the only way to know precisely where I am or the exact altitude is with a GPS.

While passing 17,000-foot-high summits of the *Altiplano* (High Plains) of Bolivia, this instrument can be vital, as there are seldom markings anywhere to tell a lone traveler what road he is on, and often there are no roads at all. The trails that can be found are dirt or sand and sometimes disoriented travelers must optimistically ride along riverbanks searching for tracks from other vehicles, hoping to find a visual marker somewhere. It's possible to cross this region without satellite navigation but just one more complication to contend with. The heck with it! Turn the page.

Again this morning's departure was in a cloud of tear gas due to more protests against the recent fuel price hikes. A ten-percent rise in fuel costs translates into ten-percent increases across the board in goods and services, a significant blow to a struggling Third World economy, and the masses are out in force expressing their displeasure. From my hotel window I can see rows of helmeted cops behind plastic shields preparing to handle street demonstrations. The countryside will be a different story though because short of violent insurrection, authorities seldom get involved in rural civil unrest.

As an organized protest, mountain *campesinos* are reported to block roads by rolling boulders downhill onto highways from above and bombarding anyone trying to pass with rocks and bottles. They don't have guns or bombs yet and I doubt they are at the stage of wanting them. But I'm not taking any chances on getting into a predicament where my trip can be delayed again.

Once out on the open road, I'm undisturbed by anything or anyone as I soar through the foothills of the pine-forested Andes. Most of the ride is at a steady 10,000-foot elevation, occasionally crossing mountain summits above the timberline of 15,000 feet where my sputtering motorcycle engine and I both gasp for thicker air. At this altitude, there's little response to the throttle or my own physical reflexes. I've spent the last several weeks acclimating at high elevations, but this afternoon, rising so quickly keeps me on the edge of blacking out.

Rocky slopes of jagged peaks provide spectacular backdrops as I corkscrew up and down narrow hairpin turns without shoulders or guardrails. Above me to the left, snow-crusted mountains shoot straight up to 20,000 feet, and a few yards to the right, dizzying sheer granite cliffs offer drop-offs to distant farming valleys below. Because of the intense focus necessary to navigate the treacherous roadway, there's barely opportunity to divert my eyes to absorb the drama. Around every bend is a scene demanding a photograph but daylight is limited. I must keep moving. I don't want to get caught up here alone in the freezing evening rain.

Blistering solar rays at this latitude and altitude, without the benefit of atmosphere to filter them out, seem able to penetrate even the plastic of my helmet. I'm bundled up against the crackling dry chill in my fully insulated riding suit with electric vest on high and still shiver at tiny currents of swirling frosty air sneaking through the zippers. I marvel at the extremes around me yet also experience disappointment that I'm unable to spend more time and enjoy the moment.

Against the backdrop of another sensational equatorial sunset, I lazily drift down into the ever-evolving colonial city of Cuenca, my last overnight in Ecuador. Before I left Quito, Ricardo mapped out interesting stopovers all the way to southern Chile and so far his foresight has been correct. I wonder what else he has planned.

Again, I awoke to the sting of tear gas and chanting students, and again I hit the road in a hurry, skipping breakfast. I'm too close to the Peruvian border to slow down and take chances. I would have preferred to take my time this morning but there's no telling where the protests might lead. Riots equal road closures.

Riding south, potholed pavement turns to gravel and later mud at times and never with any predictability. Hundreds of pigs, donkeys, and goats wander the roadway as herds of stubborn cattle force me to weave my way through with concerns of a stampede. An occasional llama led along the road by a solemn-faced old Indian provides the sense that at last, I've reached new territory.

Leaving Ecuador takes only moments and entry into Peru is even easier. All customs require is the original title to the bike and my passport. Officials complete forms behind a desk that stands outside in the warm afternoon sun. The entire formality consumes thirty minutes, including an invitation to come home for dinner and meet the sister, who just happens to be looking for a husband. Jovial officials crowd around my bike firing questions about my trip and where I'm headed next. Realizing it could take awhile to escape, I politely cut them off. It's a ten-hour ride if hustling, and sundown is closing in, so I stow my gear with a smile, nod farewell, and wish good luck to the sister.

Back at sea level again, the coastal terrain resembles the rocky Sonora Desert of northern Mexico and both myself and my motorcycle function better with a denser atmosphere. When stopping for food or gas, I'm deluged by happy, curious small-town folk anxious to shake the hand of *el Vikingo Loco* (the Crazy Viking). I hesitate to slow down because when I do, they shout at me to return and chat.

PERU

PERUVIAN DESERTS
January 11, 2002
● ● ● ● ● ● ● ● ● ●

The twelve-hour ride from the border to Piura, Peru, has cut short my time to explore the city, but luckily I find a neighborhood family restaurant downtown where they cook up a tasty meal of fresh sea bass and chips, complete with an Inca Cola.

Traffic in Peru lives up to its reputation as some of the wildest in South America. Drivers play a nonstop, nerve-racking game of bumper-car chicken. The rules: vehicles traveling in the same direction must maintain light contact, barely tapping the next cars' fenders. Amidst the synchronized chaos, horns are used in the same way that motorists in other countries use their brakes. Travel reports indicate Argentina is even worse — I can hardly wait.

My map shows solid blazing desert for the next thousand miles south. But this morning, luck is with me. For a welcoming protection, blanketing gray clouds are thick enough to shield me from the persistent radiation from above. Traveling farther from the equator, the days become longer as the sun lingers longer on the horizon, extending precious hours of light, helping to make up for lost time.

There's much to see and do in Peru, but looming foul-weather reports farther south prompt me to keep moving. Each adobe-bricked little *pueblo* along the way has a fascinating marketplace and tranquil central plaza inviting further examination. I reluctantly ignore the temptation and hustle onward, telling myself I'll be back some day.

Having lived most of my life in the California desert, I appreciate the commanding splendor and dominating serenity of desolate terrain. You either love the desert or can't stand it, there is no in-between. Gazing into the endless barren swells of sand dunes rising gently from a tan sea of emptiness, I'm overwhelmed with a fulfilling sense of isolation. To the west lie the tranquil waters of the Pacific Ocean. And to the east, jagged granite crowns of the imposing Andes mountain range rise defiantly, separating the rest of Peru from the sweltering Amazon basin. Reflecting back on the last three months, it's hard to believe I'm finally here.

Crosswinds bounce my little motorcycle around like a Styrofoam ball as I struggle to stay in one lane. Fingers of drifting sand spread across entire stretches of highway, leaving me to guess where to point the front wheel. Locked in a mood of wary amazement, images from the movie *Dune* tease my imagination. I'm awed at traversing such alien lands, ancient domains at the mercy of natural phenomena beyond my control.

With nothing to hinder the relentless winds, blurs of blinding dust spin into malicious sandstorms, ending as unpredictably as they began. The abrasive crud accumulating on the outside of my body also accumulates inside my nose and throat. This irritates my sinuses but I'm more concerned about the air filtration system on the carburetor and effects of abrasive grit on the inside of my panting little engine.

Two-man teams of bored *Transito* police inhabit scattered isolated military outposts, sporadically flagging over unlucky motorists as a means to pay their rent. They usually wave me on: I'm too insignificant to bother with. If they do stop me, it's only to ask about my journey and relate a few tales of their own travels. Everyone is amiable in Peru, even the cops.

Time constraints will confine my days in Peru to the colonial city of Cusco, the mountainous gateway to Machu Picchu, the hidden ruins of ancient Inca civilization. The rest of my Peruvian experience is limited to small talk in gas stations, hotels, and oddball roadside cafés. However, I feel fortunate to travel this amazing land by motorcycle, the ultimate opportunity to absorb the majesty of ageless treasures. In spite of my hurry — I'm one with Peru!

Guidebooks and travelers' tales warn that Lima and Cusco are the crime pits of the world. Even the locals say that these two cities are rife with underhanded thieves and vicious criminals, and to be on constant guard. Given my experiences thus far in Peru, this is difficult to believe.

LIMA
January 13, 2002
• • • • • • • • •

The city lights of Lima eventually blink into view at the end of a hectic midnight ride, lengthened by *bandito* policemen. This afternoon, I was caught at one of the numerous roadside speed traps set up on the outskirts of most towns. A triumphant local cop had me dead to rights on radar, speeding through his *pueblo*, and pretended to write a ticket while waiting for an offer. He explains this will cost 300 dollars in court but I suspect this is merely his initial bargaining position. I stand firm on the proven tactic of *"no hablo español."* I'm sure he prefers money to writing a ticket but because of my refusal to play along, he insists we go back into town and speak with *el Jefe* (the chief).

After a brief conference, the cops decide to adjust their negotiating stance by lowering their demand to 150 bucks. It's not often they actually catch someone breaking the law, especially a wandering *gringo*, and by their standards a rich man. It's obvious they have no intention of letting this slide, so I modify my position also. I don't dispute the infraction and agree to pay something, but, I explain that I only have credit cards and a small amount of pocket change needed for fuel. We're 100 miles from Lima, the desert night is pitch black, and I tell them that I'm almost out of gas. Frustrated that their prize is slipping away, they take the change anyway as partial payment, bargaining away the rest for my four-dollar sunglasses that I groan are expensive imports. If I didn't have a stash of money hidden in case of just such occasions I could have easily been stranded in the middle of nowhere.

Through it all, we maintain our sense of humor with feigned sincerity and wry smiles, but the procedure consumes a valuable hour of riding time. Although further behind schedule, and now in the time zone of nocturnal predators, it is worth every peso for the show alone. *El Jefe* and I end up laughing about our respective performances and shake hands with a hearty, *"Buen viaje."* So much for my scratched-up Korean shades.

Lima is everything the warnings claim and worse. Riding into this maddening armpit of metropolitan confusion at midnight with all the drunks and locos playing demolition derby has me longing for the hazards of desert nights. Fearing to become a statistic, I'm anxious to leave as I arrive. My senses are on full alert and remain so until back on the open road.

OVERCOMING DELAYS
January 14, 2002
• • • • • • • • • •

Tonight I meet with a friend of a friend named Louis who shows me around the treacherously overcrowded city while I follow him in his car. The metropolitan area is so enormous and sprawled out that, at times, even he must stop and ask directions. I can only imagine how chaotic this would be without a guide. Far past midnight, traffic is still jammed with maniacal drivers fearlessly challenging all in their path. Sidewalks and roadways are crammed with throngs of people, walking or riding bicycles. The rest are spilling out of packed tin-can buses, spewing vile black soot aimed at my lungs.

My bike is long overdue for maintenance and Louis arranges for a mechanic whom he trusts to do the work. The questionable conditions in which motorcycle shops operate here makes trust a significant word. I hope he can repair my collapsed rear shock absorber quickly because I'm trying to get back on the road by noon tomorrow to reach the jump-off point at Cusco — a four-day ride up into the Andes. To complicate matters, a new GPS has been Federal-

Expressed ahead to either Lima or Cusco, and I can't reach Donal Rodarte, my faithful judo student, to determine which address he used. First I must track him down, then prepare for battle with customs over the import duty.

My damaged shock receives immediate attention from the mechanic and within an hour we speed off in a taxi searching for a replacement I've been assured will be easy to find. After fours hours and countless head-shakers mumbling, *"No hay"* (There is none), we finally find a man who confirms there is no Kawasaki dealer in Peru. He offers, though, to import a shock for us in two weeks for 700 dollars.

I shiver with the distressing news, imagining the freezing winds blowing in from Antarctica. Another delay means my timing will be disrupted and I could be stuck in southern Chile waiting out the frigid South American winter. At the moment, it's questionable if I can beat the predicted early snows of Patagonia. And there are several thousand miles of rugged unpaved roads ahead that will be tough to ride without proper suspension.

We turn to plan B — finding someone to rebuild the factory shock. One man tells us to come back at five o'clock and he will have it done. I explain in broken, near impossible to understand Spanish, this won't work, it must be earlier. No problem, how about three o'clock? That's perfect. I can be on the road by five and only have a few hours of difficult night riding ahead.

Later that day, with the sun gracefully retreating below the horizon, I blast past the last tollbooth exiting Lima and ride onto the *autopista*, hoping for an overnight in Pisco. From there, I'll deviate off the Pan American Highway and spiral back into the Andes.

Yet in my hurry, I failed to inspect the rebuilt shock when we re-installed it and later discovered that all the mechanic did for the fifty bucks I paid him was clean it. Even though there was no improvement, there is still a bright side. At least toll roads in Peru are free for motorcycles and the government does something here that I found in few other countries — they repair their potholes. Still, this will be another risky late-night ride with no one to keep me company except aggressive truckers who refuse to dim their lights and stray cattle seeking warmth in the center of the road.

Soon, I am speeding back across a glowing desert landscape under an enormous blackened ceiling shot full of twinkling stars. Off to the west, a meager slice of moon rises, arcing across the midnight sky. As the winds subside, a light ocean mist deposits a film of salt on my face shield, which I stop to clear every twenty minutes. During these moments, I shut down the engine just to savor the roaring silence. Marveling at the enveloping chilly desolation, it's difficult not to linger. I love the desert as much as the mountains or the jungle, and am continuously captivated by the contrasts this planet has graciously offered its inhabitants. While a prisoner in Colombia I dreamed of these moments, knowing if I survived, I would one day complete this ride no matter how long it took. Once again, I eagerly plunge southward, overwhelmed in the pure ecstasy of feeling alive.

A TOUGH DAY
January 16, 2002
• • • • • • • • •

Because of the long ride ahead from Ayacucho to Andajeulas, I slid out of town a freezing two hours before sunrise. This high in the Andes, it's bitterly cold at night. And the lack of food in the hotel restaurant squashed any hope of a hot breakfast.

At the outskirts of town, the road immediately turns to dirt and remains that way, except when it changes into mud. There were warnings the road would be severely rutted, narrow, and cluttered with radical switchbacks. Potholes are too numerous to bother dodging so I attack them straight on while standing on the foot pegs, splashing rooster tails of brown water and mud left over from last night's rain. Glistening spray sparkles in the expanding solar rays of the approaching dawn and within an hour my bike and I are both coated in gritty pale muck.

The consistent violent jarring, worsened by the blown shock, is so intense it's impossible to focus my jiggling eyeballs and it feels as though any moment my teeth might shatter. I have serious doubts about my camera and computer surviving past noon and my long-ago ruptured cervical disks require massive doses of Motrin. The thought of a full day's ride in these conditions, alone in the Andes, makes me feel like I've just picked a knockdown, drag-out fight with multiple opponents.

There is a paved road leading to Cusco that would have been much easier to travel, so why would anyone intentionally set out into such extreme conditions? Because on a journey like this, challenges define life and make a man feel alive. Also, it's the best darn ride since departing California. Storybook Andean scenery opens like secret pages of ancient mountain marvels unfolding for only those who witness it firsthand. Grinning until my jaw aches, I peer outward through my face shield at the sharp multicolored canyons and towering peaks above — it's as though I'm ricocheting through time with little to indicate what century this is. For hundreds of miles in all directions in the frigid mountain air, no two viewpoints are alike, rendering me breathless in awe of this natural phenomenon that I've only imagined. This is the reason to experience Peru and it's worth every second of hassle and discomfort.

Andean scenic ecstasy can only be fully absorbed on two wheels, quenching my lust to discover what lies around the next bend. Never have I tasted moments like these and can't help but wonder, "Where does it go from here? How can anything top this?" In these blissful moments of breathless wonder, I want to shout my discovery to the world — to share what's rocking my senses and electrifying my spirit.

As often as possible, I stop for photos, but not nearly often enough. Time is critical at altitude in the Andes. After sundown whatever is still exposed in the empty mountain paradise, freezes.

For hours, it's just the mighty Andes and me, face-to-face. No other human life, only vast herds of grazing long-necked llamas embroidered on endless hillsides of multishaded green. The only sound is the popping of my engine and the bitter taste of harsh wind ripping across wet grassy fields. Once again, I merge with the landscape to find myself inhaling what I see. There are no fences or telephone poles and except for a rutted, thin ribbon of orange dirt unraveling before me to the horizon, there's no proof I'm not the only man on earth.

Among the chilly shadows of rocky cliffs, the single-lane dirt road hardens into a broad path chiseled from solid stone, circling and looping around mountains toward valleys nearly a mile straight down. Every turn is a blind curve and it is either heading up or down, with dizzying sheer drop-offs into granite canyons barely visible thousands of feet below. Earlier, I saw a few speeding minivans packed with tourists. Now, the entire mountain is empty and I can't figure out why.

At lunchtime, I stop at an Indian outpost for fat filets of fresh river trout, fried *pueblo* style. There are a few pickups and vans parked by the side of the road as though waiting for something to happen. This is good. I hope they stay parked. It allows more room to move without fear of collisions on the curves.

In 1989 I rented a Jeep in Kashmir and drove the cease-fire line between India and Pakistan, along the Indus River to the faraway northern city of Leh, in the province of Ladakh. At the time, I thought that was the most spectacularly dangerous one-lane road in the world, but this Peruvian corkscrew through the clouds has established a new standard. It's also the roughest ride yet, compelling frequent stops to check my gear to make sure nothing has broken loose. The time factor continuously pushes me forward and despite the lure of the scenery, there's not a moment to spare. When I ride into the shadow of a mountain, temperatures drop dramatically, an ominous reminder of what's to come at sundown. Yet so far, it's one glorious moment after another.

And today, I learned a new Spanish word — *paro*. After hearing *paro* shouted enough times this afternoon, I still couldn't determine the meaning—until after fruitless guessing and a small riot, I sort of understood. *Paro* is related to the verb *parar*, meaning "to stop." Like all Spanish verbs, *parar* needs to be altered (conjugated) according to who is addressed and in what tense. There are no stop signs here, instead there are *paro* signs.

At the entrance to a small remote farming *pueblo*, a uniformed policeman blocks the road waving a red flag, demanding a halt to produce my documents. No problem. After inspecting my papers, he announces it's prohibited to proceed farther. Assuming another shakedown, I push the issue, asking why not? He only repeats the word paro. According to the Spanish dictionary, *parar* with an "o" at the end should translate to "I stop." It's difficult to understand what he means and I insist on continuing anyway. Apparently not wanting to debate, he shrugs his shoulders, waving me on.

Farther ahead, bowling-ball size stones have been scattered across the road in between downed trees, which I easily skirt. *Campesinos* alongside the road are yelling *paro*. At this point, I'm thinking *paro* must mean obstacle of some kind, maybe a landslide up ahead. What the heck, a motorcycle should be able to get around anything.

Gradually, scattered rocks become neatly arranged lines across the road every quarter mile, which I simply weave through. I also notice people aren't smiling anymore. There's a sense of trepidation in the air, yet delay is a bigger worry. Soon there's a long line of parked vans and trucks. Disembarked passengers mill about with furrowed brows. Once again, I decide to slowly pass around them but the crowd is passionately waving their arms yelling *peligroso* (dangerous) and *paro*. Curiosity, as well as a need to continue, takes over — sooner or later I'll discover just what a *paro* is.

Suspecting *paro* means obstruction, I explain to the crowd that since motorcycles are more agile than buses, I'm not worried about any *paro*. They huddle for a brief conference and then conclude since I am riding a motorcycle, maybe I can deal with the mysterious *paro*. Their attitude changes, and they switch to cheers, with pats on my back and shouts of *"Adelante!"* (Move onward!). With a quick flip of the starter switch, I fire up and proceed.

After my horrible ordeal in Colombia, I made a decision to never again allow myself to be taken prisoner — and therefore would never again stop at another roadblock. I know the potential consequences of this resolution and accept them. So this afternoon, when I spot tree branches lying across the road and trunk-size boulders blocking the way with men standing at ready on either side, I think, "Fuck it, here we go."

While revving my engine, I kick it down a gear, and ease over the first bunch of foliage in a hail of rocks and chunks of debris being pitched in my direction. Although the wave of miscellaneous missiles comes close, nothing hits me. The first hurdle was easy, but the next is a tightly packed row of much larger boulders with no open space to pass through. I'm at a dead end with an angry mob storming down from the hillside above chanting *"Paro!"* and armed with shovels and pitchforks. Once again my options are limited, there's nowhere to go. I must stand and, you know . . . negotiate. At least no one is shooting at me.

Within moments I'm surrounded by incensed *campesinos* with focused frowns of indignation and quickly figure one thing for certain — *paro* is something serious. However, I also know the heart and spirit of *campesinos*. They are good-natured people who I believe will not harm me unnecessarily. Perhaps I'll get a chance to explain. With arms up in gesture of surrender, I inform the impatient crowd that I speak only a little Spanish and don't know what *paro* means. They calm slightly, gruffly explaining in a barely understandable dialect that *paro* is a road blockade used for the purpose of a strike, a protest against the government for high taxes and no voice.

These are significant concepts to Americans — taxation without representation! Being from a country that prevailed in the greatest revolution in human history, I have a soft spot for revolt and protests against oppressive government policies. I'm opposed to violence but sometimes that's the only alternative when the governing authorities refuse to listen to the cries of the downtrodden. I like these people, but need to win them over and convince them to like me. It's time for the magic solution.

A sly smile spreads across my face as I point to the camera dangling from my neck and bellow out, *"Soy escritor! Y quiero escribir en su protesta."* (I am a writer! And I want to write about your protest.)

A murmur drifts through the crowd erupting into cheers and shouts of approval. Wary attitudes dissipate into smiles of understanding the ignorant *gringo*. They form a line to shake hands, apologizing sincerely, pointing to my tires.

An older man clutching a pitchfork utters, *"Lo siento señor, las espinas"* (I am sorry sir, the spines), as he hands over one of the thorny tree branches to examine. They did try to warn me, he claims. Meanwhile younger *campesinos* are busy picking inch-long spikes from my tires. I hope in vain that Jimmy has chemically treated them to self-seal around small punctures as there's no time to pull the wheel off and screw around with a patch kit.

Time becomes ever more critical as the tires could be slowly leaking. There's nothing left to do but keep moving and try to finish crossing the mountain before dark. To maintain the spirit of goodwill, I request a group photo for my web site to make them famous around the world. I want to be in the picture also but there's no one I trust enough to handle my camera. The eager mountain farmers can't comply fast enough and moments later work together rolling boulders aside for me to pass. Assuming this is the only blockade, I mentally calculate time lost, thinking it's still possible to reach the next overnight while temperatures are tolerable.

But as I soon discover, this is not the only roadblock. Every few miles another group of *campesinos* has rolled down boulders from the hillside or cut down a thick tree that lies across my path. These blockades are unmanned and the boulders are easy to get around by driving between or beside them, but the sites with trees across the road present a different challenge. The trunks are two feet thick and far too difficult to move alone. However, an old martial arts slogan echoes in my mind — "An obstacle is only something you see when you lose sight of your goal." And it doesn't take long for reinforcements to appear.

Two transit cops were just finishing dragging their 125cc Honda around a shallow embankment at the first tree block. After a friendly greeting, they offer to help me do the same but my bike is too heavy, even for the three of us. We finally opt for a heave-ho maneuver, together bending the lighter tree branches to one side allowing enough space to barely clear. I take their picture, assuring them they would soon be famous all over the world. (This is getting to be a reliable gimmick.)

The next tree trunk across the road is again too heavy to move, but a young *campesino* tending his goats shows me a way to backtrack a hundred yards, drop down next to a creek, and cross a cornfield to ride up on the other side of the barricade. To complicate matters, earlier today a starter solenoid connection had worked loose and I have been push starting the bike all day. Negotiating the cornfield without running over the crop is no easy task. And after killing the engine half a dozen times and wiggling wires to get it started again, another half hour is lost.

The last tree is too long and heavy, with no way around either side. Yet I have not come this far to turn around. A short hike leads to a grain field with a few *campesinos* busy plowing their land. Two of them are young and strong, one is old and drunk, all are eager to help. The only solution is to go over the top. We find the lowest section of tree trunk and once again initiate the heave-ho, lifting and dragging the bike until it becomes stuck on the top of the log, resting on the engine skid plate. As the motorcycle momentarily teeters, I pause and consider a photograph. But the bike starts to fall to one side and the pregnant wife of a *campesino* has to come running to help us keep it upright until we lower it to the other side. After a final inspection for hoisting damage, I convince myself this has to be the last barricade.

At the next isolated Indian *pueblo*, people are again shouting, "*Paro, paro.*" Apparently it's their intention to shut down all traffic in the entire region for twenty-four hours and they are almost as determined as me. However, I cannot afford to sit next to the road for another half day. The temperature is already beginning to drop with the fading daylight, and God only knows what is going to fall out of the darkening sky.

But help arrives as an old beat-up four-wheel-drive pickup with *Comisario* written on the side speeds past with uniformed men inside shouting, *"Me siga."* (Follow me.) There are two boys in the back with bicycles and drinking beer, so I assume at least they are harmless. And since there are likely more blockades ahead, these guys must be heading for a way around them. I follow. Off we drive with spinning tires, cutting across muddy fields and small creeks the truck can barely negotiate. After a half hour's off-roading we return to the single lane road we had deviated from. I mumble a prayer that we've passed the last of the roadblocks and with no time to spare, twist the throttle.

This new path ahead points directly into ominously boiling black clouds lying low on the horizon, while freezing mountain air is becoming colder by the moment. There's barely time to stop and suit up before marble-size hail begins firing down as though I'm a moving target. I stop for a final photo as plummeting ice particles begin to whiten the landscape. The weather toggles back and forth between painful hailstones peppering my hands inside waterlogged gloves and blinding driving rain. If I don't find the summit and descend quickly, I'm in trouble.

As I ascend toward the mountain crest, the slushy muddy trail freezes solid and popcorn-size snowflakes flutter down over ruts and potholes in the road like puffy illusions disguising the threat beneath. The sky is so dark it's hard to guess the time. Hopefully there are still a few hours of light left, enough to reach shelter. One side of my electric heated grips malfunctions, allowing the glove on that side to ice up. Soon my fingers become too cold and stiff to wiggle. At this point, with the temperature inching toward zero, the only thing maintaining my core heat is a battery-operated electric vest.

Because of the blockade, there's no other traffic or other humans out in the storm. Evaluating my situation I realize if the slow leaks in the tires cause them to deflate or if I blow an electrical fuse, events will take a serious turn for the worse. Calculating how much gas remains in the tank I decide even if I can't ride any farther, it's possible to leave the engine idling long enough to stay warm. The grim reality is, if I can't ride any farther, I might only be able to avoid freezing another few hours. Another failure and survival becomes questionable. Reconsidering the changing odds, I reflect on the peculiar trials and tribulations of this journey thus far. At this moment, one tiny thorn in my tire or one small, overheated fuse will determine my fate.

As the back end of the bike abruptly begins to sway, I'm not sure if it's due to a rutted road or my rear tire going flat. I don't want to stop and find out which. The bike is too unstable to shift out of second gear and suddenly the road ahead leads downward. Yet this is a sword that cuts two ways. I'm rapidly descending but also out of control on frozen ground. My brakes are useless and all I can do is keep my legs stretched out, wildly paddling with my feet in an attempt to remain upright.

Within thirty minutes I'm exhausted from struggling for stability but at least I'm descending. As the foul weather lessens and temperatures climb, the frozen road returns to mud. Another mile down the steep grade, twinkling lights appear. Maybe a car, a truck, a farmhouse? At this point, anything means relief from shivering. My rain suit is completely soaked but my electric vest pumps lifesaving heat.

When my rear tire finally fails, within seconds, I'm riding the rim, wobbling all over the road. I could possibly continue rolling at a slower pace but would quickly destroy the tire. I opt for running next to the bike, guiding it downhill toward the distant lights.

For the last two months, people from around the world have sent emails wishing me well and praying for my safety — and maybe tonight those pleas were answered. There's no other way to explain how, on this miserable stormy night, the only other vehicle on this deserted mountain road happens to be a flatbed truck with a crew who has just finished unloading their cargo at a distant farm.

Within minutes, a grumbling diesel lorry eases to a stop and three men leap from the cab to assist; all seem amazed to see anyone out here alone in the storm. First they wrap me in a dry jacket and warm me up inside the cab with the heater blasting away on my hands and face. Ten minutes later, it takes every bit of strength from the four of us to lift the bike up over our heads and onto the back of the raised flatbed. We finally manage to wrangle it into a cockeyed position, secure enough for the hour-long ride to the isolated city of Andajuelas far below. I love Peruvians.

As we arrive at the only tire-repair shop within a hundred miles, we're mobbed by anxious children eager to help us unload, and of course, ask all the usual questions about the bike and the mysterious *gringo*'s journey. Everyone seems to appreciate the distance I've traveled in an effort to know them and their country.

CUSCO, PERU
January 20, 2002
• • • • • • • • • •

The twelve-hour trip from Andajuelas to Cusco was a repeat of yesterday, except at the end of the day I finally reached a scenic, newly paved highway during the last three hours for a smooth glide into Cusco. Well after dark, I'm cold and soaking wet as usual, but relieved to know there's somewhere to relax for a few days. After a quick loop around the city center, I find a cheap room on the fourth floor of a run-down but bug-free hostel with secure parking across the street. Just outside my window reveals a stunning view of the rust-colored tile roofs above sixteenth-century Spanish architecture.

Since real estate is more expensive in large cities, quaint courtyard hotels with big strong iron gates to lock out the evil at night don't exist. So far, my overnights in Peru are mostly in isolated cities high in the Andes, places connected only by beat-up roads too difficult to travel by car. Normally guests arrive by plane or minibus and hotel staff are not used to accommodating travelers with vehicles. I receive strange looks after stomping in late at night dripping wet and asking about parking for a motorcycle. Usually I don't bother telling anyone I've traveled from California, as few can comprehend someone riding in this region for pleasure, let alone from a country so far away.

World-famous Cusco is a cosmopolitan, colonial city populated by interesting people from somewhere else. Enterprising Peruvians migrate from other parts of Peru in search of tourist dollars, and the foreigners who live here complete a mosaic of cultures and languages from around the world. It's a worthy city for sightseeing and, of course, the jumping off point for train trips to study the most complete ruins of ancient Inca civilization at Machu Picchu.

Still, Mexico is my benchmark for rating other countries and unwittingly has raised the bar for evaluating other Latin American nations. Colombians are as nice as Mexicans. Food in Peru is as robust as Mexico and so forth. But few recognize the compliment. Everyone wants to be first and foremost, but in my opinion, only Mexico can claim that title. As in Mexico, city life in Cusco centers around the central plaza with its timeworn, ornately decorated stone cathedrals and colonial structures. In Mexico, it's *el Zocalo*. In Peru, it's *la Plaza de Armas*. When arriving in a new city, to find my bearings, I just ask for the *Plaza de Armas*. That's where budget hotels and decent restaurants are and, of course, the information conduit to the world, *Café Internets*.

When not busy chronicling events of this journey on my laptop, I take early morning strolls through cobblestone streets, engaging in my favorite pastime, yakking with locals. It's a battle of who gets to ask the most questions, them or me. I want to know about their lives and their city and they want to interrogate *el Vikingo Loco* about his adventures. Eventually we strike a balance and I walk away fulfilled, feeling good for having met someone new in a strange country.

Cusco is famous throughout Peru for its nightlife as well as its cultural attributes. But with an "early to bed, early to rise in order to beat the afternoon rains" schedule, I find it difficult to accommodate disco time. Besides, when traveling abroad, I avoid establishments serving alcohol. In my youth, I awoke enough times peeking through bars — which today curbs any remaining lust for nightclubs. Short fuses get shorter with liquor.

Yet after avoiding nocturnal activity for almost four months it's time for a break. Latin Americans are night owls when it comes to partying and I'm fast asleep as they're just starting to rock. My solution: doze off at seven and wake up at midnight with salsa feet.

By 1:00 a.m. fashionably late, luscious Latinas are strolling into the hottest clubs in Cusco. Some of the most beautiful women on the planet hail from Latin America, many of who would like to meet an American man in hopes of obtaining that ticket to paradise, a green card. Unfortunately, they are as knowledgeable as beautiful and don't fall for the "Come back to my hotel room tonight and we'll go get that green card tomorrow" routine.

After wild Saturday nights, Sundays are quiet days in Cusco. Most shops and restaurants close, but the plaza overflows with people of all pedigrees. Backpackers, beggars, Indians, and one lone Viking motorcyclist mingle in the afternoon sun. Saving the best for last, I buy my train ticket for Machu Picchu for a day at the ruins on Tuesday so I can roll Wednesday morning for Bolivia. Riding the Altiplano will mark another milestone in this adventure, keeping me awake nights, anticipating what lies ahead.

Utilizing the last of my free time, I spend the day working on my bike changing oil, fixing loose wires, and tinkering with minor deferred-maintenance necessary to remain on the road. It's important to be extra careful when making repairs while traveling. If parts break during an adjustment, or even if a bolt strips, there are no spares available locally, and importing replacements can take weeks.

MACHU PICCHU
January 22, 2002
• • • • • • • • •

Although I didn't need to be at the train station until 6:00 a.m., there was too much excitement ahead to sleep late — I'm up and ready at four. The previous evening's rains have subsided to a timid tapping on copper-colored tiled roofs, while the brown-bricked city below awakens. Encased in the dark blue glow of an approaching sunrise, as minutes tick by, scattered lights flicker on while more wink off during the predawn changing of the guard. On the dot at six, our sleek, modern train wobbles from the station to begin its winding trudge uphill and out of Cusco. For the first half hour we traverse upward through a series of cleverly designed switchbacks, past shanty towns and squalor, rocking forward and back, ascending as steadily as an aircraft spiraling to gain altitude.

It's a sluggish ascent through diverse layers of humanity, a weary rise through descending tiers of socioeconomic status connected by mud roads to the city below. The rhythms of the moaning train climbing skyward to mythical Machu Picchu lull me into passivity. Here I sit, packed in with blue-haired tourists representing the western industrialized nations. Yet for a change I view scenery unconcerned about potholes or rebelling beasts of burden in the center of the road. But accustomed to controlling the pace, already I miss my motorcycle. In this elongated glass cage I feel separated from nature while grumbling along through spectacular granite gorges. Insulated from the stunning panorama, it's difficult to refrain from constant twitching.

The thickly forested, mountainous countryside is as beautiful as anywhere in Peru, but in this benign, enclosed environment, I feel nothing. Without the wind in my face I can't smell the meadows or taste the light drizzle in the air. Merging with the landscape is out of the question. Within this cozy carriage, I don't even shiver as we snake past snow-capped peaks sparkling with the morning sunrise. I mutter to myself, "The next time I can't ride my motorcycle somewhere, I'll ride a mountain bike."

As we ramble along a canyon floor, swerving with the bank of a swirling muddy river, I long for a rubber raft to shoot the rapids the rest of the way. This tour is as sterile and predictable as California.

As the blue-hairs ooh and ah with their usual chatter, I stare into space drumming my fingers. Retired Canadians are full of blatantly sensible questions followed by, "Eh?" Stone-faced Germans on a group tour won't crack a smile to save their lives, and I suddenly realize that I am the only American.

The neatly packed train finally comes to rest at Machu Picchu station and pukes out its first load of babbling tourists. Downhill we file as an invading force armed with dollars and Nikons on a broad path lined with eager vendors and costumed Indians. For a man who loathes being one of the crowd, I am surely one today.

It's a fifteen-minute bus ride up to the ruins past jagged jungle summits and breathtaking drop-offs. After coughing up a twenty-dollar entrance fee, I'm free to roam and explore impressive ancient antiquities and, on this warm sunny mountain morning, seek the ghosts of Inca civilization.

Like enormous fingers of green, surrounding pointed peaks of rocky jungle shoot skyward as I enter the earthen path leading to the ruins. Every day in Peru has shocked me. Although I gripe about tourist trains and buses after daring motorcycle adventures, a group tour is the only way to arrive and indeed I'm glad to be here. Arrows point the way to a hiking trail winding through a perfectly matched stone pillar city. To avoid panting crowds already bunching up at scenic overlooks, I veer off in the opposite direction — a summary of my approach to life.

Coated with sunscreen and sporting a new alpaca hat, I set out to explore and wander the skeletal remains of a forgotten culture, undisturbed. All was well until halftime, when my path intersected with onrushing armies of blue-hairs sputtering more oohs, ahs, and ehs, while peering into corners of the chiseled stone maze. In spite of distractions, I manage a few minutes of solitude perched atop a picturesque overlook on a granite slab cantilevering out over a sheer drop. Anxious to sense my unique surroundings I sink into brief meditation, spiraling down quickly into nothingness.

Machu Picchu, like most everywhere on this journey, requires more time than I allot. Yet there's no controlling the lust to move on followed by a nudge to fire up and head down another road. Younger travelers I meet are from Argentina, Chile, and Brazil. Still, I encounter no one from home. Everyone is sincerely friendly and eager with questions about America and where I'm heading next. After meeting so many nice people today from countries on my to-visit list, I'm more restless than ever to jump back in the wind.

From Cusco, it's a two-day ride to La Paz, Bolivia, the departure point for crossing the *Altiplano* into Chile with a descent through the Atacama Desert toward Santiago. The wilderness of Patagonia awaits with its enchanted forests, canyon-carving glaciers, and spectacular fiords. Once again tonight I drift off to sleep dreaming in Spanish of adventure to come.

ON THE BORDER
January 23, 2002
• • • • • • • • •

I knew I'd made a mistake by accepting a riding partner when he's an hour late for the early start he requested. He arrives at the time I wanted to leave anyway, but sitting in the hotel lobby waiting prevents me from doing the things I put off. One of several reasons I prefer to travel alone.

He's an American biker living in Peru who wants to ride to Brazil. He suggests we travel as far as La Paz together, which is possible to reach in one day on a high-speed run of ten hours. I'm in love with Peru and in no hurry to leave and would rather take my time, dividing the ride into two days. In Cusco, I made many friends, and if not committed to riding with someone, I would have stayed a few more days. That's the advantage of traveling alone. You can reverse decisions on a whim without annoying anyone.

Throttle controls your mood and your mood controls the throttle, that's Motorcycling 101. My partner wants to ride eighty mph and make time for the border because he's in a hurry to get to Brazil. Four months ago I made a decision to slow down and not kill myself by running too fast in such unpredictable conditions. Besides, there's way too much to see and experience along the way to view Peru in a blur.

Even though the road is well paved through open spaces and nearly all straightaways have zero traffic, we agree to a limit of sixty mph. Back in the States this would call for ninety mph cruising but here, I'm driving him crazy riding slow and eventually, foolishly allow myself to be drawn into matching his pace.

Suddenly out of nowhere bolts one of the thousands of dogs that chase motorcycles in South America. Unaware there are two of us, El Fido attacks the lead bike traveling at seventy-five mph. Unable to match the biker's speed, he slows to a fast walk, directly across the path of my fishtailing Kawasaki 650, infamous for its poor braking ability. We're both lucky, as he barely leaps out of the way while my front tire gobbles up sections of tail fur.

Collision with anything at this speed means loss of control and a tenth of a second difference could've brought us both down. I consider how this might have ended. There are no emergency helicopters here to whisk an injured biker off to high-tech trauma centers. I likely would lie here until a speeding truck or bus rolled along to finish the job.

My companion never notices or looks back, violating a cardinal rule — to keep an eye on your partner. The lead rider should always keep track of the rider behind in his mirror, in case he runs into trouble. This distraction increases the hazard of riding lead, yet it is part of the responsibility that comes with that position, a reason I prefer to ride lead.

The rest of the day is more of the same, blasting past rural scenery demanding hours to properly digest and although I silently promise to return someday, I worry I might not. I need to stop for photos.

Lake Titicaca is off to the east. The sun is dropping beyond the glistening Royal Andes, reflecting off the ebony waters of the highest navigable lake in the world. Enormous jagged, snow-covered peaks are mirrored on the still surface, commanding a moment of silence, a gesture of homage, and a call for meditation. In the rush, I settle for a photograph on the wrong camera setting.

We arrive at the border at dark, increasing the turmoil and confusion caused by busloads of weary travelers simultaneously converging on the immigration office. A dozen giggling, excited children surround our bikes offering to guard them for us while we get our passports stamped. My partner says he has a better idea. If he comes back and finds anything missing he will hunt them down and break their fingers. I don't like this approach.

Inside the *migracion* office I start yakking with friendly officials, who stop what they're doing to fire off the usual questions about this journey. I explain how sad it is to leave but promise to return one day. After they help with my paperwork, I pull out my camera for a group shot, nearly causing a riot as everyone wrangles to get into the picture. Meanwhile my partner says something offensive to the man holding an essential stamp — who announces there is now a problem stamping his passport. He states, "There's a rule against it," and he verifies the claim by producing some obscure regulation about foreign residents needing a letter proving they are debt-free before leaving the country. The whole matter could be resolved with a different attitude or a five-dollar bill as a token apology. My partner digs in his heels, choosing to argue instead. Guess who wins? Eventually, we approach customs to clear the bikes. While I'm busy shaking hands with jovial *aduana*, my partner has another argument going. In all fairness, he's a nice guy, just burned out on the people, culture, and Third World bureaucratic procedures. After living in Peru so long he's even bored with the scenery.

He has now managed to get himself officially denied exit from Peru and we must stay another night on the Peruvian side of the border to try again in the morning. Since I already crossed, I need to go get a re-entry stamp in my passport to remain until morning. A process that should take minutes stretches into hours.

We find a three-dollar-a-night hotel down the street with no hot water or private bathroom. Even with heavy wool blankets and bedding down in a sweater, the cold dominates. At 13,000 feet, it's hard to sleep long or soundly due to an increased heart rate from lack of oxygen, and several times I wake up gasping for breath. At least the sheets are clean, and at this altitude, there aren't any bugs.

BOLIVIA

ON THE ROAD TO LA PAZ
January 24, 2002
● ● ● ● ● ● ● ● ● ●

After recalling why it's best to ride solo, I quietly slide out the patio door at the courtyard hostel and hightail it for the border. Everyone there is as cooperative as last night. The customs official on the Bolivian side insists that I strap my camera around my neck, proudly declaring, "It will soon be necessary to take many photographs." After another big hearty *"Buena suerte amigo,"* I spin into the mud roads of Bolivia and a new chapter of life to the tenth power. Each morning, I awake to what seems like another dream of the open road. Senses grow more acute, perception alters, and whatever troubled me the day before is soon forgotten. Vacillating in and out of surrealistic moments, I fee like I'm drifting through Salvador Dali's painting of the melting clocks.

The fluorescent pale glow of the morning sky is abnormally vast today, stretching across the pencil line of the horizon farther than I can ever remember. Low-lying, white wispy clouds resting gently against the overhead blue dome appear almost within reach, and I imagine brushing them aside for a better view of the mountains. It is moments like this that cause me to realize that although I live within a foggy dream, through this mist I find clarity.

Dreams and goals define life. When dreams change to goals, the small talk ends and the work begins. As I teach my students, "The easy part's done and that's the talking." There are short-term, medium-term, and long-term goals, each with their own degree of complications to test one's resolve. Once goal-oriented, you can control your life. A round-trip motorcycle ride to South America has always been a dream for me. However, when it became a goal, it evolved into an exercise in discipline and perseverance. I knew it would be a tough challenge and prepared for the inevitable obstacles. Now, my dream ride has become a test of the human spirit and personal development.

If I can survive these trials, I'll be more capable than ever of succeeding in life's challenges. This journey was never intended to prove something to anyone else. My intention was to better understand the real world and my own character, as well as to explore my own limits.

Unfortunately, in the ecstasy of merging with the surrounding wonderment, there are moments of depression and loneliness. Alone most of the time, I sometimes struggle to overcome the brain-mangling effects of captivity by thugs bent on destroying my mind, and I find my jaw clenched far too often. It feels as though my captivity occurred a lifetime ago, yet it's only been forty-four days since being freed. Three weeks ago, my stomach could barely handle a normal meal and I lacked the physical strength to do a single push-up. I have never before taken on so much, in such a weakened state.

Although it feels like I could stay on the road forever, I recognize it's not psychologically healthy to be isolated from friends and family after the Colombian ordeal. How risky is this — living inside my head with life centering around only the road beyond? My first thoughts now are in Spanish, and if I'm in a hurry there's no telling what comes out. With mental practice, I dial in localized dialects and figures of speech, which I usually don't understand until after crossing the next border. Each frontier becomes a fresh journey, an entry into a different culture, a different geography and a different political landscape. Every new country offers another lifetime. Nothing is predictable. Just another phase of a fantasy that flows from astonishment to occasional fear to toe-curling ecstasy sprinkled with bits of trepidation.

It's the tragedy of the staggering poverty that's most disturbing, along with the frustration of being unable to affect it. Some days I consider returning as a Peace Corps volunteer, other days I ponder marching back to lead a revolution. At times, the ruthless injustice of the Third World is more than I can bear.

Having grown up within a capitalist society I see little wrong with struggling harder to get ahead, but there should be limits. No human being could witness the suffering of the developing world firsthand without acknowledging the need for a more equitable distribution of wealth.

When everyone is engaged in the race, it's no sin to strive for victory, but racing against those who are crawling is disgraceful. There is something obscene about a rich man in a Mercedes honking his horn at a destitute old grandfather on a scrawny donkey, yelling at him to get out of his way.

If there is dignity in wealth, it lies in disguising it and utilizing it to help others. How there can be billionaires while masses starve is an issue that needs to be considered, now more than ever. Acknowledging the legitimate need for certain sectors of the human race to bolt to the top should also beg the question — how much is enough?

LA PAZ, BOLIVIA
January 27, 2002
• • • • • • • • • •

After three laid-back nights indoors resting in La Paz, waiting out foul weather, I'm stir-crazy once again. La Paz is a typical South American big city, with colonial architecture and museums full of Spanish artifacts. There's a heavier police presence than I've seen thus far. Gangs of scowling *Policia Nacional* outfitted with machine guns, helmets, shields, and tear gas launchers circle like predators awaiting victims. Sneering facial expressions confirm these goons are looking for trouble.

The people are a mix of races and cultures ranging from European blends to full-blooded Indian. There's little American influence in music, culture, or the media. This is fine with me; I didn't come this far to hear rap music or eat at McDonald's. The extraordinarily broad Indian women dominating the street merchant scene waddle about like rotund cartoon characters with undersized, dark felt derbies cocked to one side of their braided hairdos. Thick multilayers of petticoats they wear beneath colorful native costumes of geometric patterns make them look even wider.

As I shoot a few interesting pictures at the Alacita Fair in downtown La Paz, locals seem to resent being photographed and return my meek smiles with burning stare-downs meant to maim. I'm the only *gringo* among 100,000 Bolivians, who are out to have a good time without the presence of foreigners. The people are more tolerant than friendly, and offer polite acknowledgments in return, but it's obvious they prefer no outsiders, especially ones with cameras. Until yesterday, I resisted snapping photos of Indians even though they make fascinating studies with their native costumes and ornate headgear. Some hold strong traditional beliefs that photography is a form of stealing their soul. I try to respect this but occasionally yield to temptation and sneak a shot off with the digital camera leveled from my waist.

Streets are packed for a mile in all directions and inside it's almost impossible to maneuver through the shoulder-to-shoulder crowd. The Alacita Fair consists mainly of booths manned by indigenous people, each peddling the same cheap trinkets as the next and, of course, hundreds of food vendors cooking up secret traditional dishes that whet my culinary curiosity. Anxious to show courage and behave as a local, I boldly devour things that still have beaks, hoofs, and eyeballs intact, followed by fluffy, deep-fried, sugary pastries.

The upcoming ride across the southern half of the Bolivian Andes will cover some of the most remote and scenic regions of the country. From here on, I'll be experiencing the *Altiplano* at altitudes of 14,000 to 17,000 feet, across hundreds of miles of salt flats and deserted plateaus. Vast segments are unmapped and those maps that do exist often disagree about where, or even if, there's a road. Even my GPS shows only open, high-altitude plains of barren landscape between international borders. Mostly, I plan to follow tire tracks in sand or salt across immense, dry lake beds — tracks that may not show up in the rain.

There are several 300-mile stretches with no fuel available but my bike's range is about 260 depending on conditions. Even with a spare three-gallon fuel supply, if I take off in a wrong direction against a headwind, it could mean trouble. Temperatures drop to below zero after sundown and there's almost no traffic in the daytime and none at night. A problem with the bike under these conditions could have unpleasant consequences. Settlements with available shelter might have generator-supplied electricity but certainly no phones or Internet. For the next few weeks, I expect to be out of contact until emerging somewhere in northern Chile. From there it will be a two-day ride at sea level south to Santiago.

THE BOLIVIAN *ALTIPLANO*
January 29, 2002
● ● ● ● ● ● ● ● ●

Optimistic locals described the 250-mile ride from Oruro to Uyuni as ten hours of rugged off-road wrangling. Generally that would mean eight hours on a bike and an easier time. So far it's a miserable surprise.

Road conditions begin poor and become worse in minutes. There's nothing but open high desert, with no markings or indications which way to turn at the numerous forks in the deep-sand road. I use two maps along with the GPS. None correspond. The GPS is the most honest, as it indicates precise positions on the planet. Unfortunately, it fails to display any of the tiny remote outposts or dirt roads of the Bolivian *Altiplano*. My whereabouts is a mere black triangle on a blank screen with no reference points other than the international borders of Bolivia, Chile, and Argentina. My route for the next four days is simple — head for a mountain range I know exists 200 miles west, then follow the foothills to Chile.

From my current position, I must travel directly south to my planned overnight in the *pueblito* of Uyuni. I arbitrarily select a trail from one of the many forks in the road and ride for a while, watching my compass to see if I drift east or west. If I do, I return to the fork and try the other, hoping it leads due south. This is a frustrating, time gobbling process and each moment is critical out on the *Altiplano*. At night, temperatures drop below zero and since distance vision is limited in the dark, I'll have no way to see where I'm heading.

Soil conditions seldom worry four-wheel travelers but on a motorcycle, when riding off-road they can make the difference between remaining upright or sliding horizontally. The beat-up, battered, one-lane excuse for a trail varies in soil consistency from DG (decomposed granite) to deep coarse sand to hardened clay. All respond differently to wet or dry conditions.

An extended stretch of windblown DG quickly becomes the worst washboard surface imaginable. The cross-grooves are from six to ten inches deep and are spaced wide enough to prevent smoothing the bumpiness by riding the tops a little faster. There is an inescapable, violent jarring at any speed with no relief from the relentless punishment of eyeballs jiggling so bad I can barely focus.

When the road is not washboard, it turns to soft coarse sand, without any visible warning in advance. A firm wrenching of my handlebars as the front wheel digs in signals it's too late to slow down. What's left is to accept the new direction the front wheel is twisting into, and fight to remain upright. These stretches drag on for miles and, for the last few hours, I can't shift out of first gear without sacrificing control. Even at five mph, at this altitude it's an exhausting struggle to maintain a straight line.

At times the road dips into gullies flooded with water or mud, with no way around. I never know how deep they are, so I build speed and race through where it appears shallow. The slower I go, the farther I sink. The mud also wrenches control of the front wheel until I plant my feet to keep from tipping over. Then dark-colored goop instantly fills my boots.

I've grown accustomed to hustling early in the day and retiring by four to avoid the late afternoon storms. Today, I'm too far away from a town to quit early. I need to find shelter before dark and am on constant lookout for any kind of structure, inhabited or not. There's nothing but high-altitude, wide-open plains, with the steadfast Andes hundreds of miles away in all directions.

At a 15,000-foot summit I notice fresh fallen snow on the sides of the road and hope a squall passed ahead and maybe my luck has changed. Yet the problem now is, the snow has melted on top of the compacted clay road, making it slick as ice.

The first stretch of wet clay whisks the bike out from underneath me, sending us both sliding sideways, tearing a saddlebag off in the process. There's been no other traffic all day, so I'm alone trying to pick up the bike on a sloping surface I can barely stand on without slipping. With some serious grunting, I turn backwards, lifting with leg power, and just as I maneuver the bike upright, my boots slide and we both go down again. I use every bit of remaining strength on the next few tries until finally managing to put the kickstand down and rest for a moment before jumping back on to continue. There's not a second to waste; I'm already behind.

Another thousand feet up the road, the bike spins out again, sending us skidding upside down into a ditch and twisting my shoulder with a painful pop. I crawl back far enough to snap a photo and then repeat the process of righting the muddy machine. So goes the afternoon under a menacing sky and no sign of my destination or suitable structure for shelter. Now, after so many crashes, I can only rely on one arm to lift the bike. Amazingly, there's no significant damage to the bike. The aluminum-strapped plastic hand guards that Jimmy installed have cracked but still protect the hand levers against breakage and for some reason every time I go down it's on the left side. This means the left saddlebag gets torn off a dozen times today but due to its superb design, obediently snaps back into place. I love this equipment.

After too much guesswork in the dark, I finally limp into Uyuni fourteen hours after setting out. People in the street of this rustic *pueblo* stop and stare. Both the bike and I resemble ghostly clay statues. Nothing matters at the moment except a hot shower and a good night's rest. Anyways I find the good night's rest.

Tomorrow, I will start early for a three-day ride across the most rugged region of the *Altiplano* and down into the Atacama Desert. Thus far, it's been merely a warm-up for the real endurance test still to come. Guidebooks advise against attempting this route in the rainy season, or under any circumstances, alone. There's no way to avoid the rainy season now, but maybe one of the tour Jeeps leaving in the morning will permit me to tag along behind.

PLANAR DE SALAR
January 30, 2002
• • • • • • • • • •

Several small tour companies operate in Uyuni to take stouthearted travelers on expeditions into remote regions of the Bolivian *Altiplano*. The southern half of this country is famous for its high-altitude, salt-encrusted lakebeds. Concealed within this wasteland, multihued saltwater lagoons fill with bright pink flamingos posing against the vivid colors of mineral deposits. Since there are no airports or even railroads in the region, few travelers wander this far into the Andes. From the nearest city, it's a long, bouncing minibus ride on the partially paved road. The dirt road I took, I've named Hell Highway. Either way, if you are in Uyuni, you must really want to be here.

There are plenty of scare stories about the route I've chosen to reach Chile. For the first time, I'm going to pay attention to the warnings and take the precaution of following a Toyota Land Cruiser, also headed out this morning into the *Planar de Salar* (Salt Plains). The tour operator promised a departure at 10:30 a.m., sharp. At 11:15 we're finally exiting the small high-altitude *pueblo* of Uyuni to begin our venture into the far reaches of one of the more remote regions on earth.

The road out of Uyuni is as bad as the one leading in and like yesterday, only gets worse as the day progresses. Generally, when traveling overland it's better to ride a motorcycle than drive a four-wheel vehicle — under these conditions, it's the opposite. The stability of the Land Cruiser allows it to move twice as fast as a motorcycle and the tour operator's schedule dictates that they speed. No one, not even experienced guides, wants to get caught out here after dark.

The cherry-red Land Cruiser is packed with eight laughing, singing, college-age American backpackers, the Bolivian driver, and his wife. The severely rutted, washboard road keeps them happily hopping along at thirty mph, enjoying a mild thrill each time they hit a stretch of soft sand that sends them fishtailing slightly out of control. Yet what gives them the giggles strikes fear in me. A safe speed for my awkwardly weighted motorcycle on a road this bad is fifteen mph so I ride out of control, struggling to keep up.

The constant teeth-shattering jarring is painful misery to me and damaging to my electronic equipment. I feel beat up, broken down, and aching in every swollen joint from yesterday's crashes. I need a few days to heal up but this was the only crew leaving until late next week. Once again, it was now or never as we disappeared into a seemingly endless, ultra-high-altitude wilderness of hundreds of square miles of uncharted terrain. There are no reference points on any of my maps. With the exception of a few meekly populated outposts manned by local families catering to travel groups, almost the entire desolate region is uninhabited by man or beast. The dry rocky soil at 14,000 feet is incapable of supporting life, not even insects.

The nonstop throbbing in my twisted shoulder is a steady reminder — I can't afford to go down again. My body and equipment may have miraculously survived the previous day's thrashing, but I'm out of chances. There's no more margin for error; any damage to the bike rendering it inoperable means leaving it behind. Any damage to me, rendering me unable to ride, sends me up the proverbial creek without that paddle.

Within a few hours we encounter patches of white crust on the ground that appear at first to be ice from the previous evening's freeze. The farther we drive, the bigger the patches become until we abruptly plunge headlong into a vast, shimmering white, dry lake bed. Minutes later, there's nothing in sight but a bright, blinding surface with short jagged mountains ringing the horizon. The enveloping silence of this eerie blank world disorientates me.

It's picture time for the tour group, affording me opportunity to catch up while they stop to romp around snapping photos of each other in comical poses. It's a perfect setting for a snowball fight except this is not snow. It is salt crystallized over the eons to form a high-altitude illusion of a winter wonderland. It's also hard to believe that this dry lake bed, 14,000 feet up in the Andes was once at sea level.

Although confident I'm on solid ground and there's no water under the sodium crust, I still use caution as I lower my kickstand and dismount. I step around softly, half expecting the surface to crack open and gulp me into chilling depths. I can't shake the uneasiness, even when bending to touch the surface. It has no color and no temperature. In every breath, I'm swallowed up within an acoustically dead, benign environment where all the colors of the rainbow merge to form absolute white.

There's not enough atmosphere at this altitude to filter out the sun's piercing ultraviolet rays and when I remove my helmet, the combined reflections off the brilliant crust burn my face purple in minutes. The white is still blinding even wearing sunglasses behind my tinted face shield.

Continuing deeper into the crystallized wilderness, we discover scattered mountaintops rising out of the white are really just ancient islands too high to be encrusted by layers of salt. We stop for a meal at the biggest of the cactus-covered rock mounds. The Land Cruiser crew brought food for themselves so I find a cave where a local family of island dwellers is cooking their midday meal. A dollar buys a place at the table with dried llama meat and a lukewarm Coke.

Back on the salt flats, it's party time. There are no obstructions or soft sand to slow us down and the Land Cruiser driver and I speed across the flat surface as fast as the altitude allows our motors to breathe. There's barely a ripple to disturb the flow, and I resist temptation to drop my feet and spray rooster tails of salt into the dry mountain air.

Since the ground is crisscrossed by thousands of tracks running in all directions, it's impossible to find one consistent path. My GPS is useless; it only displays international borders hundreds of miles away. Without an experienced guide to lead me, there's no possibility of locating a way out so my survival is tethered to the vehicle ahead.

As we speed along free of obstructions, I feel confident enough to stop for a photo. Cautiously keeping one eye on the accelerating Land Cruiser and the other focusing through the lens of the digital camera, I'm caught off-guard at how quickly my newfound friends are disappearing. Within the thirty seconds it takes to stop, unpack the camera and shoot, the rapidly fading fiery red Land Cruiser has turned into a black dot. Panic sets in as I try to memorize the point where they evaporate into the silent blank wall of white.

I must recklessly increase my speed to catch up and hope the driver has not altered his course. If he did, we'll never find each other again, even if he happens to notice I'm no longer behind him. I will simply wander around in circles until running out of gas. There are no search and rescue planes. I'm on my own.

The last signals from seven orbiting satellites confirm a heading of southwest at sixty miles per hour; catching up requires kicking it up to ninety with crossed fingers. There's no choice. I slam the hammer down, deciding to hold it open until something gives, one way or another.

Whomever friends talk to when they pray for me was listening again today as the black dot grows into a flaming red Land Cruiser full of laughing, singing youngsters. When I pull up alongside the speeding vehicle, the unwitting passengers smile and wave enthusiastically. They hadn't even noticed I'd fallen behind.

The front end of the bike, my pants, and my gloves become layered with sparkling crystals of salt that shine like ice. Even my skin inside the protection of my helmet and face shield gets a light covering. In this scene of sensory depravation, I breathe the white as well as hear it.

For two more hours we roll across the colorless landscape until the process we followed to get here reverses itself. Again we encounter patches of rocky earth leading back to crumbling roads of soft coarse sand littered with small boulders hazardous enough to also slow the Land Cruiser. The stress and strain of fighting to remain upright returns and doesn't subside until sunset when we reach a tiny group of adobe *casitas* grouped together in the stillness of this Andean desert.

There's no electricity or telephone but we are issued flimsy cots in a chilly brick dormitory and given cold soup and hot coca leaf tea to relieve the effects of altitude. Tomorrow morning at sunrise, we'll kick it up another notch or three.

STILL SPINNIN' MY WHEELS
January 31, 2002
Laguna Verde
• • • • • • • •

So far out into the boondocks, there are no crowing roosters to awaken us, but we are up at 7:00 a.m. and ready to roll on schedule. I get moving earlier than the others to wash the salt off the bike and to buy some overpriced drum gas from a local boy; a bargain at any cost, considering it's the only fuel in the region. According to my calculations, I should be able to make it from here in San Juan, Bolivia to San Pedro, Chile if there are no problems.

I ask the Land Cruiser driver what to expect on the road ahead. He replies, "*Mas malo señor, mucho mas malo.*" (Much worse, a whole lot worse.) Just what I didn't need to hear.

He wasn't kidding, he was understating. The road today is mile after mile of deep coarse sand that keeps my tires spinning in first gear until noon. An incorrect air/fuel mixture in the carburetor begins to take its toll on my laboring engine as the temperature gauge hovers on the high side all day. There's a chance of piston meltdown if remaining at low-speed, high-RPM too long. Air must move over the radiator to keep the motor cool.

Slowing down to wait for me aggravates the Bolivian driver, and

I understand he has his own pace to maintain. He lets it be known with disgusted looks that his patience is gone. The original deal was he would let me follow only if I could keep up. It is clear to both of us, that isn't happening. I've been going as fast as possible and he has been going as slow as he possibly can. Something has to give and it does. I'm now on my own.

Within minutes he disappears into identical swells of sand dunes leaving me only his dust cloud in the distance to provide a direction of travel. But that too is fading and hard to follow. Just like the salt flats, there are tire tracks by the thousands crisscrossing the rocky soft-sand-covered hills. Which set the Land Cruiser might have made, I can only guess.

Even at this laggard pace, I am still riding out of control. When I manage to accelerate enough to shift out of second gear, the front wheel is invariably yanked away, leaving me fighting to stay upright, stretching out my legs and paddling with my feet. This has been going on for hours and my groin muscles feel like they are being ripped from my bones. I'm thoroughly exhausted and lost.

The GPS indicates we've been skirting the eastern border with Chile, heading southwest, and I assume if I continue to hug the base of the mountain I will ultimately reach an outpost, hopefully before running out of fuel. The air is freezing cold but I sweat profusely inside the foul-weather suit. Still, I decide to leave it on, afraid to waste a single second either changing clothes or resting.

There's no doubt that if I don't find the red Land Cruiser, I'll simply ride aimlessly until running out of fuel. The stark reality is, survival is questionable in the subzero nighttime temperatures of the Bolivian *Altiplano*. It's a no-brainer; catch up or get shipped home as a Popsicle.

Rolling over the top of one of the endless sandy mounds, I spot a faint dust cloud a mile away. This is my only chance. Again, it's now or never. The rocky trail feels somewhat firmer so I cast my fate to the wind and hold the throttle open, flying off recklessly in search of what may or may not be the vehicle's fading dust cloud.

The final bouncing blast to catch the elusive Land Cruiser lasts only seconds, just long enough to build up enough speed to kick into third gear. Instantly the front end washes out from underneath me, and I shoot forward, head first over the handlebars, straight to the ground like an arrow. An excruciating crack is followed by silent, empty black.

At first I think it's Dutch being spoken, then Hebrew, then German. Somewhere in the swirling unconsciousness surfaces a soft familiar echo . . . "I think he is still breathing." Finally, in a distinctive Kiwi accent, I hear a young New Zealander ask, "You spyke English? Can ya 'ear me, mite?"

There's background chatter in languages I think that I recognize but don't quite understand. As I strain to open my eyes, more dirt and grit falls into them, stinging. I attempt to speak but my mouth is coated in and half-filled with sand. It takes all my concentration not to cough. All I can manage is a groan to acknowledge I hear them. I must have muttered something understandable because they all begin speaking English at once, firing off questions faster than I can answer.

"You all right, mite? Can ya move yer legs? Can ya feel this? Can ya feel yer toes?"

Suddenly there's more sand in my face as they lift the bike off while the wind blows debris into my helmet. The young New Zealander shades my face with his hands because I cannot move mine.

Slowly, I begin to focus on the scene around me. There are twenty men and women huddled around, leaning in with worried expressions on their faces. One of the girls is crying. They keep asking about my legs and I moan they feel okay, then mutter, "Why, are they broken?"

Years of judo competition and previous bike wrecks have taught me that you can't always immediately tell what is damaged, because the trauma of impact alters pain sensors. If I wait, the pain will subside. It's not my legs that concern me; it's the excruciating pain in the back of my neck and inability to turn my head. I recall injuries from throws in judo tournaments; the damage was seldom as bad as it seemed at first. After landing wrong with a severe impact, you'd swear you broke all your ribs or blew out a knee. But if you waited a few minutes the pain would ease and often you'd be ready to fight again.

I ask them to wait before we try to move, maybe I can do it on my own. In the meantime a more important question — How is my bike?

"The bike is full of sand, but looks okay," the German says.

The pain in my neck is incredible, but subsiding. Sure enough, after ten minutes I feel confident enough to say, "Let's give it a try."

With a couple of hearty lads on either side steadying my rise, I'm soon standing on my own two feet and rinsing gritty sand from my mouth with a bottle of fresh water. I fight nausea with slow deep yogic breathing, and my equilibrium returns.

"How long was I out?"

"Dunno mite, we were 'ere several minutes before you came around."

They're making preparations for someone to ride my bike and start to load my ripped-up saddlebags into one of their silver Land Cruisers. "No, no, no. Thanks, but no thanks. I'll ride my own bike, boys."

"'At's not a good idea mite, you've 'ad quite a spill."

"Thanks bro, but it don't work that way, I rode it in, I'll ride it out."

"At least let us carry your bags in our wagon, it will make your bike easier to handle."

"Thanks guys, I'll manage." (A basic rule in travel is, never get separated from your gear.)

There were hundreds of square miles of unmapped high desert wilderness with dozens of alternate trails and roads to choose from today. I try to imagine why a small caravan of silver Toyota Land Cruisers, representing the only human life in the wide-open rugged plains selected the same one I had chosen. I guess it's another coincidence.

I methodically repack my gear and cautiously climb back onto the bike. There's a few parts bent out of shape, and a small clip on the saddlebag has finally given way after the numerous times it's been torn away, but it still holds in place. The GPS is scratched up and the mount is twisted, but it bends back easily. I'm shaken but ready to ride — there's no choice.

I pass out business cards to everyone and promise to write about them in my journals and apprehensively limp back into the wind. Though each bump in the road feels like someone kicking me in the head, I fight the temptation to pop a Motrin. I know I've sustained another concussion and don't want to thin my blood and risk bleeding in my brain. This new group is moving much slower and is easier to follow.

After an hour of slow, steady increase in altitude and rapidly falling temperature, we reach the 16,000-foot summit just as snow begins to fill the air. In the distance, I spot the bloodred Land Cruiser and the young Americans busily engaged in a snowball fight. As I pull over to stop, one of them asks, "Where have you been, Glen? We were worried you might have fallen off your bike."

The caravans head out again, lumbering across the rolling terrain toward Laguna Colorado, a tiny outpost of a dozen adobe buildings and another colorful saltwater lagoon. Because of the snowstorm it's hard to calculate how much daylight remains — I estimate an hour. When I ask the driver how much more time until Laguna Colorado, he says, "One hour." We both quietly realize, one hour for him is two for me.

Again he grows impatient and pulls his Land Cruiser to a halt, offering to ride the bike for me because he rode one once as a kid. Yeah right. Again he warns that he can't wait while pointing to the gently sloping hills in the distance. In Spanish, I think he says, "All tracks lead to San Juan." With that, he disappears in seconds over the next rocky knoll.

The last humans out tonight are all in front of me and I now have a new definition of what it means to be alone. It's getting dark quickly and as we descend from the summit, the swirling snow turns to icy rain and the thousands of barely detectable tracks spread out over miles finally seem to lead in one direction.

The temperature is dropping as fast as the clocks are spinning and the black clouds lower into freezing evening fog. It's another long shot and I wonder if tonight my luck has finally run out. I look around one last time before releasing the clutch. I'm again soaking wet and shivering, and again, I'm out of options.

Once rolling forward, I can't allow myself to stop; if I do, the sand may be too soft to get moving again, and I don't have the strength to dig out the bike if it gets buried. Fighting this miserable terrain has drained my arms and legs of any reserve energy and the cold is creeping in. The electric vest maintains my core heat long enough to get within sight of a silhouette of a small group of block buildings in the distance next to a darkened, mist-shrouded saltwater lake. I made it.

With no electricity and no wood to burn for heat, gas stoves boiling water for noodles are enough to keep the inside chill of the eating area tolerable. There's no running water for a shower or toilet and it's too cold to undress in the dank, stone dormitory. I wolf down some foul-tasting noodles, stumble into the dorm with a dozen bunk beds, and crumple into a pile on a lower rack. As I pull a set of grimy covers over my head, I plunge immediately into a comatose sleep only to awaken with the driver of the red Land Cruiser shaking my aching shoulder.

"If you want to follow us in the morning, we are leaving at 5:00 a.m." The remote Bolivian/Chilean border outposts are only open a few hours on weekdays until noon and closed on weekends.

"If you miss your chance tomorrow, you will have to wait until the trip next week."

"Don't worry, I'll be ready."

The best roads in South America are in Chile, even considering its infamous gravel *Camino Austral*, a road that leads adventuring motorists through a scenic wilderness in the southern half of the country. As of sunrise tomorrow I'll be within hours of motorcycle paradise. I drift off to sleep dreaming of pavement, a shower, and the hot dry air of the Atacama Desert.

LAST DAY IN BOLIVIA
February 1, 2002
● ● ● ● ● ● ● ● ●

A young, unshaven, bundled-up Bolivian man holding a candle marches into the dorm at 4:45 a.m. shouting *"Vamos, vamos."* I don't have much gear to repack, but I still would rather perform the double-check with more light than the candle he leaves to illuminate a room jammed with bunk beds. There's no electricity and no heat. It's damned cold. Time to go.

I load my saddlebags while the Land Cruisers warm up and spew enormous, billowing clouds of white vapor into the freezing morning air. Drivers quickly back out into caravan formation. No one wants to be last in case there's trouble with their equipment. The last vehicle has no support and I never want to be the last vehicle again. I want to be directly behind the red Land Cruiser and ahead of the three slower-moving silver ones. If the red wagon gets too far ahead again, at least I'll have the silver ones as backup. This is my plan anyway.

It's far below zero and the bike is hard starting but finally fires up in a weak pulsating idle with the choke full on. We're an hour from sunrise and the much-anticipated blue glow of an approaching dawn.

The motorcycle seat covering material is a neoprene type similar to a wet suit. It's great when dry, but when wet from the rain, it holds enough water to freeze solid. I sit atop a buttock-chilling crust of ice while holding down the GPS's "on" button. Nothing happens and the Land Cruisers are starting to pull out. Damn, another GPS down. As a last resort, I pull the twelve-volt plug adapter off and wiggle wires. Sure enough, it faintly blinks to life.

When it's first switched on, the GPS screen features a series of rotating balls that spin around the viewer screen to indicate a search mode for satellites. I know from experience how fast those balls should rotate. Not only does the screen fail to cycle on time to the next phase of satellite signal strength readout, but the process is in slow motion as the balls barely move. I recall reading in the manual that this unit should operate in sub-freezing temperatures. I can only guess that it must be more than ten degrees below zero. I chuckle at the thought of going for a motorcycle ride when it is cold enough to shut down an all-weather instrument like a GPS.

The connectors on the switches Jimmy installed on the bike to efficiently manage the electronics have corroded in the heavy salt air. Nothing works at first. After wiggling some wires, lights suddenly flash on, the vest warms up, and one grip heater flows heat.

The blessing now is the soft coarse sand that caused so much trouble last night is frozen hard as concrete and as long as I stay within ruts running in the direction everyone else is headed, I should be fine. Off we jiggle, bounce, and slide, following only a dim set of red taillights in the lead.

It's still too dark to see through my tinted face shield, so I leave it up, exposing my skin to the stinging, frigid predawn air. Droplets from my running nose and eyes flowing down my face instantly freeze solid, while ice builds up on my boots.

Our first stop is at the base of an active volcano for a bath in a shallow pool of natural hot springs that feed into a small lake. Everyone changes into swimsuits and wades into the steaming mineral pool for a sunrise dip while the Bolivian driver and his wife whip up scrambled eggs and toasted bread over a propane stove. I decline offers to join the Jacuzzi party but gladly accept an issue of steaming *huevos*.

The dirt track finally transforms into a real road, freshly graded and relatively smooth although still soft in places. Still, I can't risk increasing my speed and again the driver warns that he can't keep waiting. He promises the road leads to the border crossing with Chile in an hour and that there are no complications to be concerned about. Yet the unexpected patches of soft sand are undetectable until the front end dips down, burying the wheel. My head feels like it's about to explode and my neck is too stiff to turn. No way can I take another fall.

An American woman, a California forest firefighter, dislikes the idea of the driver leaving me behind. She worries about my concussion and what would happen if I should nod out while riding. She won't let him get too far ahead without checking on me. Sure enough, the road that can't go wrong has several forks and if she didn't make him pause on hilltops until I could see which way to go, I would get lost. Nice to know Americans still look out for each other.

For the last few days I've been counting the hours to the Chilean border and real roads. I love scenic Bolivia with its kind and warm people but the challenging routes I intentionally chose were a bit too tough for me. There are certain segments of this journey I would never repeat. Riding the *Altiplano* down through the salt plains in the rainy season alone is one.

The two-room shack that is Bolivia's official border station is a welcome sight. I've been told that after crossing the frontier, it would be a different world, a leap forward in time. Indeed it is. Five miles past the WELCOME TO CHILE sign I spot guardrails and an on-ramp. I fear it's a mirage. A wish is within seconds of becoming real. Solid ground! With a lighter-weight bike, functioning rear shock, and me in better physical shape, this would have been a more pleasant ride. As it is, both my bike and I are beat to hell and there's still another 13,000 miles to go!

A long-awaited moment finally arrives and I choose to savor it without merely driving onto the on-ramp. First, I pause to inspect the road ahead and double-check that it's real. This smooth asphalt highway is empty in both directions and still 12,000 feet up in the Andes. I ride a few circles smiling to myself. This is going to feel good.

As though beginning a race, I point my front wheel toward the steep mountain grade and slam the hammer down, winding out each gear, milking the last available RPM until kicking into fifth. The altitude makes acceleration sluggish but the pull of gravity from the radical downhill grade compensates, drawing me faster. The sun is blinding bright, the sky an astounding deep cobalt blue, and with such rapid descent, the temperature of the dry, high desert air rapidly rises.

There are twenty-five miles of smooth asphalt to savor en route to the Chilean customs and immigration office — no stop signs, traffic signals, or other vehicles. This is it, I'm alone and flying high as the clouds left behind. I restrain myself from tearing off my helmet and doing handstands on the grips. For skiers, this is ten feet of packed powder after days of skiing icy moguls and slushy straightaways. To Taoists, the ch'i is flowing big time.

The silky blacktop points directly downhill with barely a twist to consider a curve. The rapidly unraveling charcoal ribbon is so steep that it generates sufficient inertia to render my brakes useless — there's no way of stopping now. I laugh aloud, watching altimeter numbers drop like a clock spinning backward. Within fifteen minutes I descend 10,000 feet into the warm embrace of the waiting Atacama Desert of northern Chile.

At the Chilean immigration office, a tall, lanky, redheaded official stamps my passport with a toothy smile and rapid-fire Spanish. I think he says "Welcome to Chile" in one syllable. I say, "Thank you" using ten. Customs is a slam-dunk and after showing the bogus original copy of the motorcycle title and my phony international driver's license, I shed smothering foul-weather gear to explore the *pueblo* of San Pedro de Atacama.

My guidebook suggests this is a very atypical city for Chile. Its narrow dusty streets and charming old-world buildings teem with more tourists than locals. Too crowded for me, and if it's not typical, why would I want to see it anyway? There are no ATMs, only one money changer using that special kind of exchange rate for travelers. No thanks — time to hit the road.

It's a straight shot from here to the island of Chiloe on Route 5, the Pan American Highway. There's still a long way to go from there to Tierra del Fuego depending on how I opt to cross the Andes. Consider it like riding from Los Angeles to New York. Hell, it's 1,000 miles more just to Santiago! Once past mid-Chile the weather will likely turn menacingly unpredictable and a warm summer day will be low fifties without too much rain. The natural elements tormenting the bottom of South America are fierce and unforgiving, with horrendous crosswinds — the kind that rip and tear at small motorcycles attempting to brave Antarctic turbulence.

For now, this northern strip of Chile along the coast is Atacama Desert, the driest region on earth. The woman running her hostel says it hasn't rained in four years and even then it was just drizzle. At least I can pack my rain gear in the bottom of the saddlebags for a few days.

The Chilean countryside resembles California more than South America. At the moment, Chile has the strongest economy in the hemisphere and its citizens seem more German than Latin American. They take their rules and regulations seriously and abide by them to the letter. Drivers stop at stop signs and red lights. No honking horns and banging into one another. There's a speed limit that everyone obeys and a certain overall orderliness that one would find only in Munich. Damn, I miss Peru.

Another similarity to California is the high cost of living and traveling. It's a shock to discover those three-dollar-a-night hotels of Peru and Bolivia cost thirty bucks here, but at least they all have hot water. Food is expensive also. I eat most meals out of supermarket lunchmeat sections and at the cheapest roadside restaurants I can find. Still the money disappears almost faster than the ATM can spit it out. Normal seventy-five-cents-per-hour Internet service is three dollars, with a lengthy list of restrictions. Chile has a lot of rules and no tolerance for breaking them.

Attempting to park my bike by the sidewalk, I back it in with the rear tire touching the curb like anywhere else in the world. Within seconds police swoop in, politely instructing me to park parallel like a car. Then another cop comes along, stating the wheel is pointed wrong. After all that, another uniformed person with a radio shows up demanding a dollar for every twenty minutes parking. *Achtung!*

Still, I'm enjoying the desert scenery. The air is soothingly warm, but violent crosswinds occasionally kick up, forcing me to keep the speed down. Nearing the coast, there are long flat sections of pinkish brown sand turning to earth-tone pastels of towering dunes, with dry creek beds running across their faces like veins. My imagination goes berserk. This is how I picture Mars. The desert may lack life but soon enough the weather will turn bitter cold again and I suspect

I'll find myself missing the heat.

The ride through Chile is uneventful, but after the last few weeks of pegging the adventure/danger needle I need a break from straddling the edge so long. Frazzled nerves are receiving a much-needed rest.

This is the end of the South American summer and the beginning of high season for the tourist industry, which means higher prices. Up until this week, few hotels were booked at more than ten-percent capacity and most had been willing to bargain for lower rates. This time of year, tourists from Argentina invade Chile for vacations, but I had thought that, since they are experiencing such economic chaos at home, it would be different. Some hope. I can't tell where everyone is from, but the beaches are jammed and hotels are full.

I stop in La Serena, a place guidebooks describe as a quaint seaside resort. It's about as quaint as two Santa Barbaras back to back. Everyone wants to get to the beach at once. I seldom see the beach from hotels where I stay. When first entering a city, I normally head for *el centro* because it's the cheapest part of town, although often the seediest. It's dirtier with more crime and violence, yet generally worth it to me for the significant savings, which can be critical when trying to live within a travel budget.

Without much effort, I find *el centro*, except that *el centro* here means the upscale, ritzy part of town. Glittering rows of expensive shops and fancy restaurants dazzle my senses. There are no pimps, pickpockets, or familiar stinky, piss-stained alleyways. I'm a fish out of water.

I comb the city in search of the bad part of town, skid row, the other side of the tracks, or any other area where the poor congregate. Zero. Zip. Nada. The whole place is classy, expensive, and out of my budget.

At 10:00 p.m. I finally locate a tiny, bug-free room for thirty bucks with secure parking two blocks away, and they throw in a free breakfast and cable TV.

Back on the road the next morning, it's only 300 miles to Santiago, but I decide to cut that up after stumbling across a little seaside town catering to working-class folks near a puffing oil refinery. There is a delightfully seedy, oil-speckled beach off the main drag, sprinkled with family-owned restaurants selling delicious seafood platters of steaming *mariscos* and freshly baked bread.

CHILE

SANTIAGO
February 6, 2002
● ● ● ● ● ● ● ● ● ●

Choosing to drive slow and savor the mild desert environment, I allow four days to reach Santiago. It's a ride that even at a leisurely pace should've taken just three. The last stretch in Bolivia left the bike and my body equally battered, with both in need of rest and repair. I've been looking for a place that has motorcycle shops, Laundromats, bookstores, and a dentist to fix the teeth I shattered in the last wreck.

Santiago has all these things, but also impatient crowds and an impersonal atmosphere. Like all Latin American cities, it's overcrowded and plagued with excessive traffic. I get around faster by leaving the bike parked at the hostel and walking wherever I need to go.

I'm unsure which is more dangerous, riding the *Altiplano* alone or crossing the streets of Santiago on foot. There should be guidebooks and safety equipment available for this type of high-risk excursion. Special footwear, helmets, and maybe a whistle or other device to warn drivers that they are about to run you over. With so many close calls, I almost get splattered at every corner. If you don't wind-sprint from one side to the other, the traffic signals on the eight-lane boulevards strand you on the center divider. Motorists wait impatiently, revving their motors, and when the signal changes, it's as though the green flag has dropped at the Indianapolis 500. Engines roar, tires squeal, and everyone speeds off in foul clouds of fumes as this urban drag race changes venue to the next light. I'm sure it's just my imagination, but everyone seems to aim for me.

Back on schedule, I give myself another ten days to reach Tierra del Fuego, nearly 2,000 miles away, the halfway point of the journey. From there I'll turn around and take the long way home through Argentina, Uruguay, Paraguay, Brazil, Venezuela, and Panama before backtracking through Central America and Mexico.

The pavement will end in another 800 miles when I reach the gravel-surfaced *Camino Austral*. Then I begin crisscrossing the Andes between Chile and Argentina to reach Ushuaia on the island of Tierra del Fuego. This is the southernmost inhabited town on earth. Just off that coast lies icy Antarctica, ferociously controlling the mainland weather.

SOUTH OUT OF SANTIAGO
February 8, 2002
Concepción, Chile
● ● ● ● ● ● ● ● ● ●

I planned on staying in Santiago for three nights, but after only two, I yield to the familiar pull of the road and ecstatic rush of asphalt passing under my butt at ninety feet per second. Since the ordeal with Colombian guerrillas, the psychological aftermath has been gaining on me. I know the bullet I dodged will eventually catch up; however, I figure if I keep moving, I can stay ahead of whatever is in store. At times, the turmoil feels as though I'm charging down a mountain trying to outrun an avalanche. For now, I need to continue on so whatever is going to hit will do so when I'm safe at home. Motorcyclists know the therapeutic effects of twisting a throttle — I keep twisting mine to outrun the avalanche.

Leaving Santiago is a breeze without the normal hassle of asking for directions. A quick left at the end of the street from my hostel and it's a straight shot down to the on-ramp of the Pan American Highway headed south (Al Sur). A new day on the open road is a spiritual rush.

Since arriving in Chile, I've been unable to shake the feeling of being in California — same terrain, same roads, and same weather. I need an easier pace for a while and this is perfect. There are no afternoon storms to beat, no freezing subzero temperatures, and no blazing heat. The average high is seventy-five degrees in the day and fifty in the early mornings. There's still daylight at 9:00 p.m. and the sun rises each morning at five.

The roads are well paved and pass through luscious forested landscapes. There are no potholes or stretches that turn to dirt or mud, and all the turnoffs and highways are clearly marked. Cattle are fenced off the road, and not a single dog has chased me trying to bite my tires since crossing the border. For the first 700 miles, there were no cops, no truckers playing chicken, and no buses stopping to pick up passengers in the middle of my lane on freeway curves. The only thing to slow me down is a sporadic crosswind that kicks up with just enough punch to yank me off the road if I get caught daydreaming.

I have no concerns about highway bandits, threats of guerrilla activity, or cops jacking people up for bribes. Fees for driving toll roads are high but they charge by the wheel, so I pay half of what bigger vehicles do. Gas is expensive at two and half bucks a gallon but there are so many stations it's impossible to run out. At fifty-five miles per gallon, the cost of dead dinosaurs has little impact on my budget.

Most people I encounter are aloof. Until I make the first move they don't want much to do with me. When I stop to ask directions, chances are fifty-fifty they will ignore me as though I'm not there. If they do respond, the chances are fifty-fifty they will provide incorrect information. Correct information is any that steers me in the general vicinity of wherever I asked about. "Go up two blocks then turn right" can actually mean anywhere from one to ten blocks and maybe turn right or left. No one wants to admit that they don't know so they invent information, or maybe they enjoy sending *gringos* on wild-goose chases.

The guidebooks describe Chileans as abrupt and conservative. When talking to me, Chileans often call themselves *muy frio* (very cold). Compared to other Latin Americans, I would describe them as the opposite of friendly. At first I think it's because I'm American, but I notice before even speaking or removing the helmet, they're already flashing disapproving frowns. It must take effort to be this grumpy.

Riding the Pan American Highway south is similar to exploring central California. Smooth gentle hills and big plots of farmland appear in the distance like even squares on faraway knolls. Local farmers peddle fresh produce from rural family spreads scattered along the highways. They offer everything from spinach and corn to huge slabs of homemade cheeses.

Hitchhiking is safe and common here and the exits to most towns are lined with young, long-haired, backpacking Chilean men accompanied by their forlorn-looking girlfriends, pleading for rides. I get the feeling they wait long hours before being picked up. It's tempting to stop and offer a tip about how smiling might distinguish them from the others and create better luck.

Early afternoon, I turn off the sunny Pan Am Highway and head toward the coast. Within ten miles, cultivated agricultural fields merge into dense green pine forests beneath graying overcast skies. Chilly, damp fog blowing in off the ocean signals it's time to bundle up in sweaters and leathers. Full foul-weather gear will be needed soon and I'm ready. *El Pacifico* eases into view as a faint mist turns to light rain, and soon I'm winding down the rocky coast past crashing waves. There's an occasional lighthouse visible in the distance. Pungent ocean air mixes sweetly with the fragrance of strong scented pines and waving eucalyptus trees. Groaning foghorns warn mariners of rocks and shoals in mournful songs of greeting. I'm officially in southern Chile.

Ricardo Rocco has introduced me online to a local motorcycle enthusiast who is known to welcome and assist roaming bikers from other countries. Guillermo is waiting for my call when I reach Concepción. We meet minutes later near the *Plaza de Armas* just as the workday ends and downtown streets swell with rush-hour traffic. After greeting me with a hearty Latin American embrace, we sit down in a crowded outdoor café where grey-haired local riders congregate in the late afternoons after work. He speaks as much English as I do Spanish. One at a time he introduces me to middle-aged, neatly groomed business types rolling in on spanking new BMWs, Harleys, Ducatis, and other high-performance machines.

Due to heavy import taxes, motorized vehicles in Latin America cost considerably more than in the U.S. and these are already expensive bikes in California. Riders must generate significant income in Chile to afford hobbies like collecting *motocicletas*. One grandfather-type who owns a winery also has a collection of 160 motorcycles, including 40 Harleys.

A bearded man and middle-aged woman cruise in, each leathered up and on their own bikes. She is introduced as a recently elected senator, and he, as the mayor of a suburb near Santiago. There's the owner of a helicopter service company, several bankers, a few engineers, and one adventuring Viking motorcyclist from southern California.

Guillermo encourages everyone to meet for a ride into the country at eleven the next morning. However, for some reason none of the twenty invitees shows up. I'm unsure how to take this, but I'm choosy about riding partners myself. Any more than one carefully selected *compañero* is usually too many.

The little single-cylinder Kawasaki 650 is no match for Guillermo's lightning-swift new BMW R1200RS. At the first twist of the throttle he speeds ahead onto the open road leading out of Concepción. Aah, wanna play? He has more horsepower for the straightaways but I can lean deeper in the curves. I barely manage to keep up during our 150-mile afternoon road race through the countryside.

Biker heaven. We trace our way across seamless asphalt ribbons that wrap around seaside bays, crisscrossing estuaries spanned by concrete causeways and steel bridges. Solid forests abut the highway as we blast past aromatic seafood restaurants and roadside cafés. It feels as though I've been here before as I marvel at how southwestern Chile mirrors northwestern America. I'm riding through the Washington–Vancouver region near the coast, right down to the foliage.

CONCEPCIÓN
February 10, 2002
● ● ● ● ● ● ● ● ● ●

After staying with Guillermo for two nights, it was time to hit the road. On the morning of departure he insisted on escorting me part-way down a spectacular coastal route he selected for me to travel to my next overnight. It was a lengthy detour along the seaside inland valley, with just enough scenic wonder to tantalize me with what's ahead. One hundred and fifty miles later, a foggy forest road led back to the Pan American Highway headed south for Puerto Montt. The ten-hour deviation was worth every second.

The German enclave of Puerto Montt became a two-day layover so I could dedicate twelve hours to receiving phone calls from my readers. Again, I was overwhelmed and amazed at the outpouring of support from folks at home, and even total strangers.

Tomorrow will be a short hop from the tip of the peninsula to the island of Chiloe and halfway down the island, another ferry ride across the Gulf of Ancud back to the mainland at Chaiten. From that point, the pavement ends to become General Pinochet's famous folly of wasted tax revenues, the gravel road of the *Camino Austral.*

As usual, weather reports are gloomy with major storms blowing in from Antarctica. If there's time, I might hunker down on the border of Argentina for a few days before the final drop into Punta Arenas and Tierra del Fuego. By now, I'm undeterred by extreme weather, but there's so much to see along the way I don't want to experience it fighting blinding rain.

CHILOE ISLAND
February 12, 2002
Quellon, Chile
● ● ● ● ● ● ● ● ●

The morning began sunny and warm, but while rolling off the ferry from Puerto Montt to the island, icy rain strikes again. Does it ever end? It's the type that starts out as easy drizzle only to become full sheets of soaking misery until I am drenched because I procrastinated about suiting up. It sucks climbing into a rain suit when already shivering in soggy clothes. South American weather has turned gloomy again — chilly enough to be uncomfortable but not life-threatening like in the *Altiplano* of Bolivia. I might contend with a taste of hypothermia but freezing or frostbite is no longer a worry. After riding the Andes, all else seems a cakewalk.

Approaching the seaport of Quellon to catch the ferry back to the mainland, it hits me — the end of the trail is nearing. Quellon is the terminus of the Pan American Highway, the road that stretches from Alaska through Canada, the U.S., Mexico, Central America, and ultimately the middle of Chile. I'm finally out of pavement and nearly out of road.

Through a light fog, I pass villages with houses built over the water on stilts. The shores are lined with pastel-colored, open-bowed fishing boats lying on their sides in the low tide mud. People here are friendlier and don't appear to be in such a hurry as those farther north. Half of them earn their living through agriculture, the rest from the sea. Their robust greetings suggest a stronger spirit and a nature more to my liking — more Latin American.

There are dozens of freshly painted restaurants offering seafood dishes and shellfish that I've never seen before. After a brief pantomime session with a waitress, I feel brave enough to order *Locos con Papas*. It turns out to be a mussel that's soft as butter, but after a squeeze of fresh lemon it tastes as good as abalone. *¿Quien sabe?* It's all delicious and the table bread is always fresh from the oven.

A cheerful old woman at the ticket booth says the ferry runs every other day and the next one doesn't leave until 3:00 p.m. tomorrow. To be safe, I buy a twenty-dollar ticket in advance for the five-hour sail to Chaiten to reach the *Camino Austral*. From there I'll drift southeast toward Argentina. No road stretches without interruption from north to south in Chile because the landmass is separated by small islands and fiords. In order to reach Ushuaia I must cross over into Argentina and zigzag back and forth several times between the two countries. To circumvent the *Camino Austral* and all the border crossings, there's a three-day ferry that sails between the islands, ending up in Punta Arenas — but it bypasses too much of Patagonia.

Shortly before dark, I find a rustic two-story hotel room with knotty pine interior, hot water, and a coal heater to dry out my drenched gear. Tomorrow I'll start out dry, skipping the usual hassle of pulling on soggy clothing at sunrise. And there's still another thousand miles of gravel, mud, and rain ahead before I reach Ushuaia. According to guidebooks, the return leg up the east coast through Argentina is a monotonous road, straight as an arrow and flat as a pancake for 3,000 kilometers to Buenos Aires. Weather reports warn of several weeks of rain ahead so there's no point in waiting around here any longer. Succumbing to reality, I roll with the punches and buy a pair of rubber wading boots and plastic gloves.

CAMINO AUSTRAL
February 13, 2002
Chaiten, Chile
● ● ● ● ● ● ● ● ●

Other than the ferry being three hours late, crossing the Gulf of Ancud is uneventful and takes place in the dark. Lashed to the steel deck of the pitching ocean barge, my bike receives an intense saltwater bath while I try to sleep off seasickness. Again liquid sodium wreaks havoc on electronic connections and uncoated metal. Tomorrow I must find a source of fresh water to bathe my rapidly corroding little motorcycle.

It feels good to roll off the boat onto the dry and stable mainland. It's past midnight and freezing night air prompts me to grab the first hostel in sight. No matter how cheap the accommodations in Chile, they all have hot water and the elderly proprietors are surprised to be asked. Yet with no insulation there's no difference between inside and outside temperatures. The wooden rooms are so cold it's like sleeping in a refrigerator. But the owners do provide thick piles of wool blankets to warm up under and that's where I remain curled up until sunrise.

It's much more relaxed here without the hustle and noise of the main tourist areas. In such an amiable atmosphere, I don't feel compelled to maintain line-of-sight observation of my equipment, allowing me to venture beyond sprinting distance of thieves doing the slash and dash. With hardly a worry, I can park the bike on the street and leave it unlocked.

PUYUHUAPI
February 14, 2002
• • • • • • • • • • •

After a steaming cup of boiled milk, fresh pastries, and four fried eggs, I set off to explore the breezy wilderness of southern Chile in the crackling morning air. This is my first taste of the rugged *Camino Austral* that extends 500 miles down to the first crossover into Argentina. The farther south I ride, the more the terrain resembles Alaska, although the locals hail from the Alps. In the shadows of the Andes lie scattered settlements inhabited by turn-of-the-century German immigrants whose architecture and craftsmanship reflect an enchanting Bavarian character. It's Latin America again with the attitude and spirit of a people anxious to greet travelers. There's electricity most everywhere and some telephone, but no Internet, leaving me temporarily in cyberspace limbo.

A tiny tree thorn, probably left over from running the *Paro* blockade in Peru, finally worked its way deeper into my front tire causing a minute puncture. Fortunately the tire flattens within a half mile of a remote valley *pueblo* with a repair shop. For a buck and a half, a young European-looking Latino patches the tube and sends me on my way with a variety of farewells.

After enjoying a giant slab of fresh grilled salmon and French fries in a gingerbread-style restaurant, I'm back on the dusty gravel road rolling south. Although relatively smooth compared to off-pavement rides in Bolivia, the loosely packed gravel causes a squir-relly feeling in my handlebars. It's difficult to go much faster than thirty mph and the turns are slower still. Ahead lie several 150-mile, eight-hour rides, so I mentally readjust my arrival date in Tierra del Fuego.

Entering Patagonia, the *Camino Austral* cuts between solid blocks of forest surrounded by towering, snow-laced peaks and sheer gran-ite walls shooting straight up like jagged skyscrapers. Numerous rickety wooden bridges over aqua waters built decades ago worry me at first, but hold firm, and I get used to them. In this thinly pop-ulated frontier region, few travelers are willing to venture this far. Only the most dedicated choose to endure the poor conditions and Spartan accommodations. Possibly once per hour, I pass a four-wheel-drive vehicle with camping gear loaded on the rooftop. The rest of the time I drift in my favorite place and state — alone in the wilderness, daydreaming in blissful solitude that I am the last man on earth.

PATAGONIA
February 15, 2002
Coyhaique, Chile
● ● ● ● ● ● ● ● ●

This morning, I discover what it's like for a six-foot-three man to take a shower in a bathroom with a five-foot ceiling. The only hostel space in Puyuhuapi is a small corner of a converted upstairs loft in a local farmhouse. But my needs are few — clean sheets and hot water.

It's taken eight hours to ride 160 miles to the Patagonian town of Coyhaique, the last stop with Internet access for a while. Still woozy from my last concussion in Bolivia, my brain can't take another crash so I ride slowly and cautiously, knowing tomorrow is more of the same. The surrounding wonderment of Patagonia is tainted by fear of another head injury. After all, I don't want to come home drooling.

The scenery is more spectacular than the big city travel posters that prompted me to take this route. Once past the last pueblo, the countryside opens into the vast spaciousness of the Chilean wilds, and except for the crunchy gravel road, the infinite environment appears untainted by humans. Crisp mountain air pops with cold, like early autumn in Alaska. Deep passages through glacier-carved canyons remind me of an endless Yosemite National Park. Mighty rivers leap outward from massive sky-high granite bluffs, spewing giant waterfalls. Foaming water cascades down gray cliff faces to crash hundreds of feet below over house-size boulders. Spray from the pounding vaporizes into sparkling clouds of mist that the morning sun transforms into rainbows above faraway treetops.

The road, still rough and dusty, serves as a barrier to all but the most resolute adventurers. I try to imagine the first thoughts of Charles Darwin as I retrace his tedious steps into this pristine wilderness. Together, we marvel with a land of bubbling blue rivers, sparkling turquoise lakes, and glacier-lined mountainsides solemnly guarding serene valleys.

Since early this morning, I've seen no other human for a hundred miles and little else to remind me of what species I belong to. Existing within this heavenly awe as a mere speck in an endless reverberation through geologic time — yesterday becomes only a moment in an ageless eon. Kneeling to touch the earth in reverence to this magnificence, I rocket back a billion years.

LOST
February 16, 2002
Aisen Region of Chile
● ● ● ● ● ● ● ● ● ● ● ● ●

Shortcuts are always a crapshoot. Just after sunrise, in an effort to make up for time lost after missing a turnoff for the first southern border crossing into Argentina, I roll the dice. The map shows a dirt road connecting to a paved road, a shortcut that should avoid backtracking to a junction some twenty miles behind.

On the two-by-three-inch screen of a GPS it's difficult to tell the difference between lines that are roads, rivers, or international boundaries. As I ride farther east, the black triangle on the screen indicating my position reveals that I'm rapidly approaching a black line. I assume this line is the highway I'm intent on reaching. To better guess my location, I use three maps at once, combined with the GPS, to determine where I should go. None of them correspond precisely. In poorly chartered regions like Patagonia, there's lots of speculation. What I can't figure out is why the black triangle indicating my position has not only intersected with a black line appearing as a highway, but is now well past it and I haven't seen any highway.

Meanwhile, the dirt road ahead narrows to a rough footpath ending in a barbed wire fence where there is a sign stating, CAMINO CERRADO (ROAD CLOSED). On the other side is a hundred-yard-wide rocky riverbed with water flowing two feet deep. Since it's taken forty-five minutes to come this far, hopefully the sought-after road is on the other side. I cringe at the thought of having to turn back in defeat.

After another twenty minutes of struggling across the river spinning my tires through the bog, I reach the other side. Now, I find another hundred-yard strip of loosely packed river rocks the size of bowling balls. I must ride over these rocks to reach a distant farmhouse where I can ask directions. What the heck, I've come this far.

Bouncing over scattered rows of boulders halfway across the field, I'm greeted by the rancher's angry pack of dogs. They are telling me, with bared fangs, that I've violated their space and shouldn't go any farther. More snarling persuades me it's better to wait. Within minutes, a curious old Latino smoking a pipe saunters up with a puzzled look on his face. I call out, *"Hola señor. ¿Donde estoy?"* (Hello Sir. Where am I?)

He takes a long drag off his glowing tobacco bowl and casually replies, "Argentina."

This is a significant problem. Crossing international borders without passing through official immigration and customs procedures is a serious criminal act. I'm certain to be jailed if caught.

Although I would probably be freed with a fine, I don't want to find out how many months in an Argentinean prison this is going to take.

I ask what's the best way to return to Chile, hoping at the end of his driveway is a smooth road back. After another casual drag off his pipe, he replies with a smirk, *"De donde vino."* (From where you came.)

This means I've lost half a day of what was a full day's ride to the only outpost within a hundred miles. At least this close to the South Pole, it stays light until 10:00 p.m.

DIRT ROADS TO ARGENTINA
February 17, 2002
Puerto Bertrand, Chile
● ● ● ● ● ● ● ● ● ● ● ●

Because there are no hotels in small Patagonian towns, I overnight mostly in *hospedajes*, the equivalent of a bed-and-breakfast elsewhere. Locals rent out rooms in their homes and include a breakfast. Additional meals are negotiable. *Hospedajes* are enjoyable because it's a chance to meet Latin Americans and see how they live and think.

Tonight, good fortune is with me when invited to join a local family in their small country cottage. For further delights, this cozy wooden cabin is also occupied by a traveling group from Buenos Aires, happy to meet an *Americano*. Late into the night, we play games on my laptop and take photos together to mount on digitalized calendars and magazine covers. Amidst stinky blue plumes of cigarette smoke and above the blare of accordions from crackling loudspeakers, we swap stories about where we've been and where we're going.

In the morning, we feast on oven-baked bread, homemade gooseberry jam, goat cheese from the cellar, and four fried eggs compliments of the chickens in the front yard. My bedroom was cold enough to hang meat in, but the red-hot wood-burning stove in the kitchen adequately thaws me out before I jump back into the Patagonian wind.

Enjoying a taste of morning sun, I'm reluctant to think about the weather for fear of jinxing it. Patagonian weather changes in an instant. Clouds can move across the sky like a video on fast forward. It's been unusually stable the last few days, warming up to the low sixties with barely a breeze to cause ripples on the dozens of lakes along the road. At times I stop near massive pine forests so thick, it's impossible to see into them. Wallowing in bliss, I relish the silent symphony of the wild with no thought of when this will end.

My maps indicate I've now ridden the *Camino Austral* as far south as possible, and finally I cross into Argentina at a seldom-used border outpost. The lone immigration official living here says that no one has passed through in four days but he is expecting a supply truck next week.

On the Argentine side, the Andean terrain immediately turns into barren, rocky desert. Temperatures flare into the nineties as a deteriorating surface slows me to a crawl. The mangled gravel road is spiked with hard-to-spot patches of loose dirt, making riding difficult, and I nearly crash a half-dozen times before noon. I average fifteen mph and if able to click into third gear, consider that speeding.

Numerous shallow rivers continually impede my way. After stripping off my gear, I must first wade through wearing knee-high rubber boots, poking the river bottom with a stick to find the best route. Once past these rivers, accelerating through long sections of finely ground dust sends the rear of my bike fishtailing out of control. My spinning tires kick up beige clouds of talcum that swirl into the openings of my clothing and baggage. This is as far off the beaten track as I can get without a helicopter. But my goal was to cross the southern Andes off pavement, and here I am.

At times, the road diminishes to a mere cattle trail with dozens of forks and no indication of which way to go. The latest preprogrammed memory chip in the GPS displays no roads, rivers, lakes, or towns — only the Argentine frontier behind and a black triangle on a blank screen. All three maps indicate the proper direction to head is east for seventy miles. Using dead reckoning, I must reach Route 40, a single lane, pea-graveled road, considered the main north-to-south corridor in western Argentina.

One small problem — a line designating Route 40 doesn't appear on the GPS. And the precise direction of east on the maps varies between northeast, due east, and southeast — so my compass is useless. Other than the border guard I met hours ago, there's likely no other human within a hundred miles. I can't even find a lone rancher to ask which way to turn on any of the numerous forks. It's been hit or miss since the border. Most of today is spent lost in the hot, desolate, high deserts of Patagonia.

At sundown and exhausted, I finally reach my destination of Hotel Bajo Caracoles in the province of Santa Cruz. The name is more impressive than the place. Bajo Caracoles is a lone settlement of thirty-two people on Route 40 with the only fuel in the region and a ten-room hostel run on locally generated electricity. A welcome relief for eleven bucks a night. The next town south is another 320 miles. Since this is beyond my tank range, it will be necessary to haul extra gas.

There are warnings of strong headwinds. Headwinds affect mileage. Even with extra fuel, I'll likely be coasting into the next stopover on fumes. Tomorrow will be a long haul to Tres Lagos and El Calafate — at least the pea-gravel road is straight and well marked.

From there, my route veers back into Chile at Puerto Natales to visit Torres del Paines National Park and on to Punta Arenas. A short ferry ride across the Straights of Magellan should dump me onto the island of Tierra del Fuego, Argentina, and the turnaround in Ushuauia. If luck continues, the ride home begins in nine days.

ARGENTINA

● ● ● ● ● ● ● ● ● ● ● ●

Since those unfortunate events in Colombia, this journey has taken so many bizarre twists and turns that I've lost track of what's normal and what's dangerous. If I'm not scrambling for safety or concerned for my life, I think something is missing. The intensity of the perils and pleasures I encounter is never predictable. Spectacular scenery under the most extreme riding conditions on earth is par for the course; the weather is the wild card.

Worse than predicted, the ride south on Route 40 becomes a steady fight to remain upright for 320 miles. My average speed is twenty-five mph while I'm on the edge of control the entire time. The gravel is deep and loose, forcing my front tire in directions I don't want to go. There are twelve-inch-deep tire grooves carved down to solid clay. If I remain within them, employing total concentration, it's possible to hit third gear.

It's hard to believe what is happening as the fiercest crosswinds imaginable blast in laterally. A gas station attendant casually remarks, "I'm lucky — the wind is not too bad yet." Still, it's as though enormous, invisible hands randomly slap me across the road without warning. With each explosive gust, I veer off uncontrollably across the deep ridges of gravel with outstretched legs, wildly wobbling back and forth.

Yet I grow accustomed to the exhausting maneuvering and settle into what feels like a safe pace. Soon, a treacherous patch of sand snatches the front tire and nearly pulls me down. There's just no winning, and no relaxing to enjoy the scenery. What scenery? The horizon appears as a slim line encircling the barren, high desert landscape. A few armadillos occasionally scurry across the road. But by the time I stop to chase them down for a photo, they're busy burrowing into the ground. Wild horses gallop into view from out of nowhere, and within seconds disappear into clouds of dust along the range.

Small herds of brown and white guanacos, long-necked cousins of the llama, trot along at leisurely paces. When they spot my approach, they abruptly sprint off, zigzagging in unison toward some unknown refuge. They are magnificent animals, like mini-giraffes bounding along as graceful as antelopes. Then, for no apparent reason, a lone guanaco drifts in by my side — pacing me as together we glide across the plain. It barely acknowledges my presence for several miles before vanishing into the desert. I've heard of dolphins behaving like this but never land-based mammals.

Mid-afternoon, an ominously darkening South American sky begins to tease me with a few plops of rain but doesn't muster the will to let loose. Mother Nature finally takes pity on a hapless motorcyclist, realizing I need a break today. I don't lower my guard though; this far down in the southern hemisphere, weather turns to hell in an instant.

In the last fourteen hours, I've encountered four cars and three trucks heading north to Brazil but have seen none in my direction. After spotting the dust cloud of an approaching vehicle miles away, I ride off the single-lane road, allowing them to pass by at a safe distance. In Latin America it's expected that motorcyclists get out of the way of cars and trucks if they want to remain intact.

I'd love to say that today has been something other than long and miserable but the fatigue is overwhelming. In this constant test for survival, the obvious question arises — is the hassle worth it? Even after all the trials and tribulations so far, there is still no doubt, I am glad to be here. The avalanche continues to follow but I remain ahead. Through it all, my most effective tool is still that every morning, with a big smile I hum Willie Nelson's "On the Road Again."

MORE WIND
February 20, 2002
Torres del Paine National Park
• • • • • • • • • • • • • • • • • •

Refreshed and rejuvenated after two nights in the touristy Argentine town of El Calafate, I depart to visit Torres del Paine, one of the most famous national parks in South America. This requires re-entry into Chile via a short stretch of pavement on Route 40 south, and then back to gravel. When a local commented yesterday during an extraordinarily violent windstorm that it was not that bad, I couldn't imagine how it could be any worse. Today I find out what he meant.

Although the road is solid enough to support speeds up to fifty or so, incredibly ferocious winds blasting in off the prairie force me to slow into a second-gear crawl. If someone had described these conditions earlier, I wouldn't have believed them. Even in the midst of a vicious gust, it's difficult to comprehend turbulence of such intensity. Leaning to the right as far and hard as possible, raging wind currents not only hold me up, they lift the bike off the ground, shoving us sideways. As the wind snaps my neck from side to side, I feel like a crinkled paper bag being smacked around the landscape. Why I've not been blown across the desert is beyond me. It's so crazy I laugh out loud.

At lunchtime, I park the bike in the shelter side of a lone, run-down café located in the middle of this desolate prairie, and sit eating a piece of dried-up chicken. Outside the window, my bike rocks wildly in powerful gusts, its weight rocking against the anchor of the kickstand. I shudder with the thought of diving back into this insanity for another three hours.

In spite of incredible winds, the sky is clear and the jagged peaks of Torres del Paine and the massive canyon-carving glaciers beyond are looming into view. At the park entrance, a lone federal ranger holding onto a post to keep from blowing over warns, "It gets real windy up ahead." Cyclone strength gusts are sufficient to make waves big enough to body surf on the scattered lakes along the way.

Pushing as hard as I dare, it takes three hours to ride the last twenty miles. Finally, I reach the far end of the park to find the solitary hotel is not only radically overpriced, but also full. Nearby, there's an old wooden, two-story shack with dusty pads on the floor for campers with sleeping bags. Since I don't have one, I bundle up in my foul-weather suit, munch down a chunk of packaged ham, and call it a night. Falling asleep with howling winds shaking the dilapidated old building, I dream of calm weather and smooth asphalt.

February 21, 2002
Torres del Paine
● ● ● ● ● ● ● ● ●

In the morning, I met a driver who slept in his bus last night. He explained that another bus had blown over the day before and he didn't want to take any chances with his. The wind was forecast to be lighter directly after dawn but kick up again in the afternoon; judging from the howling outside, it's as bad this morning as last night.

Not wanting to gamble further, I decide my sightseeing in Torres del Paines is over, and even after the hassle to get here, it's time to cut my plans short and get the heck out while it's still possible. It's only 6:00 a.m. and while I type today's journal, my flimsy wooden shelter is again under Mother Nature's violent assault. The walls shake and shudder as menacing winds build up again, spitefully challenging the integrity of the roof — a good enough sign for me to hit the trail.

Park roads wrap tightly around icy lakes and rivers, with little margin for error in the form of shoulders. If I get blown off the road, it will be directly into frigid water. The powerfully sculptured peaks of the Horns of Paine compel a pause, and while my bike rocks on its stand I gape at the awesome display of geologic magnificence.

The tortured peaks appear as enormous twisted shards of granite rammed upward from the center of the earth, towering above the surrounding steppe. In spite of the wind, I manage to balance my camera on the handlebars for a self-photo in front of this everlasting spectacle of nature.

Finished betting on the weather, I launch back on the road for Punta Arenas and decide to skip a planned overnight in Puerto Natales. Another hour delay could make the difference between escaping or becoming stuck for a week. From now on, I ride while the wind permits.

ALMOST TO THE END OF THE WORLD
February 22, 2002
Crossing the Straights of Magellan
• • • • • • • • • • • • • • • • • • •

The ferry from Punta Arenas to Tierra del Fuego sails across the Straits of Magellan at nine every morning but officials insist that passengers arrive an hour early for loading. It's a long hour. There are only four trucks and one other motorcycle on board the ferry; its capacity is ten times more. I wonder what the locals know that we do not.

In 1520, Ferdinand Magellan discovered this inland passage while searching for a shorter route around the turbulent Cape Horn, one that would avoid its tumultuous seas. As he passed between the mainland and this island, he discovered tribes of Indians barely clad in animal skins keeping warm by constantly maintaining fires, even in their canoes. Thus the island's name, Tierra del Fuego or Land of the Fire.

After European conquerors later disputed ownership, the island was split evenly between Chile and Argentina, with the latter instituting a penal colony in the 1800s for political prisoners and petty criminals. This former prison town is now the southern seaside city of Ushuaia. Because it is the southernmost inhabited space on earth, I chose to make this my turnaround point. It sounded good last year.

How about a ride to the end of the world?

But, rather than a destination, Tierra del Fuego is merely a marker, the halfway point of my journey and the start of the long haul home. This is only the seventh round of a fifteen-round fight, and as I teach my students, champions are determined by who perseveres to the finish line.

The spirit of twenty-three years of intense martial arts practice has carried me this far, providing strength of heart to continue past obstacles that included everything from unusually foul weather to captivity by bullying rebels in Colombia. I prepared for this journey as diligently as for any of my bouts in the ring and utilized every bit of knowledge accumulated over a lifetime. Battles are won in training and preparation, and like my favorite instructor, Gene LeBell, teaches, "You get beat by what you don't know so be ready for everything."

Ahead, just to exit Argentina, there are 2,000 miles of unfamiliar roads and questionable weather conditions. In Buenos Aires, an unstable political climate has recently resulted in mass rioting and the death of a hundred people. This morning, I met a Brazilian man who warned of constant heavy rain in his country for another three months but not to worry, the temperature in the steaming Amazon jungle is forty degrees Celsius (105° F).

News reports claim Venezuela is on the brink of civil war because their population is tired of the strongman president smothering their economy. I haven't decided how I will return to Panama from there, by air or by sea. Whenever there's trouble anywhere in the world, the most popular cry is to blame the United States. In troubled regions, I will be the closest representative of Yankee imperialism for anyone to get their hands on. But I don't need any more complications based on someone else's politics. I still wrestle with sporadic waves of depression that I suppress only by keeping the throttle open and remaining fixed on my goals. Still, some question my judgment.

Critics wish me to fail, just to say "I told you so." One journalist cited my desire to continue traveling after being released from the ELN as borderline madness. But I'm certain that my students and those close to me, although somewhat frustrated, understand my reasoning. Only time will tell how this has changed our lives.

Win, lose, or draw, a man could not have asked for a better backup team of true believers and although sometimes we've spoken by phone, I often wonder what our reactions will be when I finally return to California. When interviewed about this journey by reporters, I do okay until I describe those who have stood behind me — my voice cracks with emotion and I can't finish speaking my thoughts. Indeed, while sitting in this dimly lit, lonely South American hotel room typing these words, tears tumble down my cheeks.

HOMESTRETCH TO THE TURNAROUND
February 22, 2002
Crossing Tierra del Fuego
● ● ● ● ● ● ● ● ● ● ● ● ● ● ●

A twenty-foot-wide rusted steel ferry ramp slams down onto the cement landing with a heavy clang of certainty. After almost five months of a tumultuous journey, I've reached the island of Tierra del Fuego. Rolling onto dry land under a bleak gray sky, while hunkered down against the biting, frigid winds tugging at my scarf-covered neck, I debate whether to stay the night and leave early tomorrow. Should I risk crossing the island to Ushuaia immediately, hoping to make it before sundown? Depending on weather conditions, the 240-mile ride could take from eight to fourteen hours. It's high noon on the bottom of an unpredictable planet. The one thing that is predictable is the weather. It can switch instantly from bad to freezing hell.

My guts warn the total season is about to change any day, or any minute for that matter. Even if I reach Ushuaia, I may be trapped if the winter snows arrive early. It's now or never and there's no time to eat; every second counts. The road is hard-packed gravel, the type that lends itself well to stability under motorcycle tires. It's two and a half hours to the Argentine border and another six from there to Ushuaia, not counting customs and immigration delays.

The sun and the clouds are slugging it out to see who will prevail but there's enough light drizzle to keep the dust down. The fickle wind can't make up its mind and never subsides as it switches direction every half hour. First it's a strong headwind, which allows me to settle into a set, forward-leaning riding position. Then without warning, powerful gusts smack in from the side as a violent crosswind jerks me laterally, forcing me to slow down or get blown off the road. There's no consistency and I'm wishing Mother Nature would make up her damned mind.

When gale forces revert to a tailwind, the silence sweeping in from behind evolves into a spooky tranquility. A light pressure against my back indicates the wind blowing faster than I'm moving forward. My curiosity aroused, I slowly increase my speed to seventy mph, trying to determine how fast the forward air is blowing. Equilibrium is reached at seventy-three mph in a still pocket of air. If I'd wanted to, I could've kept a match lit. I raise my face shield and feel nothing. Dead calm.

Normally when driving at a rapid pace and spotting the shadow of a cloud on the ground ahead, it takes only seconds to overtake and pass through it. Today the shadow remains a few feet beyond my front tire as we travel at the same speed — continuing in unison until the wind shifts, then the shadow flashes behind me in an instant as though the world suddenly skipped ahead.

I'm wearing everything that fits under the insulated foul-weather suit, with the electric vest and heated grips turned up high. Still I shiver whenever I tilt my head in either direction as it creates a slight opening for the stinging icy air blasting in from Antarctica. The weather never lets up, only promises to get worse as the sun arcs farther across the sky.

Inside the first page of my passport, the Colombian Federal Police hand-wrote an explanation why I have a new passport issued in Bogotá with no entry visas, only an exit stamp. Sometimes immigration officials notice this when thumbing through my documents and question me about it. But more often, they are in a hurry and don't look.

Today, at the border crossing, after standing in a long line of bus passengers waiting to be processed, they notice. Naturally, this is followed by questions about being captured. How I was freed, and how much did we pay? It only makes it worse telling them, we paid nothing. Then they want to know why. That answer could consume much travel time. I don't know what weather surprises lie ahead, only that the weather is deteriorating as minutes flip by, and I don't have a moment to spare for small talk. But if I'm short with them and they consider me rude, I could suffer additional scrutiny. Where is my rear license plate? Or why does my phony international driver's license look fake?

I give them the answer military guys all appreciate, leaning forward and whispering in my most serious, just-between-us voice, *"Negocios secreto."* With this they nod knowingly, finish stamping my papers in silence, and send me on my way out into a savage wind that slams the door behind and almost blows me over.

Once on the Argentine side of the border, I spot one of my favorite road signs, *PAVIMENTO ADELANTE.* PAVEMENT AHEAD. Fighting atrocious weather is challenging enough, but driving on unpredictable surfaces only makes matters worse. At least now firm asphalt will provide a solid field on which to do battle.

Although the brutal winds give me a hard time, I maintain a decent pace with my guard up. On the horizon, dark clouds curling into massive charcoal knuckles are preparing to clobber me with some type of moisture and, judging by how fast the temperature is dropping, it will likely be solid.

Snow flurries swirl across the road ahead that now changes back to gravel. At least it's not rain. Rain would soak me within an hour, then freeze my boots and gloves. While in Chile, I coated them with grease, but the seams still leak and can fill with water.

The terrain unfolds from flat grassland to a thickening forest as I rise onto the menacing mountain summit. I can no longer determine altitude as the GPS's cigarette-lighter plug shook apart last week. While stopping one last time to snap a photo, I find my fingers too numb to unzip my suit and pull out the camera.

One good thing about reading mileage signs in kilometers is the numbers get smaller quicker than if in miles. Almost twice as quick because a kilometer is only six tenths of a mile. I mentally convert to miles by multiplying times six and dropping the last number. Sounds complicated but after a short while this can be done with a glance. When riding under these horrendous conditions beneath darkening skies, I develop a tendency to count kilometers more than I should. As the weather worsens, it's necessary to reduce speed, so the clicks drag by painfully.

There should be two hours of light remaining but as I reach the black clouds, it turns completely dark and begins to snow heavily. My face shield has iced over. As fast as I wipe it clean, it freezes up again, providing only occasional glimpses of what's ahead.

Near Ushuaia, the gravel road turns back to pavement. City fathers of Latin American towns always manage to get their federal governments to improve roads with asphalt near their boundaries. Ordinarily this would be a welcome relief but tonight it only represents more threat. The pine-tree-studded hillsides are laced in fluffy white powder, but since asphalt retains heat more than other surfaces, it melts the snow as it lands. This is great for a short while, as it keeps the road clear and passable for the bike.

The problem is, with plummeting nighttime temperatures, wet pavement freezes solid and the game comes to a screeching halt. Actually, I prefer my tires to screech and halt rather than slide out from underneath as they do the second they hit ice. Two-wheels are better than four — except in deep sand and on ice.

Already wary of the deteriorating weather conditions, I slow to a first-gear crawl, hoping to make it to the city without going down. Dropping the bike in the mud and sand of the *Altiplano* was bad. But those surfaces were relatively soft and not as lethal as sliding across hard, abrasive asphalt late at night with speeding logging trucks behind me. As a last resort, I take to riding the narrow dirt shoulder, but it too eventually freezes solid — although it still provides more traction than icy pavement. At this pace, kilometer signs grow fewer and farther between and I consider stashing the bike in the woods and hitching a ride into town. But soon, faint lights in the distance pop into view and immediately a sign appears — EL CENTRO 6 KILO-METERS, or 3.6 miles. At this pace that's another half hour.

Eventually I manage to arrive downtown where the first open business I encounter is an Internet café. Not caring if it violates local ordinances, I ride up on the sidewalk and park outside the café — even jail right now would be a welcome relief. Flinging the glass door open, I'm shoved backward by a blast of hot, dry air as I stumble inside, barely able to walk with legs so stiff that I can't use my toes for balance. I'm too cold to talk, so I point to an open station and the proprietor nods sympathetically. He then comes over, takes my gloves without asking, and heads toward the kitchen to dry them out. He is speaking in a runny Argentine accent that sounds more Italian than anything else, but I'm in too much of a daze to understand. I just keep mumbling as I shiver, *muchas gracias señor, muchas gracias.*

Shaking small chunks of ice off my collar into a pool of water that's accumulating under my chair, I mistype my username and password a dozen times until finally logging on to the Internet to see who wants to say hello and ask about my day. I have a festering fear in the back of my mind that getting this far, to Ushuaia, was the easy part.

NORTH!
February 24, 2002
Ushuaia, Argentina
● ● ● ● ● ● ● ● ● ● ●

Argentina is famous throughout the world not only for its meats but for generous portions. The *Asado* (barbecue) is a favorite national event. After a subdued but triumphant arrival in Ushuaia and a partial thaw in the Internet café, I step outside, now craving food. The first restaurant I see has a big open pit in the window. Inside, a blazing fire with sizzling quarters of beef and lamb dangle on chains from above. Being both cold and hungry, this is a sight to behold. I immediately postpone a hotel search in order to feast.

This is an elaborate buffet with a sign in Spanish reading, "All you can eat for ten pesos" or, at the current exchange rate, five bucks. The setting is fancy and, like most restaurants in Argentina, California-clean. I've been lucky to eat twice a day lately so it's time to make up for missed meals by wolfing down all I can eat.

Yet later that night my earlier splurge became my barnyard pal's moment for revenge. For the next two days more fluids flow out of my body than I thought existed. After finally mustering the strength to shuffle downstairs to the hotel restaurant for the complimentary continental breakfast, the clerk tells me I don't look so good.

Yes, I explain, I ate some bad food the other night.

"¿Cordero?" (Lamb?) he inquires.

"¿Si, como tu sabes?" (Yes, how did you know?)

"No se" (I don't know), he mumbles as he returns to his book-work.

It was hard not to roar out, "Well if everyone knows the meat is bad why the hell are you still selling it?" But grumbling bowels keep my temper in check.

The CNN weather forecast predicts two more days of showers, then rain for another three. Outside it's already pouring and it doesn't seem wise to stick around and see what real rain is like. Between intestines in revolt and wanting to see more of the town, I'm reluctant to load up and hit the road this morning. Waiting isn't an option either. Although it's bitter cold, it's still above freezing and I know it will only be colder and much wetter tomorrow.

It's like having to choose between jumping into an icy river today and being miserable for the next twelve hours or putting it off until tomorrow, when it will be much colder. I opt to get it over with, knowing that soon enough, I'll be farther north sweating it out in some sizzling Amazonian jungle.

Technically, the moment I set foot on the island of Tierra del Fuego two days ago, I could have claimed partial victory as having reached the most southern land mass. But I wanted to make sure there were no shoulda, coulda, wouldas later popping up to haunt me. Ushuaia is the city I was intent on reaching, but there's still one other geographic spot, famous in travelers' photographs. It's also twelve miles south on a dirt road, in the national park. I'll delay my departure for warmer weather by two hours if I choose to ride down and snap a picture next to the engraved wooden sign reading "This is the end of the road." What the heck, I've come this far.

This hand-carved sign states it is 17,848 kilometers to Alaska. Before leaving California, in order to plan tire changes, brake pad replacement, and servicing, I needed to compute how many miles were involved. The common claim was that from Tijuana, Mexico, to Tierra del Fuego, Argentina, it is 8,000 miles traveling straight through. If riding back on the east coast of South America, another 12,000, for a total of 20,000.

After taking the longer route through Mexico and wandering around Central America, the mileage I accumulated by the time I was captured near Medellín was 5,200. The boys shipped me a bike with 3,400 miles on it. Today, after zigzagging back and forth through the Andes, the odometer reads 11,361 miles. This is a total of 13,161 miles ridden in just under five months through thirteen countries. The "Ride for the Heart Team" did it a few years back with readings in the 14,000 range but no return mileage as they sold their bikes down here.

My original estimate of 20,000 miles is way off and it appears I will be closer to 25,000 by the time I reach the U.S. border. Upon completion, this ride will include approximately 5,000 miles of gravel, mud, or sand. You could liken that to riding a bike from Los Angeles to New York City and halfway back again, without pavement.

Exiting Ushuaia, I must ride back over a mountain summit, descend into the plains of Tierra del Fuego, and cross the international borders twice more before settling into the next month of mainland Argentina. In view of the last few weeks, I eagerly look forward to rolling my tires north up the coast of South America.

Exiting Ushuaia, mountain passes turn cold and wet, but within a few hours after descending into the open grasslands, dark clouds lighten and temperatures trickle upward. This is too good to be true — I am defrosting. Soon splashes of blue appear as the sky recalls its fearsome puffs of white and the sun shines down, drying the last of the mud puddles and wet grasses of the soggy rangeland meadows. After a time, I shed my insulated gloves and unzip my foul-weather suit to dry moistened sweaters and release rapidly accumulating body heat. I was beginning to wonder if I would ever see the sun again. The wind still bangs me around a bit — it doesn't matter, I am finally warm.

The crowded ferry ride back across the tranquil channel takes only fifteen minutes, and one hour later I pass the last customs point into Argentina. With new batteries in the GPS, the compass heading finally reads what I've been longing to see, NORTH!

Sunsets linger forever this far down in the southern hemisphere and the enduring burst of radiance in my mirror stretches my shadow a hundred feet forward. The gravel in the road resembles crinkled tin foil. Intermingled with a rising, smiling three-quarter moon, the few distant clouds remaining turn a shiny silvery-platinum. To the east, a squall over the Atlantic dumps its final load of the day as a last gesture of peace. Roaming sheep in the meadows appear as scattered tumbleweeds. In a grand finale, the sinking sun sets the brown grasses ablaze in an orange yellow glow. I flip up my face shield for a blast of warm fresh air as Mother Earth murmurs to me in a comforting embrace: Welcome to Argentina!

ARGENTINA
February 26, 2002
Rio Gallegos, Southeast Coast of Argentina
● ●

My first full dose of Argentina begins this morning. Previously I've only crossed the border for a day or two at a time while winding south through Chile. Riding steady, it'll take a week to reach Buenos Aires for bike repairs and maintenance, then I'm off to explore for another month. Hopefully, the local dealer will have tires, brake pads, and oil filters for this tired little motorcycle.

The people in Argentina reveal a hearty, festive nature, often describing themselves as *"muy loco"* (very crazy). Their passion for life shines through in everything they say and do. I receive a warm welcome wherever I go, and the people seem pleased that I ask so many questions. One morning while waiting in line for the ferry, a father in the car ahead whispers something to his young son and moments later an eight-year-old-boy climbs out of the back seat and walks up to offer me a cookie. Next, his giggling little sister brings a cup of fruit juice, asking in English a well-rehearsed, "Waas yoo nam?"

I've mostly met small-town folk thus far and they are usually friendlier than big-city dwellers but there's no telling what lies ahead. I might get mugged in a riot in Buenos Aires or have the time of my life. The country has everything from tropical jungles to open plains with Andean glaciers in the distance. Argentina has absorbed the best of Latin culture and continental architecture. So far the country feels more like Europe with a classic Latin pulse.

Finally, I wake with an appetite. My stomach screams for food but my brain warns, "Don't try it yet buddy." It's a five-hour ride to Puerto San Julian to visit the penguins and city restaurants, but I decide to wait until settling into a hotel before starting to experiment with the local cuisine. Southeasterly winds provide a comfortable tailwind, locking me between two storm fronts. If I ride too fast, I'll catch the storm ahead, too slow and the other storm will grab me from behind. We all move at an even sixty, so I stay dry.

Before returning to the road, there's a chance for a quick boat ride to an island bird sanctuary. I promised a friend back home to pose with the penguins. That pleasant obligation fulfilled, I saddle up and prepare for the onslaught ahead. The wind pounds unmercifully from all directions from the first moment I launch into the turbulence until stopping to eat in a desolate gas station.

The angular headwinds switch directions unpredictably, flinging me about while I struggle to maintain lane position. On the plus side, there's no traffic and the road is paved. Even with the throttle wide open, the seventy to eighty mph headwinds keep me at fifty. Gas mileage drops from fifty miles per gallon to the low thirties. I crouch behind the fairing, throw all my weight toward the gale-force blast, and hang on. When slowing down to stop for fuel, the moment I pull in the clutch, it's as though I squeezed the front brake. Once, I came to a complete stop without braking and actually started rolling backwards, blown by the wind. It's far too intense to ride more than six hours at a time, but there are 1,200 miles left to Buenos Aires, and I want out of this madness.

Waiting at a small-town traffic signal, above the sound of the engine's idle, I hear the dreaded noise that sickens hearts of motorcycle riders — metal to metal contact. The low-pitched grinding noise, barely audible above the roar of the wind, compels me to stop and inspect, hoping it's my imagination. Perhaps something caught in the fender. No such luck.

Motorcycles are not popular in South America and outside of major cities there are few shops that sell or repair them. Even in capital cities, Kawasaki dealers are rare. Argentina is more up-to-date and I keep my fingers crossed while asking around for a repair shop. Yes, two blocks down and turn right — a small miracle. Close enough to push and coast. A lucky day after all. The owner is a professional motocross rider who also builds motors, and is about as good a man as you'll ever find. We unbolt the top end to check the valves and work downward from there. Finally we pull the timing chain and alternator to discover an ear broken off the crankcase and the balance chain tensioner — shattered into five pieces. No parts available in the hemisphere.

LONG SHOT
March 5, 2002
• • • • • • • •

The motocross team shows up to assist. Amazingly they reassemble the components in the correct order with no shop manual for technical guidance. To remanufacture the broken part, they saw off the end of a case-hardened wrench and weld it on to what's left of the original balance chain tensioner. Then they countersink the bolt hole inside the crankcase for the broken ear and use a longer bolt to hold it. The balance chain has stretched too far and won't adjust any farther, leaving excessive slop. Add to that, the alternator is missing a magnet and out of balance. Still, I'm going to give it a shot, hoping it provides enough charge to keep the bike running.

A few hours later, I make it farther north to the city of Trelew where the lone motorcycle dealer only handles Yamaha. He says I may be able to order Kawasaki parts up ahead in Bahia Blanco, another 450 finger-crossing miles. The engine noises are getting louder, but I opt to roll those dice again and take a chance.

BUENOS AIRES
March 5, 2002
● ● ● ● ● ● ● ● ●

The last few days with the rapidly failing KLR have been precarious. Metal-to-metal sounds increase, compelling numerous stops to pull off my helmet and listen to evaluate how much engine life remains. This makes for slow progress, but I try to push it as far as possible, hoping to catch the last clank just before the engine blows.

Farther north, the wind subsides, with temperatures increasing enough that I can stow my cumbersome foul-weather gear. With nothing but tropics ahead, I won't need it again until the Central Highlands of Mexico on the way back to California. Small towns are still a hundred miles apart, and brown, windswept, low grasslands have changed to cool green orchards and manicured farms. There's a marked increase in traffic. Earlier, I met a car once an hour, but there is now a steady flow of weekenders returning home after holidays in the country.

I love the people of Argentina, but they uphold their well-earned reputation as the most dangerous drivers in Latin America. Long, empty, well-paved straightaways invite motorists to relieve their boredom by exploring the capabilities and limits of their cherished automobiles. A hundred plus is the norm and apparently without consequence, as I've yet to see a cop anywhere. Speed seems to be a popular though perilous pastime, despite the vehicles being packed with families. When cruising at 100 mph and encountering a vehicle in the distance they wish to pass, drivers accelerate to 120, get as close to the rear fender as possible, and then barely drift to the left to overtake at the last second.

Used to zero traffic, I allow myself to be lulled into ignoring my mirrors. Suddenly, out of nowhere, a two-ton rocket blasts by, close enough to buff the bugs off its bumper, using the rubberized fabric of my saddlebags as a rag. In Argentina, this type of driving is the rule, not the exception. Everyone drives this way as if this maneuver is taught in school. I ask myself if these maniacs are the same helpful folks I met earlier in roadside cafés. They had been so friendly. What happened to these wonderful people when they got behind the wheel of a car?

It's just as crazy in the city. When two vehicles approach an uncontrolled intersection, both accelerate and aim toward one another until one backs down. Motorcyclists lose this game and must be on guard in all directions. When nearing intersections I ride close to buses or big trucks, letting them run interference. It isn't so appalling to see a car speeding through downtown traffic at ninety mph; the shock is that no one notices. Earlier, I scoffed when advised to park the bike in Buenos Aires and take taxis. Now, I'm relieved it's dismantled on a workbench waiting on parts, so I don't have to make that choice. Besides, strolling the sidewalks provides opportunity to study the opposite sex.

The head-turning beauty and classy attire of Argentine women are legendary. No matter how they are covered, they appear mouth-wateringly sexy. Maybe it's the economics of the way they dress, using less material and leaving their midriffs bare. Stores that formerly sold pants, apparently peddle only cans of different pastel-color spray paint that, when dried, faintly resembles fabric. It's outrageous. Men walk around in a constant state of heat gawking at the eye candy.

At first I try to be cool and not stare while every few minutes nonchalantly wiping off my chin, but it's unavoidable to be mesmerized by such remarkable beauty. The women seem used to the attention but realize if they reveal as much as a smile or allow eye contact, they won't reach the end of the block without being followed by panting suitors. *Señoritas* never stroll down the streets in Buenos Aires. They march purposefully with face down, gaze focused on the sidewalk ahead or with eyes cast upward at the sky, never leaving that opening. I of course want to document this spectacle with my trusty Sony digital to satisfy my curious Internet readers, but it's difficult to persuade the women to hold still.

It's nearly impossible to greet them with a *"Buenas tardes"* before they strut halfway down the block. I resort to stopping in stores along Florida Street in *el centro*, pitching sales girls in fancy shops to pose for a quick picture. Once they allow me a moment and hear my American accent, a brief conversation becomes possible, but little else.

No surprise that the tango is the most passionate dance ever invented. Purposeful steps to a commanding accordion pace explain with musical intensity the cultural roots and passion of a nation's past. One can't merely watch the tango performed without sharing the experience. It doesn't cause you to tap your feet or rock your hips, but you will find yourself mentally mirroring the expressions and fervor of the couple locked in precise motion. Gliding and strutting across the floor while whipping in and out of impassioned poses that reflect their alternate personalities makes an observer feel voyeuristic — as though enjoying a private act in public.

Last year, the currency exchange rate was one peso for one dollar. Recently that doubled to two pesos for one dollar, making Argentina a bargain travel destination. Actually, prior to this radical devaluation, the country was overpriced and the economy out of control. At present, costs are slightly lower than they should be when compared to similar goods and services in other Latin American destinations. Overall, I find Buenos Aires the most pleasant capital city yet.

However, a complicated banking crisis is alive and simmering dangerously as citizens fume. Because of government austerity measures, account holders are able to draw only small amounts of money from banks on a weekly basis, and the frustrations are escalating. Most banks have been covered in steel plating. Platoons of helmeted police guard them in the daytime against aggressive and angry mobs. Nightly news programs show protesters banging pots and pans together while in some areas the looting of supermarkets reveals the desperation of the people.

In an attempt to save their political hides, local officials blame the world banking community. The international economic powers blame corruption and mismanagement while ordering the Argentine government to get its house in order before providing any further assistance. I don't know who is to blame, only that Argentina is much too important to let slip away.

BACK IN THE WIND
March 12, 2002
Buenos Aires, Argentina
● ● ● ● ● ● ● ● ● ● ● ● ●

My ailing Kawasaki has finally been repaired and a much-needed week-long R&R was enough to rejuvenate me. Once again, I'm ready for the open road. The mangled little motorcycle received new tires, brakes, and a tune-up. The balance chain and tensioner have been replaced along with missing bolts that vibrated out weeks ago. A Progressive Suspension rear mono-shock gives the bike a new feel, and since bumps and potholes are unlikely to affect me anymore, I can already sense my back pains subside. The carburetor is finally jetted and adjusted correctly, providing new life to the tired motor. A depleted battery, sucked dry from the high electrical loads of heated grips and vest, is topped off and full of juice.

For the last few days, I've been studying maps and guidebooks, but still lack a clear picture of what lies ahead. Within the next month I'll ride across the entire country of Brazil, which occupies the majority of South America. Due to severe seasonal rains, many roads are washed out, so I plan to cross part of the northern country via a river barge on the Amazon River. The mighty Amazon is nearly as long as the Nile, cutting across Brazil from its main source, the Andes in Peru. That segment of the journey should take a week, but I can haul my own food and sleep out on the deck at night in a hammock. Brazil will be a unique adventure. There's much to look forward to and I am again sleepless with anticipation.

No matter how anxious I get to cross the next border, there's always a last-minute melancholy crush, but this time, when exiting Argentina, it's doubly depressing. Like always, I talk about returning someday, yet I probably never will. Battles with the elements have been tremendous experiences but ones I don't need to revisit. The thought of never seeing South America or my old nemesis, the *Altiplano* of Bolivia, again is disturbing. However, the thought of letting go of Argentina breaks my heart more.

I've met people I sincerely liked in every country but I don't want to say goodbye to my new friend in Buenos Aires. Saying *adios* to her in person is too tough. I chicken out and do it on the phone after convincing myself it's time to drift on.

As I travel around this distant world of alien cultures and mystifying people, I'm saddened to realize I won't see them again, but I will miss her forever. I reflect on the images of families and individuals who have shown me such kindness. They've had such a profound effect on me; I wonder what effect I've had on them. This time, moving on is painful. It's as though I'm never supposed to return to California but rather am destined to roam the world forever.

Freeways exiting Buenos Aires remind me of Los Angeles. After an hour of wrong turns inside a maze of crisscrossing streets and vehicular confusion, the concrete trail finally turns into the deserted highway north. I've been off the bike for six days, almost forgetting the feel of a firm wind against my chest, a wind just cool enough to relieve the subtropical heat. On a freshly repaired bike, it's like starting out all over again.

Gone are icy mornings and fears of sudden snowstorms. Frigid, gale-force winds have become gentle breezes. It's T-shirt weather for as long as the sky remains dry, and leather jacket time only if it rains. I have two and a half months to cover the next 10,000 miles of coastal plains, broken-down roads, and sultry Amazon jungle. It's a brand-new life, and I hardly remember what occurred only weeks ago.

ALONG THE BORDER OF URUGUAY
March 13, 2002
● ● ● ● ● ● ● ● ●

The bleak, barren landscape of southern Argentina has finally given way to varying streaks of deep green pastures in the temperate north. Mild country mornings offer refuge from the harsh climatic challenges left behind. With temperatures in the mid-nineties, high humidity cools the rushing air and a pleasing wind wraps around my body, assuring me it's okay to relax and enjoy the ride. Plush, subtropical farmland stretches out to the horizon, and with cattle in the fields safely fenced away, I find little to worry about. Most roads are paved in Argentina and were built right the first time so potholes and missing sections of roadway are no longer a threat. No more managing unpredictable surfaces.

Traffic is nonexistent as I roam blissfully north along the border of Uruguay, confidently eyeing squalls along the mountains. For once I'm relieved when a torrential downpour flashes in. Within seconds I'm doused by hearty blasts of rain that wash my face shield clean. I flip the shield up just to enjoy the stinging droplets rinsing my open mouth. As quickly as the squall clobbers me, it moves farther west to nurture a farmer's thirsty orchard in a place where the sun is about to set. The air is still warm, causing a satisfying shiver while gently tugging my soggy clothes dry in minutes. I find myself hoping Brazil will be this kind to me.

At the approaching fork in the highway near Posadas, Argentina, I must choose between a direct route to Iguazu Falls and Brazil, or a one-day detour to Paraguay for an overnight in the capital city of Asunción. The road through Paraguay is rumored to be plagued by bandits. My time is growing short and every hour counts from now until Panama. As I ride northward, closing in on the Tropic of Capricorn, daily riding time diminishes with less sunlight. I delay the decision until the last possible moment when the fork appears. It will be one of those yes/no moments that I won't be sure of until well past the junction.

LAST DAYS OF ARGENTINA
March 15, 2002
Iguazu, Argentina
● ● ● ● ● ● ● ● ● ●

It's fascinating how time distorts when traveling. Yesterday morning seems like the week before and the departure from California five and a half months ago was from another lifetime. Constantly waking up in strange places has made me accustomed to being unaccustomed. I've learned to savor forgetting where I am until stumbling bleary-eyed out of the last hotel room and hearing a foreign language tickle my thoughts. This always makes me smile. There's no hesitation any more, I respond automatically in Spanish. The next few minutes are always the same — a methodical repacking of miscellaneous gear, accounting for articles of clothing and toiletries. After strapping down the saddlebags, I perform a final double-check and it's time to ride. Even with meticulous precautions and careful under-the-bed inspections, too often things get left behind.

Usually, I remember the forgotten item just as I'm rolling away from the curb but other times it doesn't hit me until a hundred miles down the road. Then the question becomes whether to ride back for a guidebook I left on the restaurant table or just buy another in the next city. I lost my last *Lonely Planet* book in Chile and could not find another for 6,000 miles despite searching in dozens of bookstores. I should have gone back to look for it.

Buenos Aires had more bookstores than any other city on this trip, with vast collections of guidebooks, but none on South America in

English. The number of bookstores a city has says things about the people. Not only that they enjoy reading, but also that they have time to read. In poorer countries, people are far too busy trying to feed themselves and lack time or money for books. Books are a luxury wealthier nations take for granted.

Nothing surprises me anymore. What was before considered bizarre is now the norm. Sometimes while lost in thought, I realize there is no baseline anymore. I'm no longer certain of who I am but, more important, who I'm expected to be. Nothing is written in stone and I feel as free as the winds of Patagonia. Reality is still foreign to me. It wouldn't surprise me to wake from a dream still a prisoner of the ELN in the mountains of Colombia. In moments of depression I still wonder if these are the final seconds before death. Am I awake or asleep? The avalanche is still closing in, and in times of open-eyed nightmare, I seek the only refuge I know — a twist of the throttle and another new town. At times, I sprint to outrun the lunacy.

I spent five weeks in Colombia accepting that I could die in the next minute, and when I was finally released, I refused to go home to let the reality of freedom sink in with familiar surroundings. Even now, I am still too afraid to believe I'm free. Pondering my fate became normal — nonchalant — speculating about death had grown old. I learned to ignore the intense reality and carry on moment to moment as though it no longer mattered. It's becoming painfully obvious that mental processing of this nature does not wear off easily.

When lost in the high-altitude plains of Bolivia, I accepted that there might be serious problems ahead and I set off every morning in a mechanical trance like a robot with preprogrammed thoughts. It's as though nothing can shock or scare me anymore as I try to figure out what is worth worrying about anyway.

Rolling out of Posadas, I still have not made up my mind what to do at the upcoming fork in the road. The desk clerk at the hotel warned, without being asked, that Paraguay at the moment is *"Muy peligroso."* (Very dangerous.) *"Hay muchos ladrones en el camino."* (There are many robbers on the highway.) At the final moment I consider the omen and choose the safe road to Brazil. I've had enough drama for a while.

Temperatures have cooked into the muggy low hundreds and when I'm locked in city traffic the humid air becomes a hot, wet blanket sticking to my body. Even the open road provides little relief until I spot charcoal rain clouds in the distance slowly crossing the black line of asphalt ahead. For a change, I find myself racing toward the torrential fury just to cool off. Within seconds, I'm drenched and basking in the chilly relief of a tropical squall.

When roads are wet, stopping power for a motorcycle diminishes dramatically. At the moment, however, there's no traffic, potholes or animals roaming the highway and thus no reason to stop. I don't even bother to slow down as my heat-scorched body drinks in liquid relief cascading down with the intensity of a waterfall. The air is sweet and clean and I smell the wet with my mouth as well as my nose. It's 200 miles to Iguazu Falls. Yet I want to take my time, savoring the delicate green countryside whooshing by me in bright flashing colors that rub off on my skin. This is how it should always have been — except for the cops.

Latin American countries are exceptionally security conscious, thus military checkpoints dot the roadways with a frequency bordering on the absurd. In Mexico, motorcycle riders are usually waved on and are stopped only when bored soldiers want to make conversation. They likely figure, how many machine guns and hand grenades could a biker be carrying in his saddlebags anyway?

Motorcycle enthusiasts in Argentina are not so fortunate. We get stopped more, not less. They never search me; just ask for my passport while inquiring where I'm headed and where I'm coming from. I'm tempted to ask them, "Why, did someone that looks like me just rob a bank or start a revolution?" Every ten miles there's a soldier or *Policia Nacional* waving me over to inspect my documents. They are invariably polite while rifling through my papers, trying to convince me they know what they are looking at. Most have never seen an American before and none know what customs documents should look like. After all, how many people a day do they meet who are riding the continent on a motorcycle?

It says a lot about a country when they have so many security checkpoints. It must mean they are insecure, and I wonder why. Other than their own people, who has angered them or frightened them so badly that they need all this security? If a country has so many enemies within, they must be doing something wrong to their people. When soldiers are given police authority and national police are assigned to interrogating civilians, it is a recipe for abuse and corruption. Unbridled authority soon rages out of control. If an authority figure carrying a weapon is unaccountable for his actions, no matter how noble his beginning, he soon becomes a tyrant.

When flagged over for the twentieth time today, I'm asked for another type of document no policeman in Latin America has ever requested, *documento de seguridad* (an insurance card). I sense this demand is unusual and that nobody else is being required to produce this paperwork. The creepy demeanor of this uniformed thug doesn't seem right from the beginning. Maybe it's the pus-filled sore under his eye or the crooked, rotting teeth; either way, I sense evil. Maybe it's a stereotype, but every time a cop has shaken me down, he has had bad teeth. Crooked teeth, crooked man. I don't know for certain but I'm always looking for patterns, and nobody who looked like Mel Gibson has yet jacked me up for a bribe.

Almost immediately I'm placed under arrest and ordered to a run-down cement building 500 feet back from the road. It stinks of stale cigarette smoke and urine. In the interrogation room where another half dozen older uniformed men are sitting around a wooden table, Señor Snaggletooth officially informs them that he has captured a major violator with a serious problem and states the charges. I pretend to not understand. In an obviously rehearsed move, the officers sadly shake their heads in unison. The spokesman declares the fine is 300 U.S. dollars for such an offense and produces a poorly typed form to prove it. Even with my weak Spanish I can see they have misspelled some words.

Of course there's always a helpful cop offering a solution. Maybe I can pay a lesser fine here of, say, 200 dollars and be on my way. They assure me the judge would approve and there will be no further action needed.

"Sorry guys, I don't speak Spanish," I reply in English with a big happy-go-lucky smile on my face, "and I don't understand what you want." This approach has always worked before and after a few minutes of bantering, I have been let go with a handshake. I'm confident they will give in, yet this situation grows sour. These jerks are digging in and insisting. The price keeps getting lower but they also become angrier. The fat man at the end of the table is *El Jefe* and the scary thing about this deal is how many are involved at once. Usually it's a lone cop or maybe a pair, but seldom this many with a commanding officer present. When the boss is overseeing this crap in plain sight, it is ugly.

El Jefe stands, raises his voice, and, in a move meant to intimidate, unholsters his nine-millimeter pistol and lays it on the table in front of him. With clenched teeth he asks, "*¿Cuanto tiene?*" (How much do you have?)

I ponder for a moment — are these the same soldiers that only a decade or so ago were arresting opposition political enemies to later toss them out of airplanes, alive, over the ocean? How far will they push this obvious hustle? I'm not going to argue if I should pay: I simply cannot pay because I don't have cash. I call his bluff with some intentionally poorly pronounced Spanish.

"*No nada.*" (Nothing.) "*Yo no tengo dinero, solomente una tarjeta de credito.*" (I have no money, only a credit card.) My cash is of course well hidden in the secret pocket sewn in the back of my pants. Before the situation reaches the level of them searching me, I innocently turn my other pockets inside out and lay my wallet on the table, out of their direct reach.

"How do you buy food?" they ask. Knowing they won't dare to create a paper trail, I show them my traveler's checks. "*¿Quiere estos?*" (Do you want these?)

They huddle for a moment to grumble, and the crook who originally stopped me walks up offering a handshake. "*Toda bien. Adelante señor.*" (Everything is fine. Go ahead sir.) Declining the confrontation of refusing a handshake, I hold out a flimsy paw, the direct opposite of the hearty Latin American respectful clasp, meant for friends.

Normally while climbing back on my bike, I'd chuckle about such a victory, smugly triumphant that sneaky cops didn't get away with squeezing me. But a criminal act like this here was shocking; and like Chile, after sustained public outrage, Argentina prides itself in having extinguished these practices. I am not so disturbed about an attempted shakedown, but what turns my stomach is that it has occurred in a modern country, whose people I love and respect.

Once back on the road, the stifling heat intensifies while the terrain returns to full-scale tropical jungle, reportedly for the next 8,000 miles. The only good thing about the extreme cold climates is there are hardly any bugs. Insects must not like to freeze any more than I do. In the tropics, I return to waking up mornings bearing multicolored welts from nibbling pests that lurk invisibly under hotel bedsheets.

Leaving a modern little *pueblo* after lunch, I encounter a long line of buses, cars, and trucks parked in the middle of the road. As usual, I white-line it to the front, only to be stopped by armed soldiers. Beyond them I see a long banner stretched across the road with writing on it indicating some type of protest. My heart gasps with disappointment — another *paro*. This time with the military standing by, who I hope only intend to keep order and allow the townspeople a peaceful blockade.

A smiling soldier with a machine gun politely inquires, "*¿A donde va señor?*" (Where are you going sir?) Time for the magic words. "*Voy a Brazil señor porque soy un escritor y estoy escribiendo un libro sobre la gente de Sud America.*"

He ponders for a moment as I follow his gaze to a gap between where the banner ends and a group of trees begins. It's wide enough for a motorcycle but not a car. Yet it seems as though his orders are to stop cars, buses, and trucks, maybe not motorcycles. He points to the path shrugging his shoulders and waves me on.

Another soldier, farther up, blocks my way by pointing a rifle at me. I tell him the other man said it was okay. "*El me dijo esta bien señor.*"

He shakes his head adamantly. "*Imposible. No puede ir.*" (Impossible. You cannot go.)

The first soldier walks up, discusses the crisis for a few moments, and they agree to allow me to pass. As I do, the small crowd of protesters set up in the roadway look surprised and angry as though this is not part of their deal. With no time for further delay, I don't hesitate until riding safely away from the roadblock and then discreetly unpack my camera for a parting shot. A few soldiers point at me warily and the crowd is clearly unhappy that I was permitted to pass. Time to move on. Next and final stop in Argentina is Iguazu Falls, and after that, a departure from a land that has become part of me.

BRAZIL

BRAZIL
March 16, 2002
Foz do Iguazu, Brazil
● ● ● ● ● ● ● ● ● ● ● ●

This is my last morning in Argentina so I take my time rolling out of the border *pueblo* for a day at Iguazu Falls. Skipping the hassle of money changers, I spend the last of my Argentine pesos on junk food; their value is declining so fast they won't be worth much, if anything, in Brazil. At last count yesterday, the exchange rate was two and a half pesos to the dollar and heading for three. This is great if traveling with greenbacks, but a disaster for the people of Argentina.

Soon I arrive at a nearly empty national park. Tourists are apprehensive about the political climate, and concerns about violent demonstrations keep them away. The park resembles Disneyland, highly organized with legions of uniformed staff supplying information. After a short hike on a genuine jungle footpath, a tramcar hauls me up to the 1,000-meter-long catwalk leading to the most thrilling section of the falls. The Devils Throat, with a 230-foot drop-off, is the largest of all the Cataratas. A quarter-mile away, heavy clouds of fine mist can be seen rising above the exploding water below. Standing directly above, looking down, it's impossible to see the bottom through the swirling, sparkling white.

In order to spend a few minutes alone, I hustle ahead of the crowd at the end of the catwalk that cantilevers out over the daunting precipice below. Immediately, I am seized and shaken by the powerful roar of millions of gallons of water tumbling down to collide on the boulders. Intrigued, I must get closer. Riverboats take visitors to the bottom of the falls, where the water detonates into smoky thunder. A mild climb down leads to a rocky promontory jutting out over the riverbank. Giant rubber rafts scoop up thrill-seeking travelers for a shower in the drenching mist beneath the foaming storm.

We're issued life jackets and plastic bags for our cameras and warned we will get very wet. At the final moment before submersion into the hydraulic tunnel under the falls, our guide signals to stash our cameras in the bags and hunker down. I wait until the last possible second and then some, for a final photo. Too late. A tumbling surge from above soaks both my faithful Sony digital camera and me as though we had been tossed overboard. Back on dry land, my apprehensive examination reveals no damage — even the memory stick is unscathed — my lucky day. Time to swap countries!

Exiting Argentina and entering Brazil is nearly painless, with only a thirty-minute delay while Brazilian customs officials fill out the vehicle importation documents. This is a significant leap into a new country, new culture, and new language — one I don't speak. Coupled with the loss of my *Lonely Planet* guidebook, and not understanding what people are saying, I'm one lost soul. After crossing the border, it's soon apparent that I don't even know how to ask directions in Portuguese and I have no local currency. The sun is going down and I don't want to get stuck looking for a hotel after dark so I follow road signs to the first town. Some of the words in Portuguese are written similarly to Spanish but pronounced differently. Relieved to find a sign reading, *Al Centro*, I follow the arrow hoping it leads to something familiar.

Soon, I find a cheap hotel with air conditioning, a must in the sticky evening heat, and then head out to inspect the town. Brazil is a distinctly different world than Argentina, more casual but also seedier. Maybe it's just the part of town that I settle into, but it seems the men lurking on street corners and alleyways are looking for victims. Most locals are friendly enough, and being so close to the border, some speak Spanish as well as Portuguese. Still, I feel uncomfortable without the ability to communicate or understand what is going on around me. I know little about Brazil, except what I've read in guidebooks and from a two-week trip to Rio de Janeiro twenty years ago.

ROCKIN' RIO
March 20, 2002
Rio de Janeiro, Brazil
● ● ● ● ● ● ● ● ● ● ● ●

Despite the numerous warnings describing the dangers of motorcycling in Brazil, so far, the gentle countryside is a biker's paradise. Main roads are well paved and engineered with smooth banked turns through rolling hills. Most are double lane, and motorcycles are exempt from expensive tolls, but gas is three bucks a gallon. Even truckers are polite. If they inadvertently cut me off or switch lanes too closely, they smile and wave apologetically.

Sunday traffic is surprisingly heavy with long lines of rumbling semitrucks moving fast in tight convoys. It's intimidating to ride in between them — caught up in their hot forceful wakes and knowing how easy it is to get sucked up by powerful currents and drawn underneath their enormous, grinding wheels.

The initial ride through this fresh green jungle, with pines and palms intermingling along the roadways, is uneventful. Warm, damp air demands a stop every hundred miles or so for cold coconut milk and sweet tropical fruit at the thatch-roofed roadside stands. Two bucks buys a plastic plate of diced mango and two husked coconuts stored on ice — a ready meal for a wandering Viking. Although food is cheap, it lacks in quality. I don't understand the menus, so I walk around restaurants casually inspecting other people's plates to see if something looks decent. If so, I point at it to tell the waiter that's what I want. My first words in Portuguese are *sem cebolos*, or in Spanish *sin cebollas*, without onions.

Ricardo Rocco is still emailing travel recommendations from Quito and has yet to make a bad suggestion. Since we parted last

January, he outlined an itinerary of the best places to see and overnight throughout South America. I have deviated twice from his counsel and was sorry both times. He advised me to avoid the densely populated, endless city of Sao Paulo and instead head farther south to Santos, by the ocean. I would if I could.

But I was unprepared for how fast the sky darkens while nearing the equator from the south. My ride timing is off. By seven at night, it's pitch black and starting to drizzle. My little motorcycle is experiencing another electrical failure as the motor cuts off at idle and won't fire up again. Without much problem, I push start it and plan to keep the motor running all day. If I need to stop at a restaurant, I'll find one on a hill for an easy coast-to-start. In case there are delays in finding repair parts, I want to reach Rio as quickly as possible — better to wait there instead of Sao Paulo. And trouble persists. Instead of getting brighter when revving up the motor, the lights now go dim. At least I'm still moving in a forward direction. Riding with fading lights after dark in the rain makes it difficult for truckers to see me, and I often nearly get squished between them. Distant lights of Sao Paulo appear over the next hill but I decide to take no more chances and exit on the nearest off-ramp to troubleshoot the battery.

At the first intersection, I holler from within my helmet at a motorcyclist on a small Honda next to me, asking where to buy a battery. He nods, beckoning me to follow. We find an equivalent to a Kmart store that doesn't sell batteries. He speaks no Spanish or English. I speak no Portuguese.

He is enthusiastic about helping me find a battery, insisting through an interpreter we meet that he knows of a place nearby with batteries. Off we ride, blasting across Sao Paulo's crowded highways and side streets. I'm lost within moments. My only hope is to try and keep up with him as he boldly white-lines it through traffic on a much lighter and considerably narrower bike. I'm grazing fenders with my fully loaded Kawasaki trying to keep up with a faint red tail-light disappearing between cars. Two hours later we've hit half a dozen stores but no battery in sight.

My new pal offers a place to sleep for the night. I enjoy spending time with locals but I'm uncomfortable staying with strangers. I like to come and go as I please, eat the food I want, and enjoy my privacy. It's almost midnight, and my first choice is to get a hotel and meet him in the morning, yet he assures me there are no problems or complications. I say, "Okay but let me buy us some pizza first."

After we visit several houses, I realize that he's just taking me around to his friends and family asking them to put me up for the night and really has no clue on what to do with me. It's past midnight and I only want to check my email and go to sleep. He insists that there is an Internet connection at the next house, where there is also a man who speaks English. So there is, but while attempting for the fifth time to log on to his ISP, the man of the house blurts out that my new friend wants a visa for his son so he can move to the U.S. Would I go with him to the Embassy tomorrow and help him get it? I tell him it isn't that easy and I would be busy fixing my bike early in the morning anyway. Okay, how about in the afternoon? Can we swing by and pick up a visa? No, that won't be necessary, I'll just call the president and have the ambassador drop one off. He seems disappointed and so am I. Most of the time locals do nice things for strangers for altruistic reasons, but sometimes they want an impossible favor in return. I suggest grabbing the next hotel we see and to continue battery seeking tomorrow. He never shows up again.

After a quick search the next morning, I find a back-alley bike shop packed with rusty machinery. I need to work on my bike but their only tools are pliers and a screwdriver. They get creative with tapping and pounding. Eventually we replace the battery and blown fuses, wiggle some wires, and an hour later I'm on my way out of Sao Paulo on a long, complicated freeway system jammed with commercial vehicles.

After six hours of waffling, I opt to stop over in Rio de Janeiro. Big cities are seldom representative of what the rest of a country is actually like and generally they are miserably crowded, dangerous, and difficult to navigate. But I was told it would be a sin to ride through Brazil without visiting Rio. So here I sit in a pleasantly air-conditioned little hotel room in Copocabana watching the rain.

When the sun appears, sprawling empty beaches instantly fill with tourists and barely clothed locals, all trying to gobble up as much sun as possible before it rains again. The women wear close to nothing and are probably the most flirtatious I've encountered yet. I don't know if those enticing, bright-flashing smiles are a come-on or a tease, but it seems like sex is on everyone's mind in Rio. Mine included.

On the universal scale of ten, most of the women here vary between eights and nines but their exotic features, accompanied by sultry smiles and near-nakedness, elevate them all to solid tens. After a few minutes of small talk on the beach, I invite a young olive-skinned beauty who'd been playing eye-games with her pair of sparkling emeralds back to my room to help me with my Portuguese over a bottle of rum. She smiles in return but tells me the rum won't be necessary. She seems as mesmerized over blue eyes as I am over green. Once in the room she flips on the television to a music station playing Brazilian songs and proceeds to dance a seductive samba as I lie on the bed with an imagination on overload.

Her steamy touch is delicate enough to transmit a sensuous energy through her fingertips as she lightly brushes them across my face. I shiver with anticipation and flush with desire. Long black curly hair veils the grapefruit-sized double treat about to be revealed with the tug of a string. She turns to me for the honors. Today it's great to be a *gringo* in South America.

I feel at home amongst Brazilians. My arms are cluttered with sinister looking tattoos and so are many of theirs. When traveling, I wear long-sleeved shirts to avoid alarming people. Here, tattoos and tank tops are the norm and the local tough guys roaming the streets at night seem equally worried about me robbing them than the other way around. I find this amusing and everywhere I go, I'm greeted heartily by curious street people with dozens of questions. I discover that if I mispronounce Spanish and speak rapidly, I can make myself understood and if they repeat their sentences enough times with different tones, I almost understand them. The *Lonely Planet* guidebook has a few phrases and pointers for speaking Portuguese, but it's hard to put much effort into learning a language I'll only be using for another month.

In the morning I'll continue north for a two-week ride along the eastern coast to one of the wettest regions on earth, Belem. The road ends there so I plan to hop a barge headed northwest 1,000 miles up the Amazon River toward Venezuela. After the boat lands in Manaus, it will take another few days to ride to Caracas and then on to a northwestern port city for shipping back to Panama. There's malaria and dengue fever outbreaks along the equator so I'll be coating my body with bug spray laced with DEET, a chemical the label advises will melt plastic. There is controversy over which malaria drug to use, as some are no longer effective against new strains, so this will be a last-minute decision.

MARTIAL ARTS
March 22, 2002
North on BR101
● ● ● ● ● ● ● ● ● ●

Since I only have two full days in Rio and most of it will be consumed with bike repairs and Internet matters, I saved the jiu-jitsu school visit until last. There are several to choose from but Carlson Gracie is the most famous and the closest. Off I go to meet one of the legends.

My first encounter with the Gracie family was while training at L.A. Judo in Los Angeles during 1988. One day my coach pointed across the mat to a clean-cut looking young man wearing a judo uniform cluttered with sponsorship advertising and said to me, "I want you to fight that guy."

"No problem, Coach," I said confidently, and strode across the mat to meet my opponent for the day.

He looked like a walking billboard and spoke with a funny accent but he also smiled with self-assurance. I'd heard rumors about a clan of fierce Brazilian fighters, the Gracie family, rapidly making a name in the U.S., but no one I knew had met any of them yet. My throat kind of dried up as I looked him over a little closer. "By any chance is your name Gracie?"

"Yes, my name is Royce Gracie" (pronounced like Hoits), he replied with a big friendly smile. The legend was before me. The worst thing any man can do before we fight is to scare me. I'm never embarrassed to admit being scared. Fear is not a sin. It's how you deal with fear that determines character. I choose to face what scares me and that formula has worked well over the years. Many times, I defeated men who scared me the most because I took no chances and gave it my all. Royce Gracie scared me so I gave him my all.

Yet I remember being surprised at how easy he was to throw several times in a row. The first hour of judo practice consists of standing throws and takedowns followed by ground fighting or mat work. Each technique is practiced separately, so after one judoka executes a successful throw, they start over again from a standing position. Royce, one of the best ground fighters in the world, had come to learn judo throws and takedowns.

He was being a good sport about everything, until after the tenth time I tossed him, he whispered politely, "Next time we continue on the ground?"

"Sure why not?" Couldn't be that bad — I thought.

That was my first introduction to Brazilian jiu-jitsu and the devastating art of joint locks and strangleholds by one of the premier practitioners on the planet. Each time after I threw him, he had me so twisted up I felt like a rubber pretzel. Later he admitted to me that he had two older brothers who could easily defeat him.

After practicing together, we became friends, and once when he visited me in Palm Springs, I taught him how to ride a motorcycle. That day he told me about a televised tournament being organized for an "anything goes" fight, without rules, called the Ultimate Challenge. Was I interested? But I had already experienced his technique enough to know that it was impossible to beat a grappler unless you were a trained grappler yourself. And I had no intention of getting thumped on national television so I declined. The Gracies knew they

had the drop on everyone, and were confident there were no sufficiently trained grapplers outside of Brazil, making any fight a sure
bet for them. This was a game the world of martial arts had never
seen before, and no one was prepared for what lay ahead. Judokas
and wrestlers were the strongest competitors because they were more
familiar with hands-on fighting and more proficient at throws and
takedowns. But the problem was, mat work dominated this contest,
and they won hands down.

There was tremendous rivalry between judo and jiu-jitsu, each
discipline claiming superiority. But I never got caught up in the
argument of which style was superior because I was more concerned
with any gap in my technique and felt that anyone who could beat
me could also teach me. Over the decades, whenever I looked for a
new school to train in, I always sought the toughest. If I beat everyone in the room, I was bored and continued searching until I found
a school where I got my butt kicked. They had something to teach
me and that's where I would make my new home for the following
five years. I didn't have to be the toughest, but I had to be among
them.

My motto became, "To teach me, you had to beat me." A few
months later at a judo team tournament, the Machado brothers
(cousins of the Gracies) showed up to fight the local judo teams.
Naturally, the judo men wanted to fight from standing positions
where they had the advantage, and the Brazilians wanted to fight on
the ground where they had the advantage. Consequently each fighter
was trying to direct the fight to his own turf.

My first match was with a big strong Brazilian called Rigan
Machado, captain of their team that day. He also scared me, and I
wound up executing a mediocre throw on him. I had watched the
judo fighters all day scrambling to stay on their feet while the jiu-
jitsu fighters tried to keep the fight on the ground. That annoyed me
and I wondered, just how bad could this guy be anyway? I surprised
him when I deliberately took the fight to the ground in an effort to
see how good he really was. I recall clearly that, within ten seconds,
he had my arm bent backward at the elbow joint and ready to snap

apart, immediately forcing me to submit. It was so one-sided we both had to laugh.

When we got up he gave me a big friendly hug and said, *"Obrigado"* (Thank you). Later his teammates walked up, shook my hand, and said they had never seen a judo man want to fight on the ground with any of them and would I be interested in training at their school?

Indeed I was, but at the moment, I was in the middle of my competition judo career training for the Judo Nationals and, later, the U.S. Open at the Olympic Training Center in Colorado Springs, Colorado. I could only dream of jiu-jitsu for a few more years but it was definitely on my agenda.

Four years later I walked into Joe Moreiras's jiu-jitsu class in Orange County, California, introducing myself as a former judo competitor who was interested in learning the famous Brazilian art. I just wanted to work out and was not interested in competing anymore with men half my age and made that clear to Joe. Within six weeks he had me back in the ring representing his school at local tournaments and several years later at his Brazilian International Tournament, winning all of them. I could never say "no" to a coach.

Today I'm standing in one of the most prestigious martial arts schools in Rio de Janeiro, at the heart of Brazilian jiu-jitsu, in a school that trained legends. So many injuries over the years prompted me to retire from tournaments while I can still walk. But I can never still the yearning to compete. I arrive in the middle of the last class of the day, too late to join in, but decide to stay and watch. It's great to be back in a dojo again — a sacred place of learning. I smile at the familiar, funky stench of sweat and the sight of banged-up equipment. Carlson is in Chicago training his son, but there are several competent black belts teaching an advanced class and they flash tricks I've never seen before.

This is the most homesick I've felt since leaving California. I forgot how much I love and miss the arts. It all comes back once I step into the room and sense the flowing energy of ground fighting in progress. I miss my school. I miss my students.

I was introduced to shotokan karate two decades ago in a strict Japanese environment with traditional behavior. There was always a reason to bow. My sensei, Takayuki Kubota, was a very serious man. You bow before you enter the dojo. You bow to the mat where you train. You bow before the opponent you are about to fight. Respect runs deep and lasts a lifetime. The Brazilians, although respectful, are much more casual and seem to have abandoned many traditional practices. Their culture is reflected in their art. I cannot help myself, I automatically bow before entering anyone's school. It's an ingrained reflex that gives me away as having trained somewhere before.

The mat space is surprisingly small, with a dozen men plus instructors working out in traditional Japanese *gis* (uniforms). The hallowed dojo walls breathe martial arts history with trophies of past victories lining shelves above the floor. This is the home of numerous world champions, but you don't need to see the awards to know that. You can smell it in the air.

There are several boys wrestling together who remind me of my own students back home, full of enthusiasm and eager to learn. Nobody invited me onto the mat and I'm relieved they didn't. If I had said no, it would have been the first time in twenty-three years. If I said yes, I would likely end up with an injury from being so far out of shape. After class we all shoot the breeze for a while and I return to my hotel for a sound night's sleep, grateful for the reminder of who I am.

There is much to keep me in Rio: martial arts, women, and an easy paced lifestyle. I want to stay longer but weather patterns are changing, and even if I leave right now, there will be solid rain ahead to the equator. I consider extending my journey a few more months, but that puts me into summer riding through Central America and Mexico. This means traveling through heat and hurricanes for the last 5,000 miles.

This morning, it is a hard ride out of Rio. The traffic is horrible, the exit route is long and complicated, and already I miss the action. An hour down the road, and almost on the main highway, I look back and notice that my rain suit is missing. This is an absolutely irreplaceable item and I'm inviting serious regret without it. There is no alternative except to backtrack to the hotel. Now I've lost two precious riding hours and don't find BR101 North until noon, assuring that I won't reach my overnight 300 miles away until well after dark. Most Brazilians, and all the guidebook authors, warn against being out past sundown. After my experience in Colombia, I take such warnings seriously. The road leads through the most impoverished states of the country and no matter how good people want to be, as Johnny Cash laments, "The devil walks with a hungry man."

People are friendly here, but crime is dangerously out of control. In Rio, I went for a walk with a camera dangling from my neck in broad daylight and everyone on the street stared at it. I saw no one else with a camera, or anything else of the slightest value in plain sight. Most of Brazil has a bad reputation for violent robbery and that includes the highways. Some of the worst criminals are the police, who go beyond shakedowns for traffic matters and are known to plant drugs on foreigners, then turn around and arrest them for possession. Like other problems anticipated on this journey, there's a contingency plan for this, but not a good one — pay the bribe.

Riding through the countryside, I'm concerned about the numerous police at checkpoints who wave motorists over for bogus infractions. These are plainly excuses for graft. My bike is missing its rear license plate because it vibrated off somewhere in Bolivia. I glued on plastic numbers to the tail box to resemble a license plate and also have a phony international driver's license created on a computer to replace the one that the ELN confiscated. It's unlikely that any of these locals will know the difference between the two, but I'm hesitant to find out. I doubt they'll stop at the *nao falo portugese* routine; they might demand my camera or computer.

The way north is inhabited by the kind of people who are approachable if I smile at them, yet I also feel they might turn on me in a second, given the chance. I'm not comfortable anymore. I don't speak the language, and the locals don't often see Americans riding through their turf on a motorcycle. They are more wary than anything. The open road is where I feel safest and that's where I want to be.

Life is good today, gliding over a black asphalt river flowing across green velvety carpets of grassy hillsides. To the west lie endless fields of sugarcane plantations undulating in the robust tropical breeze. In this dream state I want to ride forever. Warm showers tumble down off and on all day in relieving cycles, drenching and drying my clothes at random. The weather forecast predicts five days of rain with increasing severity the closer I get to the equator.

Dingy, open-air restaurants along the way invariably serve the same food: dried-out hamburgers and greasy French fries. I gag this down while sweating in the oppressive humidity, swatting at hundreds of flies around my head. My stomach holds up to the wide variations in diet and I attribute that to drinking small amounts of the local water. So far, I've only had food poisoning once from the bad meat in Argentina and one bout with dengue fever from a mosquito bite. Pound on wood!

Soon the sun drops to the west over the mountains beyond the cane fields. To the east, a cool draft of fresh sea breezes rolls in from the Atlantic, brushing aside the stifling tropical heat. While thinking about what lies ahead, a slight shiver wiggles up my spine as a speeding semitruck thunders past, kicking up a suffocating cloud of road dust. I'm starting to believe that I will survive this journey after all and, for the first time, wonder what it will be like crossing that final border from Mexico back into California.

SALVADOR
March 25, 2002
Salvador, Brazil
• • • • • • • •

Although much of the South American tropical scenery is identical, the cultures, customs, and language dialects vary greatly, even within Brazil. This is a journey through the solar system on a two-wheeled rocket, landing on a different planet every few weeks. Each country is a new world to discover. My only wish is for more time. Eight months are spinning by too fast. As much as I wanted to meander, there is always a weather front to beat or shelter to find before dark.

Each country warrants a full year of study to become a part of. I do the next best thing and see as much as possible, stopping in the small towns that I pass and yakking with locals at every opportunity. This short ride through Latin America hasn't made me an expert on anything, but I do develop more insight into the hearts and spirits of the people, along with a strong desire to travel again. While trying to imagine what to do when I return to California, all I can think of is preparing for the next ride.

The northeast region of Brazil is home to the descendants of black slaves and consequently dominated by traditions and religions from Africa. This cultural combination forms a fascinating blend of Catholicism and ancient tribal beliefs, synthesized over the centuries so that believers worship saints as well as animals and spirits. Across the plazas of Salvador, Congo drums beat through the night. Sensuous samba music reverberates down cobblestone alleyways throughout the Pelourinho district, sparking street dancing and spontaneous festivals that last until sunrise. Locals live to party and don't need an excuse, just a drum or a few simple instruments. Soon crowds are swaying and rocking out in trance-like orgies of glistening, black wiggling bodies locked in rhythm to the music.

In spite of constant pollution warnings, the beaches are crowded with vacationing Brazilians. There are few foreigners and I spend many frustrating hours trying to decipher city maps that show different names for the same streets. Brazil borders on eight Spanish-speaking countries. I fire off questions for directions first in *castellano* (Spanish) leading people to think I'm from Argentina. I appreciate the compliment and when I explain that I'm actually an American traveling through South America on a motorcycle, they grow even more confused. No one speaks English outside of large cities, but even if a person speaks Portugese, they talk with a strong local dialect that's difficult to understand.

Endless admonitions and warnings about robbery and murder are getting old, and I wonder how I will feel after returning home to a place where it's not a suicide run to go for a walk at night. Everywhere I venture in this section of the country, predatory eyes are fixed on me. Mobs of idle young thugs hang out in gas stations and on street corners like vultures circling for victims. Salvador is unsafe in most areas. Everyone wants something and locals find endless excuses why you owe them. If I stop to take a picture of a church, people demand dollars because they may or may not have been in the background. Just pulling the camera out is risky. As they spot it, their eyes remain hypnotically transfixed, and it's obvious they are figuring a way to get their hands on it. Slash-and-dash kids shadow me so often that it's not worth the trouble to expose my camera for photographs.

At times they close in so fast when I pull into parking lots, I don't dare get off the bike. I would be picked clean in seconds and probably several knife blades stuck in me for good measure. Once outside the safety of the heavily guarded tourist quarters, the outlying areas are spooky places to travel alone or, for that matter, with a small army. The masses are hungry and without work. But I wonder what I might do differently if I walked in their shoes.

There are half a dozen cities left to visit in the two weeks before venturing up the Amazon. This part of the country is still technologically backwards. In most towns there is no Internet service or, when it does exist, outmoded computers make it too difficult to log on.

Vast areas of this region have remained the same for the last 500 years. It feels as though I've gone back in a time machine. Twenty bucks rents a small, fluorescent-lit room with a rattling air conditioner and an old antique television with rabbit ears to pull in snowy signals from some faraway major city. I don't need to ask about hot water. The tap is always lukewarm and provides a refreshing way to eliminate accumulated road grime.

I travel relatively light for this journey; my total gear weighs only seventy pounds. I use everything I carry and want for nothing that I didn't bring with me. At the end of the day, after lugging my saddlebags up several flights of stairs, it's nice to go for a cruise around the city, whipping in and out of traffic without the bulk and sway of a full load. The bike finally handles right with the new mono-shock, and there is a seat-of-the-pants difference in acceleration, making it feel like a new toy. This morning, after a three-night layover, I pack up and turn north on BR101, heading toward the Amazon basin and farther off the beaten path. I've lost track of the world beyond where my front tire rolls, yet often think of my loved ones and how great it will be when I see them again.

MACEIO
March 27, 2002
Maceio, Brazil
• • • • • • • • •

Although the roads are getting rougher and more chewed up the farther north I ride, they are still decent enough to average 400 miles a day. Even with an early start, I often end up riding the last hour in eerie darkness. The coastal cities where I overnight are far from the main corridor of BR101, the only route to Belem, which runs through thousands of square miles of sugarcane fields. No matter how much I hustle, lately it's hard to get back to this main route until noon.

It's a typically confusing morning exiting Salvador. Five centuries ago, the city was built by Portuguese settlers on two levels, connected by steep winding roads that are seldom equipped with road signs. Locals provide conflicting directions. I stick with the best two out of three opinions and monitor the compass on my flickering GPS.

I don't understand the locals much anyway. Portuguese to me sounds like a series of vowels being mumbled rapidly with an occasional consonant thrown in for variety. Once in awhile, a familiar word pops up like *esquerdo* (left) or *direita* (right). I ask them, *"Cuantos cuadras?"* (How many blocks?) and they invariably reply *"Dos"* which could mean anything from two blocks to several miles. Even if they don't have a clue, they say something to avoid appearing ignorant.

Most of the hassle I encounter is my own fault for failing to learn Portuguese and thus I miss out on many of the interesting events around me. When I'm tired, confused, or in a hurry, words from three other languages bounce around in my head and come tumbling out in a mash of confusion. Much of my time is spent in silence for fear of appearing stupid by mispronouncing words.

The most important thing to remember when learning a new language is to be bold and practice. Most Spanish speakers understand this and speak at my level after recognizing my limited vocabulary. Others are not so patient, like Hondurans and Chileans — cutting me off in mid-sentence and shattering my confidence.

I'm forever asking Spanish speakers, "*¿Cuando estoy hablando castellano entiende mis palabras?*" (When I'm speaking Spanish, do you understand my words?) Those who want to encourage me lie, exclaiming, "*Perfectamente!*" Those who tell the truth politely reply, "*A veces.*" (Sometimes.)

Although written identically, Latin American countries have different ways to speak Spanish. Argentineans sound more Italian. Not only is the pronunciation and speed varied but certain expressions mean different things. Ask for *helado* in Mexico, you'll get ice cream; in Chile, a cold drink. I wish they would get the verb *coger* straight so I wouldn't almost get slapped in some countries. Had I spent six months in one city, I'd be fluent by now. However, with all the variations I've experienced every two weeks changing countries, it's more like learning a dozen different languages at once.

Even the computers at Internet cafés are confusing. Usually the printed letters on the keys are rubbed off. There are three different types of keyboards in Spanish alone and an entirely different one for Portuguese, both with unfamiliar letters. The space bar usually sticks and the caps keys are always broken. Writing emails — no problem; editing takes hours. Sitting in hotels tapping away on a little half-size Sony keyboard in English with oversize hands just adds to the confusion. It takes several hours to record what occurs each day, spilling out my innermost thoughts for the world to read and judge the next morning on the Internet.

There are a hundred miles of back roads to ride today while hunting for the connection returning to BR101 north. The road is poorly patched and narrow, snaking through a luxuriant jungle. This is a fine opportunity to ride and think. That is what I am doing when, over the popping of my engine and the wind whistling past my helmet, I suddenly hear a high-pitched grating sound. It's the kind bikers are always on alert for and dread.

My heart sinks while I hold my breath, straining to hear and identify the noise. It's definitely getting louder. I pull in the clutch to see if it subsides when the revs drop. No luck. I hear the grating more clearly. Oh no, I think, what the hell else can go wrong? When applying the brakes there's no discernable difference in volume or pitch until coming to a complete stop with the engine shut down. I tear my helmet off, and the muffled sound becomes a roar. Zillions of crickets, locusts, or giant bugs of some species are rubbing their legs, grinding their wings, or just talking loud in their unique pulsating rhythm. The sound fills my head. It's coming from every direction, yet I do not see a single insect anywhere. If somebody were standing next to me, I would need to shout to be heard.

Suddenly, something knocks loudly in the thicket of towering bamboo poles. Abruptly, with a rustle of crackling leaves, an enormous multicolored bird flies up, grazing the top of my head, screeching what must be an insult in some obscure bird language. The brilliant orange and flaring purple of its flapping wings are in bright contrast to the cloudy sky above as it ascends into the treetops. In retaliation, I fire up my bike, rev the engine, and beep the horn a few times. Rolling back onto the road smiling, I hear a verse of a song echo through my head, "Welcome to the jungle . . ."

NATAL
March 29, 2002
Natal, Brazil
● ● ● ● ● ● ● ●

Since I have less than a month to see one of the largest countries on earth, I must make specific choices on where to spend that time. I previously selected five cities, allotted four days to each, and then added whatever time the Amazon River segment entails. The first stops were Rio and Salvador; now the third is Natal, the capital of the drought-stricken state of Rio Grande do Norte and a regular large town.

Most major South American cities have spectacular ancient cathedrals and plazas lined with chiseled granite statues and musty museums filled with Spanish and Portuguese historical artifacts. Suits of armor and weapons used for butchering millions of naked Indians are on display, along with instruments of torture and dank stone dungeons. Towering above it all stand grandiose, ornately decorated churches in whose name these deeds were committed.

With all this selective history, you could almost forget that another race of people lived here first — a people who were systematically exterminated like cockroaches in the name of economics and God. It's not that the early explorers were without their reasons. They needed gold and silver to support mercantilism in Europe and came to the New World hoping to find it. Later, when Europe demanded different commodities, many more died over rubber and sugarcane.

So if you are wondering why I don't write more about all the fabulous ancient architecture and fascinating ruins, now you know. I am sickened by what they represent. The idea that men have been slaughtering each other over religion and economics for thousands of years is bad enough. However, when I catch a glimpse of international news, it's still all about men slaughtering each other over religion and economics. Sometimes I wonder if anyone in power reads history books.

Natal and Fortaleza have little historical significance and are primarily vacation spots for young Brazilians plus a few visitors from other South American countries. There are seldom tourists from outside the continent. In this almost private setting, I get to see firsthand how locals play. Eight hundred thousand people live in Natal. However, nearby lies a soothing turquoise sea and a ten-kilometer strip of fluffy, white sandy beach lined with cheap hotels, overpriced restaurants, and open-air bars. You can surf, swim, go for hair-raising dune buggy rides, or just lie on the beach and take it all in. This afternoon,

I choose the latter. I enjoy the other activities, but not here.

The last time I swam in unfamiliar water while paradise-hopping was when riding a motorcycle through Malaysia along the Indian Ocean, just off the Straights of Malacca, on a gorgeous desolate stretch of virgin beach. My first, and fatal, thought was, "What a beautiful spot for a dip." After plunging headfirst into enticing crystal-clear waters, I was immediately burning from head to foot, a result of acidic stings from hundreds of tiny, barely visible sea creatures. Even now, I don't know what they were, but the burning welts lasted for days, and the memory forever. On this trip, one tiny mosquito gave me dengue fever and another bug laid an egg inside my flesh, an egg which later turned into a larva and ate its way out of my body. Bearing in mind similar tales of pesky tropical critters, I decide to leave whatever else may lurk beneath the surface of this peaceful ocean a mystery.

And tonight the moon is full. As overhead puffy clouds drift apart, reflected sunlight from the other side of the earth radiates down, illuminating curling tops of ocean swells. In an eerie fluorescent glow, tips of breaking surf flash like silver coins tossed from inky black liquid, disappearing into soft silky sand. The tide is nearly full as I pull off my boots and socks for a wade. I stand just beyond reach of pawing breakers that with each hissing stroke creep closer to the shore. The warm swirling around my feet coaxes me to follow by drawing out grains of sand from beneath my soles, softly tugging and beckoning to learn the secrets of its depths. I breathe with the rhythm of the waves and drift into nothingness.

Time has become irrelevant. This moment has transformed into an infinite landscape, while realizing that I have come full circle. The past has become the future, and I am but a tiny speck on a massive oil painting of an enormous rock spinning through the universe. Except for this elongated single thought, nothing else matters and, once again, I dwell within the grace of solitude.

MOVING WEST
April 1, 2002
Fortaleza, Brazil
• • • • • • • • •

People ask me what I miss most while traveling — without a doubt, a balanced diet and exercise. For more than two decades, I've trained in martial arts six days a week, religiously. Even when roaming through Asia many years ago, I managed to practice at a school somewhere or found a workout partner with similar skills. In South America, during multiday layovers, whenever there is opportunity, my exercise regime has been limited to walks around a city. This can hardly compare to gasping for air while pumping out wind sprints around a track or building up the focus and intensity that a gym or dojo can inspire. Today I worry that I'm too young to get old.

Over the years, because of intense training for competitions and eating right to maintain optimum body chemistry, my cholesterol count was low and my cardio was always on the cutting edge. Slacking off and gaining weight were never options. Life on the road causes laziness, and I feel the difference. Readily available food is usually fried in animal fat and seldom in correct nutritional proportions for sustaining athletic conditioning. Meals are either tasty but with too little protein like in Mexico, or total protein as in Argentina, where chefs add fried eggs on top of monster steaks.

In Brazil, you never leave the table hungry. There's always a shovelful of rice accompanied by a second plate of French fries cooked in bacon grease to go with a generous slab of overdone chicken, meat, or fish. Other than excessive amounts of salt, there isn't much flavoring added.

Farther north, I discover Churascorarias, a type of all-you-can-eat steakhouse next to gas stops along major routes. Customers are issued large plates to fill at a salad bar while roaming waiters with four-foot-long steel skewers offer varying cuts of sizzling beef fresh from open-pit fires. With a beverage, it's four bucks.

To save money I stay in *pousadas* (guesthouses) and even the least expensive of them offers a buffet breakfast of scrambled eggs, fresh fruit, breads, and juices. Downtown restaurants and ice cream par-lors sell meals by the pound — they simply weigh your plate of food to determine the bill.

In other Latin American countries, Sundays are the best days to travel because most everybody takes the day off or sits in church, leaving roads open and deserted. In Brazil, for reasons I haven't determined, professional truckers are out in force on Sundays. This morning, the highway is jammed with long lines of semitrucks spew-ing nauseating black clouds of soot and vacationers returning home after *Semana Santa* (Easter Week). Double-trailer trucks bunch together in mile-long, bumper-to-bumper convoys lined up behind the slowest of the pack. A string of impatient car drivers in under-powered mini-size vehicles follow these creeping caravans. And none have the will or horsepower to pass such an intimidating parade of monstrosities.

The highway is single-lane in both directions on a beat-up sur-face, with frequent dips through rain-washed gullies. There are so many road chunks missing that I spend most of my time weaving around potholes and other hazards I rarely see until the last moment. At the moment, none of us road users are happy as this whole procession grumbles along at a frustrating twenty miles an hour. At this pace, I'll be riding through the night in the rain until sunup trying to reach the next city. It's a moment for serious choices — gamble in the light or gamble in the dark.

The road from Natal to Fortaleza leads away from the coast and inland, then meanders back again to dump me near another beach resort at the end of the day. The entire region is supposed to be in the midst of a drought, but abnormally severe rainstorms are attacking today, with more on the way. The intensity of the rain reduces my visibility to blurred red taillights ahead and obscured, water-filled, potholes too numerous to dodge. The squalls last several hours, and I remain soaked for the entire day.

The Kawasaki KLR is underpowered, and the combined weight of my 210 pounds and bulging saddlebags even further reduces my ability to accelerate or dodge road hazards. If I maintain high revs and wind out in each gear on a long stretch, I can build up enough speed to pass. The lane markers are double-lined because the road often disappears behind dips and knolls. Oncoming traffic appears unexpectedly. There's a small paved second-chance shoulder on one side for cooperative drivers to use in tight situations, and Brazilian motorists are fairly accommodating, even the truckers.

Following this string of lumbering boxes is maddening. I can't wait any longer. Truckers operate on narrow margins, with only three-foot gaps between front bumpers of one to the rear of another. Once taking on the pack, there will be no room to return to my lane if another vehicle approaches from the opposite direction. What the heck, here we go.

I kick it down a gear, hang the throttle open, and pull out of position, determined to pass a mile-long convoy of fellow frustrated motorists. Oncoming traffic forces me to weave in and out of my lane until I reach the front of the line of cars and the back of the monotonous procession of trucks. It's another now-or-never moment. I make it past the first dozen grinding monoliths okay, when suddenly an oncoming car appears over a slight rise ahead, closing in fast. There's no chance to brake, return to the rear, and get back into the correct lane. My only option is to nuzzle my right rear saddlebag as close as possible to the trucker's massive spinning trailer tires and hope for the best.

The approaching car manages two wheels on the shoulder, barely grazing my left rear bag while I fight overpowering hot-air currents sucking me under the trailer's belly. The deafening moan of the semitruck's mighty engine is like a roaring animal inside my helmet, yet I seem to be in one piece. It's only a hundred miles more.

ONE OF THOSE DAYS
April 2, 2002
Piripiri, Brazil

● ● ● ● ● ● ● ● ●

In the middle of particularly bad days when everything is going wrong, I remind myself that a better day is coming. Soon life will improve more than ever. Today, life must be about to get a whole lot better.

In Spanish, *seis de la mañana* means six in the morning, but the man who promised to have my laundry ready today is trying to convince me it means six in the afternoon in Portuguese. What he really means is, it isn't ready yet and I will have to wait for his delivery truck to arrive. Okay. I'll get some cyberwork done at the Internet café down the block. No problem, except the line is down, not just there, but everywhere in the city. After an hour of unsuccessful log-on attempts at the most promising café, I establish a connection. There is just enough time to type a reply to an important email before the screen goes blank and reduces an hour's work to a blinking cursor.

After picking up the laundry at noon, I remind myself that I have six and a half hours before sunset to cover 400 miles on a questionable road. I optimistically calculate that by riding at an even seventy for the next six hours, there will be time for a quick bite along the way with a half hour to spare.

To estimate travel times, I refer to bus schedules and note travel time for express buses. Although they drive faster than I do on the highways, I move through city traffic quicker so it averages out to beating their time by about ten percent. Their schedule today indicates twelve hours to complete 400 miles of straight road, with two cities to pass through. This tells me that there is something along the way to slow them, and I get to find out what.

First, I have to gas up. Motorcyclists don't like gas station attendants fiddling with their motorcycles. We prefer to fill our own tanks, believing we use more caution than the daydreaming youngster drinking a Coke. Brazilians are not accustomed to self-service gas stations and it often takes a bit of polite convincing before I'm allowed to pump the gas myself. Although I grab the pump handle first, this dedicated teenage attendant is determined to do his job. Not in the mood for a long debate on the subject, I reluctantly concede.

Most gas pumps have automatic shutoffs that stop the fuel flow when the backwash of a full level is detected. My friend's automatic shutoff isn't working, nor is his brain. Before I can yank his hand away from the pump handle, a good half-liter has gushed over the top of my tank, flowing down the front of my pants.

Gas on my hands is not a big deal, it can be easily washed off. Gas on normally less-exposed parts of the body burns like salt in a wound, especially when there is no water to wash it off. *"Agua, agua por favor, agua!"* I yell at whoever can hear. There's no hose, but another boy runs up with a small bucket used for cleaning windshields and pours it over my tank while using a greasy rag to wipe it off.

"No, not there. Here. *Aqui!*" I shout, pointing to my blistering crotch. He smiles, shrugging his shoulders, and hands me the bucket with a quart left in it. I yank open the front of my pants, douse my simmering flesh with the small amount remaining, thinking, at least it's not as bad as bee stings.

It's depressing to describe the details of being ripped off, so I won't. But the quick story is, one of my saddlebags has been stolen. I know that when people are desperate to feed a hungry family, they do things against their character. The frustrating part for me is that the thief peddling the items from that saddlebag will likely net only the equivalent of twenty bucks. If available, the contents important to me would cost a few hundred dollars to replace, but out on the road it's a $1,000 inconvenience. The bag was specially designed to attach to uniquely fitted side racks made just for the Kawasaki 650. It's possible to rig up something to get by with, but that will consume several days.

While assessing damages and calculating replacements I shrug it off as part of the experience and consider what is missing: a full medical kit including malaria pills and other medications, guidebooks, spare parts, extra tubes, rubber boots, elk-skin gloves, and assorted clothing. I could restock in a day in California; here it will take much longer. I lighten the disappointment by convincing myself how lucky I am they got the left side bag. Had they stolen the right, they would have the electric vest, spare half helmet, leather jacket, and other more valuable items. What if they had snatched the aluminum tail box containing my computer, camera, and vital documents? *¿Quien sabe?*

It requires intense focus and exhausting concentration to safely ride a broken-down road. It's a constant strain making a continuous series of split-second decisions: when to brake, cut, or weave in an effort to dodge bone-jarring potholes and road hazards. If I take my eyes off the space ahead for a moment, it could be too late; the front tire could plunge into a two-foot-deep chuckhole.

Motorcyclists eventually develop an increased sense of awareness of potential disasters coming at them from all directions. On a road this bad, today all of that awareness is focused on danger ahead, leaving other angles unguarded. While focused on an endless series of close calls, I am aware that if I ride into one of these jagged holes, the game changes.

Trapped in such conditions, it's not surprising that a couple of cops closing in from behind go unnoticed. And over the whoosh of the wind in my helmet, I don't hear the faint whine of a sputtering siren either. For two policemen in a notoriously dangerous area, I am a fleeing criminal with no license plate, ignoring their pursuit and trying to outrun them.

When glancing to my immediate left, I nearly fall off my bike when seeing a man dressed in uniform hanging out the window of a four-wheel-drive truck, screaming with a pistol leveled at my face. I also observe the hammer is back and have the feeling he is about to shoot.

It's time for a split-second decision. Is this a legitimate traffic stop over a misunderstanding or are these guys dressed up like cops out here in the middle of nowhere intending to rob a lone motorcyclist? Being taken prisoner by rebels at gunpoint is an experience I've been unable to forget. That time in Colombia still flashes through my mind every day. At this moment, those thoughts again race to reality. These men have guns and appear too likely to do me harm, and I recall a pledge to never be taken prisoner again.

I quick-scan the woods on either side of the road for a direction to flee. But before I can act, the driver jerks his steering wheel to his right, forcing me off the highway. The next second is a fight to remain vertical while fishtailing on the shoulder of the road. As I come to a stop in clouds of swirling red dust they bail out of their truck with guns aimed at me, yelling orders that I don't understand. Here we go again, angry men with guns barking away. I must decide — if they are real cops, I need to comply. If they are bandits, I'm going for a gun when they get close enough. Surely I can grab one of their pistols. Tense moments are about to go one way or the other, quickly.

Yet, their uniforms do look authentic, and there is radio chatter blaring from inside their vehicle with a flashing light bar overhead. But this is also a notoriously lawless region of Brazil. The dice are rolling. I throw up my hands, shouting in English so they will know I'm a foreigner, "I didn't see you, I didn't see you." There are a few phrases in Spanish that correspond in Portuguese. *Disculpe me* means excuse me or I'm sorry, as though I know I'm at fault.

"*Disculpe me, disculpe me,*" I say to them, pointing to my eyes and ears while tapping my helmet. "*No veo, no oigo!*" (I did not see, I did not hear!)

Still wary, they keep me covered with their weapons drawn while briefly exchanging a few words with each other until one of them asks, "*No Portuguese?*"

I respond, "*No señor, no Portugues pero hablo Castellano.*" (No sir, no Portuguese but I speak Spanish.)

"*¿Aleman?*" He wants to know if I'm German.

"*No señor, soy Americano.*"

They seem to relax a bit but the passenger with the pistol demands, "*Documentos!*"

"*Si señor aqui tiene.*" (Yes sir, here they are.)

Two days ago, I was hassled by a full squad of beach police in

Natal over the lost license plate. To avoid further hassle, I went to a police station in the next town and filed a police report about it. It's a good thing, because after I show him the paperwork they relax.

Brazilians use a lot of hand gestures when communicating. One is a thumbs-up if they are in agreement with you, saying hello, good-bye, or just showing they like you. In a conversation of one minute they might give you one or two thumbs-up accompanied by a series of toothy smiles.

As the first cop scans the customs-issued vehicle importation permit and passport, I repeat again, *"Disculpe me señor."* He continues to read without looking up but smiles, giving a thumbs-up. His partner stuffs his pistol back in his holster with an approving nod and walks away, climbing back in the truck to drive it off the road.

The man with my paperwork then asks where I'm going. While pointing at the map on my tank bag, I tell him, Teresina.

He shakes his head, stating, *"No posee."* (Not possible.) Pointing to the setting sun, he rambles on about *perigro* and *ladrones!* (Danger and robbers!)

He stares sincerely while slapping his gun with one hand and gesturing with the other a simulated pistol firing, repeating, *"Perigro, muchos ladrones."* He tries to explain something about hotels in a closer city called Piripiri, saying again, *"Perigro, muchos ladrones en la noite."* (Danger, many robbers in the night.)

I consider that this warning comes from two men wearing sidearms low off their hips in quick-draw style, with each carrying a second boot pistol and who knows what else concealed. Imagining this must be an extraordinarily rough area after sundown, I decide to take his advice.

"¿Cuanto tiempo a Teresina?" (How much time to reach Teresina?) I ask.

"Tres cientos kilometers." (Three hundred kilometers — 180 miles.) *"Pero Piripiri es novena minutos."* (Piripiri is ninety minutes.)

With this he offers a handshake along with one more *perigro* and something that sounds like *bon voyage*.

From here the road turns to straightaways of fresh-laid asphalt passing through thickly wooded forests, perfect for wide open jamming to make up for lost time. Perfect except that after sundown every wandering donkey, cow, or goat decides to seek comforting warmth of the roadway and comes trotting out of the forest en masse. And none are remotely intimidated by a motorcycle. I pull up close to an empty-faced donkey staring with squinty eyes and twitching floppy ears and nudge him with my front wheel to see if he will respond. Nothing, nada, zip, zero. He just continues his blank gaze. I spend the next two hours weaving my way through a maze of hundreds of roaming animals converging on the narrow strip of pavement ahead in the pitch dark of the Brazilian countryside.

LIVIN' IT UP AT THE HOTEL CALIFORNIA
April 4, 2002
Northeastern Brazil
● ● ● ● ● ● ● ● ● ● ●

Piripiri is a typical tiny rural town that in Spanish would be called a *pueblito*. The main drag is paved; the side streets are mud when it rains and blowing swirling clouds of dust when dry. Every town south of Texas, if it is big enough to have a hotel, has one named Hotel California. Piripiri is just big enough to have its own Hotel California, and I decide to follow the numerous signs leading to the fabled shelter.

Piripiri is so small and far off the beaten track for foreign travelers that it only shows up on local maps. It's unlikely they've had many Americans pass through before, let alone an American riding from California on a motorcycle. Nonetheless, the disheveled owner of the Hotel California appears to have been preparing for this moment his entire life. The song "Hotel California" is rumored to be about a mental hospital, and today I discover that this is appropriate. I'm unsure about the other inhabitants of this Hotel California but the owner, although he may have both oars in the water, has placed them on the same side of his boat.

Because the first language I use in Brazil is Spanish, most people assume I'm from Argentina. If I speak English, they think I'm German. No one ever asks if I'm from the U.S. When I inform the proprietor that indeed, I'm an authentic *Americano* from California, he explodes with bug-eyed excitement.

From out of cabinets and cubbyholes he flings piles of worn magazines ranging from vintage *TV Guide* to *Sports Illustrated*. He frantically stacks dozens of them up on the counter, begging me to look at every one. All the while he is ranting and raving the Pledge of Allegiance with one hand over his heart. As I stand there dripping wet from the torrential downpour raging outside, I am more focused on drying off and finding a hot meal followed by a comatose sleep than rifling through his collection of yellowing periodicals. Yet not wanting to tarnish his concept of the friendly American, it seems best to play along. I smile patiently while politely sifting through a few of the tattered magazines hoping to pacify him with some oohs and ahs. But this only excites him more that I might be familiar with the content — now he wants translations of everything at once.

"*¿Habla ingles?*" I ask.

"*No, pero, parlais vous Français?*" he inquires in return while whipping out his next series of showpieces — an assortment of American flags. He has all styles and sizes right under the counter in front of him, ready to display at any moment. Without actually pronouncing the words while marching in place, he rambles into mumble-humming "The Star-Spangled Banner." Even Americans can't sing this on key so you can imagine how his version assails my ears. Without skipping a beat, he drags out photographs of his motorcycle taken from a hundred different angles, all with him posing proudly, wearing American flag T-shirts. Suddenly, he ceases rambling and looks dead at me in earnest, stating solemnly in a low voice, "The Beatles!" Then, he breaks into lyrics from a variety of Beatles songs starting with "I Want to Hold Your Hand" to "Hey Jude." Within five minutes he takes me through an anthology of tunes with intermingled stanzas while simulating guitar playing with a broom. I don't have the heart to tell him this was a British group.

It's clear this entertainment extravaganza might take awhlle. So with my hands full of road gear stuffed up under my arms, I slowly shuffle backward toward the stairs and hopefully the tranquil solitude of a quiet hotel room. Although he doesn't seem to be following, he increases the volume of his vocalizing, which has switched to Bruce Springsteen's "Born in the U.S.A." He continues even louder while saluting and marching in step with upward-thrusting knees. I return the tribute as best as possible while trying not to drop any of my cargo, and slowly retreat up the stairs.

Since I'm always behind in my journals, tonight I'm determined to write for however long it takes to bring my readers up to speed. Hopefully, I'll find an Internet café in the morning to upload a new story. Most of the time I try to document what I was thinking during the day, and attempt to make sense of it at night. I want to describe places and events that have become normal to me, yet likely alien to readers back home. I'm seldom sure if my thoughts are being communicated effectively and often wonder if I appear a madman to those who read my words.

Maybe other writers are more focused, but I need silence to work. I can't write with radios, TVs, or people around wanting to talk. I require solitude to generate a rhythm and, at times, it takes as much as a half hour to get my mind channeled into a creative mode. No sooner do I slide into that elusive state when there is a loud hollow pounding on the door. "*Señor Haystat, Señor Haystat,*" my friend calls out. I try to ignore him and hope he will give up and let me tend to business.

Following a relieving silence, there is the clicking of a key sliding into the lock as Señor Loco bursts into the room babbling words to the effect that he hopes he isn't disturbing me. He plops down at the foot of the bed that I'm comfortably writing from and begins to recite the name of every state in the Union beginning, of course, with "*Caleeefornia.*" Thinking maybe if I just let him finish displaying his knowledge of American geography, he will eventually run out of states and maybe just go away.

I set my computer aside and fold my arms while trying my best to smile and act entertained. He gets through almost pronouncing twenty states when I realize he is repeating the same twenty over again and probably has no intention of stopping anytime soon. And I definitely don't want to alert him that there are actually thirty more.

By now, it's almost eleven and I need to write for another two hours and hopefully get a good night's rest before tackling the foul weather in the morning. *"Por favor señor, tang que escribir, es importante."* (Please sir, I have to write, it is important.)

"Oh no problema," he gushes, *"silencio,"* and gestures with his fingers to his lips as he reaches for my laptop.

I have to draw the line somewhere and this is as good a place as any. *"No señor, no toca por favor"* (No sir, please don't touch), I say, trying to be firm. He looks a bit hurt with the reprimand as I gently take his arm, guiding him toward the door. Abruptly he turns to me with his bewildered gaze and starts with a recital of American presidents from George Bush to George Washington while we make it slowly toward the door and out into the hallway. *"Hablamos mas tarde amigo"* (We'll talk later my friend), I assure him.

He continues his monologue as we reach the stairs when he again turns to me very seriously and whispers, "George Patton, Douglas MacArthur, Dwight Eisenhower." I manage to cut him off with a question about when is breakfast and he says, at six. I give him a funny look and he says okay, seven. I raise my eyebrows and he shouts, okay, eight; with that I smile, give a thumbs-up, and close the door.

The next morning, after a quiet and surprisingly uninterrupted buffet meal of fresh fruit and breads, I start packing my gear, preparing to hit the road. I'm just about to lock the aluminum tail box when in bursts Señor Loco, dressed in full riding gear, sunglasses, and helmet, repeating how we have to hurry before the rain starts. He rifles through my gear, holding up various articles for inspection, asking what they are for. I repack things as fast as he pulls them out and finally get ahead enough to slam the box shut and snap the lock. I'm about to make a clean getaway only to discover when we get downstairs that, in my haste, I have locked the motorcycle keys in the box. I always stash spare keys somewhere, but my emergency keys were in the saddlebag that disappeared yesterday.

I often make preparations to protect me from myself, and have also stashed a set of extra emergency keys in a place on the bike that requires removal of the tool kit and a little work to access. So much for an early start. All the while my *loco Brasiliano* is striding around the yard in knee-high step waving a huge American flag and once again singing the national anthem.

I don't want to seem unappreciative so I keep smiling while slowly wheeling my bike out to the street. Señor Loco has other plans, ordering me to stop and wait. He wants to provide an escort to the highway and is scrambling to pull his bike out behind mine. I try as best as possible to explain that I must hunt for an Internet place first and that I will need time to work once I get there.

"*Eeenternet?*" my new sidekick asks. He then tries to say he has Internet in his office and grabs my hand, pulling me down the hall. Maybe I've lucked out after all.

Once in his office he proudly points to a fax machine exclaiming, "*Eenternet!*" A woman who appears to be his secretary says something in Portuguese to him and he nods knowingly, "*Oh, Internetch. No problema.*" He seems like he has an idea on where to go, so off we ride through the dusty avenues of Piripiri in search of *Internetch*.

A series of side streets and crisscrossing alleys delivers us to a small brick building housing a radio station with a lobby full of bustling employees. My friend announces to anyone who will listen that this Americano needs *Internetch* right now and it is very important that he not be kept waiting.

Somewhat embarrassed, I'm thinking he could have asked more politely but everyone seems to be familiar with my new sidekick. They flash a wink and a smile as they lead us back to a small office with a new computer and an Internet browser already up and running. The manager points to a chair and gives us the thumbs-up.

It's hard to believe such good fortune but he emphasizes that I only have ten minutes before they must return to their work. I upload a journal, check email, and manage to send a quick message to Don Hinshaw, my webmaster, before the manager signals that my time is up. I offer a few bank notes to show my appreciation but they refuse and instead hand me a business card saying something like, "Remember us."

After a Fourth of July parade through town, my friend and I finally reach the city limits. Without coming to a stop he yells over that he can't go any farther because of the police inspection station ahead and must return home. He turns out of control, thrilled when I signal him to pull over for a photograph. I explain to my ecstatic *compadre* that I need a picture of him to show the world via the Internet this famous honorary American I met in Brazil.

This is a must-have because, without it, no one will believe the story. So here we stand by the side of the road somewhere on the edge of a Brazilian jungle, my pal and his American flag belt buckle, T-shirt, and helmet, posing next to my bike with Hotel California stickers plastered all over it, as we somberly salute goodbye in the rain.

FRIENDSHIP
April 6, 2002
Belem, Brazil, at the mouth of the Amazon River
• •

After two more days of fighting continuous rainstorms I finally reach the departure point for the Amazon River boat ride. Visibility, due to the pouring rain, is close to zero. Guidebooks refer to Belem as one of the wettest regions on earth, which exacerbates existing electrical problems. Constantly soaked, my bike has developed more problems. When the downpours intensify, an electrical short occurs and shuts down the engine. Add to that, I'm still worried about the cam-chain support ear that broke off inside the case and wonder if that bolt will hold. It's discouraging to lose confidence in a motorcycle while still 6,000 miles away from home.

Every time the engine coughs or clinks, I think, "This is it, here we go again, another breakdown." In order to catch a boat that only sails every two weeks I've had to establish a schedule. If I miss that boat, I'll be stuck on a much slower-moving barge to Manaus. The plan after reaching there is to ride north in another ten days, across Venezuela, in order to airfreight back over the soggy marshes of the Darien Gap to Panama. But updated procedures for airfreighting are incredibly complex and expensive ($2,700). I consider selling the bike in Venezuela and buying a replacement in Panama to complete the trip, but that also seems difficult.

A simmering situation with the leftist government in Caracas led by the staunchly pro-Castro strongman Hugo Chavez is unpredictable at the moment, and I'm apprehensive about riding through an area known for its support of the rebel movement in Colombia. There are rumors of impending violent civil war. I won't rest until I'm riding safely back in Panama again.

CBS News's *48 Hours* television documentary has just aired, and it included my web site address, so I've spent the last eight hours reading and attempting to answer as many emails as possible until my eyes give out from staring at a screen so long. The emails number well into the thousands, with an even split between the U.S. and Canada. The documentary's producer told me the program will show again later, with a sequel. I'm astonished at the number of people taking time to write profoundly inspirational words of encouragement — and intend to answer them all. At last count the number rooting me on is nearing 15,000. I save and file each message.

A THOUSAND MILES UP THE AMAZON
April 9, 2002
Upriver on the Amazon
• • • • • • • • • • • • • •

After a moment of reflection on the last few months, I slap myself to be sure it's all been real. Have I just boarded a boat headed up the Amazon River while cruising back from the tip of South America on a motorcycle? Even today, I still have trouble believing that this is actually happening.

This morning I catch another wave of the fantasy from the last seven months, once again venturing into territory beyond what I once considered reality. The mighty Amazon River, as big as an ocean in parts, surges relentlessly from the Andes in Peru to Belem, at the eastern seaboard of the Atlantic. The mother of all rivers is here to greet and coax me onward. The ship is about to sail, and at long last I'm only moments from experiencing a magnificence that took a hundred million years to create.

The Amazon basin is home to the largest tropical forest on earth, with 55,000 of the world's 250,000 known species of plants and trees, earning its title, the lung of the planet. Hundreds of major river tributaries remain unexplored, and perhaps as many as fifty native tribes have yet to lay eyes on another human being, black or white. The rain forest is home to 3,000 species of fish, 1,622 species of birds, 520 species of mammals, 517 species of amphibians, and 468 species of reptiles. To keep things properly balanced there are also an estimated fifteen million varieties of insects, creeping, slithering, or flying. I catch myself itching just thinking about them.

Scores of boats head upriver daily, but only a few hug the shoreline making stops at villages and outposts along the way. This boat is a good one because it cruises the riverbanks and allows locals to latch on with their canoes, hitching rides as they peddle jungle goodies to munch on.

Accommodations are cramped, with 100 double rows of sleeping hammocks suspended from pipes attached to the low ceilings and arranged so close that they constantly touch one other. Each of the three decks has ten small bathroom-shower combinations with barely enough room inside to turn around. Backpacks and luggage lie on the floor beneath and must be continuously guarded.

I buy an upgraded ticket to access a higher deck, hoping it will also include an upgrade in the notoriously horrible food. No luck. Breakfast consists of a few slices of watermelon, a dried-up hamburger bun, and a cup of hideous-smelling coffee. I keep thinking this is a primer and later a few rubbery eggs will be included, but nothing else appears. I could handle the rest if they would just provide a few eggs.

Lunch aboard ship consists of the greasiest noodles with the foulest-tasting chicken imaginable. The main ingredient for seasoning in Brazil is enormous amounts of sodium chloride, and the chicken is so salty it makes me wince and gag with every shriveled bite. I think, this can't be an accident; someone has to try hard to make a meal this disgusting. The locals, however, gobble it down in huge platefuls oblivious to what's making me pale. As we travel farther inland and away from the cities, scattered thatched-roof huts and broken-down shacks along the river come into view. Stone-age Indians selling fresh exotic fruits and boiled shrimp paddle out to hook on to the side of our boat. Fifty cents buys more than I can eat and is a refreshing break from the memories of the last meal.

The brown muddy river narrows in places to a hundred yards but widens so much later that it becomes impossible to see either shore when sailing in the middle. We pass riverbanks close enough to reach out and touch the giant bright purple water lilies lining the water's edge. There is a heavy overcast today, with too much rain dribbling down to permit lounging on the outside deck. Everyone stands around inside, shoulder to shoulder, smoking and talking about the weather. I was warned that five days on a boat with little to do but watch the jungle pass makes people stir-crazy after the first three and ready to swear off boats forever by the last day. I'm glad to have a computer and camera to fiddle with and stay busy, because boredom sets in quickly for me.

THE MIGHTY MUDDY RIVER
April 10, 2002
The Amazon River
● ● ● ● ● ● ● ● ● ●

This morning, we stop briefly at a remote river town to load supplies and more passengers. They allow us ten minutes to walk around on the docks to buy bananas and cheese. It's still dark out so no stores are open, thus curtailing my plan to hunt down eggs. There will be a longer stopover at the halfway point in Santarem with an Internet outlet for important communications and opportunity to fire off a journal. It's the second biggest city in this isolated region, with only one seasonal road connecting it to the rest of the country. The Amazon River is the only steady supply link.

The farther inland we travel, the more abundant the wildlife — no jaguars or giant snakes yet, but thousands of vibrantly colored birds in all sizes flutter and flap their wings along the shoreline. The jungle is far too dense to peer into beyond a few feet but we occasionally sail by a clearing full of water buffalo wallowing in the muck.

According to the GPS, we're cruising along at an even 10.6 mph with a fairly accurate display of where major tributaries blend in from the sides. There is a constant drizzle with ninety percent humidity, and we have yet to experience the famed Amazon sunset. A steady breeze keeps the insects at bay — a good thing since my antimalaria medication was stored inside that stolen saddlebag.

I count a half dozen male travelers on board including me, one from Spain, two from Israel, and two brother Vikings from Denmark. The rest of the 250 passengers are Brazilians sailing upriver either to return home or to visit family. The locals politely keep to themselves except for a few giggling Brazilian girls who pop up wherever us guys sit to swap stories.

CHURNING WESTWARD
April 12, 2002
Midway up the Amazon
• • • • • • • • • • • • • •

We awaken at 4:00 a.m. to a loud blast of the ship's horn announcing our arrival in Santarem. I have only been half asleep anyway, anxiously anticipating spending every second in port roaming the streets and alleyways of this famous little riverside town. It has been a remote outpost of human habitation for thousands of years, surviving even the rubber booms and gold rushes of the early twentieth century. The captain is supposed to allow us twelve hours on land but that is based on a 2:00 a.m. arrival, for which we are already late. This being Latin America, there is no telling if that will lengthen or shorten our designated stay in Santarem.

In Spanish I ask a plainly dressed Brazilian man wearing an official looking hat, "*¿Señor, a que hora estamos a salir?*" (Sir, what time are we to leave?) Sometimes the message gets through like this and I guess it does because he holds up four fingers saying, "*Cuatro.*" (Four.)

That sounds simple enough but I can't forget, he could just be answering that way because he thinks we might leave then but doesn't want to admit he doesn't know. He may not have considered the current time because a few hours before, we crossed a time zone and lost an hour. I must keep in mind, he may have bought the hat as a souvenir and is merely another passenger. There is no way to be sure so I plan to return at three to be safe.

The captain always blows his long low steam whistle for thirty seconds when approaching a dock and the same when we shove off, giving last-minute stragglers only a few moments to scramble aboard. Most of our stops are limited to a few minutes to take on or let off passengers. Other stops last up to an hour for unloading cargo and supplies for scattered backwater towns accessible only by boat. I never know for sure how long the stop will be, nor does anybody I ask. Caught up in the fascination of river life, I hop off at every landing, straying as far from the boat as I dare to snap as many pictures as possible while trying to find a small café that might quickly cook some eggs. Twice I had to sprint to the end of the dock, leaping to catch the deck rail at the last second as the boat was already untied and drifting back into the channel.

At 4:00 a.m. in Santarem nothing is open in town. But sometimes this is an interesting part of the day anyway, watching a sleeping city emerge from its twilight slumber. Merchants snoozing in wooden stalls at the marketplace are waking up groggy-eyed, tending to crying babies or jabbering with one another about the business of the upcoming day. Street sweepers and garbage trucks are busy clearing rubbish and preparing for an additional onslaught of trash makers soon to come.

Having secured a new *Lonely Planet* guidebook in a trade with another traveler, I consult it for directions to an Internet café and a decent restaurant, but nothing will open for another five hours. I just wander a few miles up the road in the warm muggy dawn, enjoying the feel of having solid ground under my feet and empty streets with roosters crowing in the background. After three days on the boat I've grown accustomed to the gentle rocking and rolling of river swells and it seems like I am now living aboard. I even slip when I see one of the other guys from the boat downtown and ask him, "What time are you heading home?"

The Internet service is painfully slow and there are several hundred emails from well-wishers, along with essential business matters to tend to. I spend five and a half hours straight, reading, classifying, and answering the urgent messages before my blurry eyes give out. The data line is too clogged with afternoon users to load photos, so I ask the owner how much for him to send digital pictures to Don from a floppy later that night when the pipe is clear. He agrees to do it for the equivalent of two dollars. I give him five and tell him it is very important. (I found out later that he could not send them either.)

One of the many things I love about Brazil is that it is a pleasantly casual country. You can never be underdressed. Life centers around coastal beaches or inland rivers, and most people saunter around in shorts and sandals like they are on vacation. It's day four on board and I'm relieved to notice that, except for a few of the giggling girls, there are others wearing the same shorts everyday.

When we stay moving on the river, a steady breeze keeps the humidity bearable. But when we are stationary in port, that switches to sweltering sticky heat with little to do but stand around sweating in clingy clothes and wait for the next whistle blast indicating we will soon be churning our way westward again.

Brazilians are difficult to compare with other South Americans, but I do know they are my kind of folks. The women are sultry and sensuous without being slutty and even the most beautiful females will always smile back. They are masters of the eye contact game and will play it enthusiastically for hours.

The men are ruggedly stout by nature, whether large or small, and carry themselves with a friendly enough air that comes with a "don't mess with me" attitude. A street guy would pick up on this immediately as the admonition, "not to mistake kindness for weakness." There is no doubt about it, Brazil can be a very rough place.

The only relief from the wrath of the relentless tropical heat is a twice-daily shower in one of the cramped toilet closets with barely enough room to raise my arms. River water is sucked up and piped into the taps and I can't help but wonder how much of this root-beer-colored fluid remains on my skin after bathing.

There are 250 passengers on board and the single mess hall on each level has only five small, six-sided tables to accommodate everyone for each meal. There is always a line formed outside running next to a row of five bathrooms. Several days of constant use, combined with the stifling dampness in the air, makes it abundantly clear from the outside what transpires inside these tiny bathrooms.

Dinner consists of what everybody refused to eat for lunch, and the last meal aboard is everything left over from the past few days ground up. In another setting, providing this type of food would be considered cruel and unusual punishment. I finally find fresh eggs in a small crowded market at the last stop and buy a dozen to cook later on the boat. My Israeli buddy sets up his miniature portable stove to boil them and at last I have an egg stash. Life is complete.

THE SUN SETS ON SOUTH AMERICA
April 13, 2002
The state of Amazonas
• • • • • • • • • • • • •

The drizzle finally subsides long enough to witness the renowned but elusive Amazon sunset as a pale indigo sky is soon ringed by huge billowing clouds. My favorite star in the universe sets creamy puffs ablaze into flaming orange with cotton-candy trails of flaring gases erupting outward from the depths of hollow canyons burning somewhere in the heavens. If I had to envision the first moment life sparked on earth it would be one exactly like this. The cosmos joins in this fiery, roaring silence while the heavens make love in the shadow of the earth.

Teakwood decks brim with spellbound voyeurs standing shoulder to shoulder in solemn reverence to the commanding solar array beyond. Each mumbles tribute to their God for a gift of such majesty. Children stop playing, babies cease crying, and lovers grow closer as all are equally awed by this mesmerizing otherworldly scene.

Gradually daylight fades into black velvet night as the finale of this cosmic orgasm subsides. Suddenly the overhead sky pops with diamonds cast magically across the void — precious sparkling jewels from far away, yet near enough to caress like raindrops on the tips of my outstretched fingers.

MANAUS
April 14, 2002
• • • • • • • • •

Brazil is the fifth-largest country on the planet and makes for serious long-distance riding. Yet somehow, in five weeks, I have managed to cover thirteen states stretching from the southern border with Argentina to the north, just three degrees below the equator. Before realizing it, I had passed through the twelve states of Parana, Sao Paulo, Rio De Janeiro, Espirito Santo, Bahia, Maranhao, Ceara,

Sergipe, Alagoas, Rio Grande do Norte, Paraiba, Para, and only seconds ago glided sedately by riverboat into Amazonas, the grandest in size and natural beauty of all the states.

In a few hours, we will reach Manaus, a city that is famous for the rubber boom of the nineteenth century, after Charles Goodyear discovered the vulcanization process to make rubber more durable and John Dunlop patented the pneumatic tire. From then on it has been a struggle of human exploitation with the boom and bust of fluctuating markets that led to the sorrowful heartbeat of this severely poverty-stricken region.

In three days, I will seek a transit point back to Central America, marking the end of the South American saga of this odyssey and the beginning of a new adventure, one I will share with my best friend, Brad Neste, who is flying down to meet me in Panama. We've planned for a year to ride the final leg to the sunny peaceful mountains of southern California together. Lately, I'm overwhelmed at the contrast between my home there and my present surroundings and wonder if I will ever be able to readapt.

While making preparations for the departure to Panama, I am sad to realize that the most significant experience of my lifetime is ending. It isn't the amount of time I spent in South America. It's the intensity of that time, from enduring the continuous onslaught of some of the worst weather conditions this planet could conjure up, to surviving whatever the darker side of humanity could thunder down upon me. Through it all, there have always been people and places to make the journey worthwhile.

While seeking the pulse of mankind, I encountered spirit-tingling extremes tempered only by the blind justice of Mother Earth. I came to experience life as South Americans do, and in times of despair, often recalled the saying: "Be careful what you wish for." I still would not trade this experience for anything.

In life's bleakest moments we should search for silver linings, now more than ever. The time I spent in the vengeful hands of a terrorist organization was like holding my finger in a light socket for five weeks. That brain-frazzling experience taught me as much about myself as well as the world around me. There is a lesson in everything — often the greater the pain, the greater the lesson. The hell my tormentors inflicted upon me can only be answered by one of two attitudes: vile hatred and desire for revenge, or patience and understanding for those born into the misery of poverty and exploitation. Once again, I have learned that living well is the best revenge. Yet while I am free, the rebels are still prisoners of their own misfortune and misguided deeds in the mountains of Colombia.

I realize now that had I chosen hatred, this would have damned my soul forever — planning and implementing acts of vengeance. During tumultuous moments of the first three days after my release, I locked myself in that closet, pounding on my own head knowing I had to make a decision. To let it go — to release myself from the shackles of rage — to continue with my goals and dreams no matter the obstacle. Such decisions don't come easy. There is a price to pay for the self-indulgence and reward of perseverance. My only regret is over the agony endured by my loved ones during those five grueling weeks, uncertain whether I was dead or alive. And none of us will know true peace until I arrive home to those much-needed bear hugs.

What I discovered about the world and my country is that when there is an attack by terrorists on one of us, it is an attack on all of us. After making the announcement in Colombia that I would continue my journey, I was overwhelmed at the level of support and the amount of heartfelt correspondence I received from total strangers. I am saving every one to reread in moments when I may again need the inspiration they once provided.

I learned much about my abilities as a man and how to overcome unfamiliar challenges. I told myself endlessly while I was a prisoner of the ELN and while enduring horrendous conditions in the Andes, "If I can survive this, I can achieve anything." Now, I believe in myself and others more than ever and can readily confirm that obstacles are only what we see when we lose sight of our goals.

I am certain of one thing — there is already more than enough hatred in this world; none of us needs any more. We cannot stand any more. And what have I done with my fury and hostility? It now blows free across the windswept plains of Patagonia and turns into the light of an optimistic South American sunrise. My weapon for revenge turns out to be the healing sword of compassion. There is no choice but to let it go. I know that I still love Colombia and all of its people — yes, all of its people.

At times, at the peak of frustration that travelers in strange lands so often endure, just when I thought I couldn't stand anymore, it was the sparkling eyes of a laughing, soft-haired child, the kindness of an aging Indian woman, or the stunning splendor of the Andes that rocked my spirit and tugged me back eagerly into the wholesome embrace of a land of many faces. When I needed a friend most, one always appeared. There had invariably been someone or something to restoke the fire of passion for this continent of such intriguing mysteries and sullen tragedies. My body and soul bear the fingerprints, bruises, and caresses of this magical kingdom, and although I will soon be on a plane out, I know my heart will never leave.

THE LONG ROAD HOME

"Madness is rare in individuals —
but in groups, parties, nations, and ages it is the rule."
— Friedrich Nietzsche

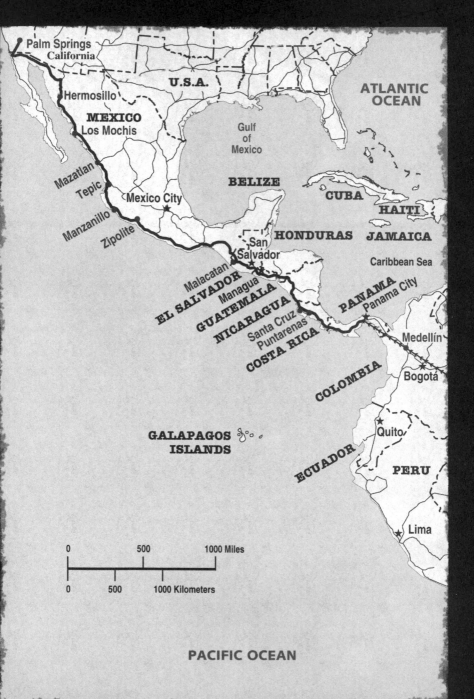

HOPPING CONTINENTS
April 18, 2002
• • • • • • • • •

Complications arose quickly in Manaus as the political situation in Venezuela deteriorated and, according to local reports, was headed for civil war. Several warnings from the FBI via email convinced me to fly out of Brazil directly into Panama. Problems of lengthy red-tape delays and a 2,700-dollar cost to ship a broken-down, 3,000-dollar bike didn't make sense. With a tremendous amount of clever footwork by Whitney Parsons from the Aspen Silver Company, my limping KLR was transformed into a bright yellow BMW F650GS in Panama City.

Even better, Brad flew in on time with his motorcycle so the two of us could ride back to California together. Although we had communicated only by email for the last seven months, we were finally ready. When we met in the Panama City airport, I squeezed him so hard I nearly broke his neck. He is the reinforcement I needed. The cavalry arrived just in time.

Brad soon realized I was off balance and pretended not to notice. I knew that I was rambling and short-tempered. He loved me enough to be glad I was in one piece and patiently nudged me from the lunacy. I struggled to convince him I was well. I was not. I was in denial and still running downhill from the avalanche but I believed that everything would be fine now that Brad had arrived. I refused to acknowledge that the psychological damage inflicted by the ELN was still festering like a time bomb ticking inside my head. Because of pride I could not face up to it. I didn't want Brad to know how bad it was. I feared to let him down.

Only moments before meeting up with him, I was still too unstable to even speak to anyone about how the team at home had supported me. After seeing Brad, I felt like Popeye after swallowing a can of spinach. I could feel myself settle and was at last convinced that I was truly free. Yet there was still a long way to go.

Just as the mighty hands of fate uplifted my mangled spirits, they reached back down, slamming me into the mud. I woke up one morning ready to write a journal, only to discover with increasing horror my laptop was missing. It was gone, vanished. The visual records of the last seven months had disappeared. Two thousand high-resolution digital photographs stored on the hard drive, several thousand bucks in equipment, and twenty-some-odd tattered pieces of sweat-stained, crumbly paper with hand-scribbled letters — all gone. The diary I risked my life to write, the most valuable item in the bag, will surely be flung in some Dumpster on the way to the pawnshop.

THE GREEN FLAG DROPS IN CENTRAL AMERICA
April 24, 2002
Panama City, Panama
● ● ● ● ● ● ● ● ● ● ● ●

Normally, I never look back in life worrying about things that might have been, but the diary loss hit hard. I risked execution to record those events of captivity. Ironically, had I been caught with it, I would likely have been beaten to death for writing it. For months after being released, I kept that black plastic bag on my body, occasionally pulling it out to stare at it, waiting to read it with Brad when we met in Panama. I know there is a message in misfortune and somewhere in that silver lining is something that will make me a better man. I just can't imagine what it is, yet. Onward through Central America!

GUATEMALA

SALESMEN OF GUATEMALA
May 2, 2002
Guatemalan Highlands
● ● ● ● ● ● ● ● ● ● ● ● ●

Last night was a kick — bargaining with two ten-year-old Indian boys peddling traditional blankets and shawls. They were the most persistent salesmen we'd met, following us for hours with dozens of reasons why we needed to buy their "hand-woven genuine Indian stuff."

Most local Indians didn't speak Spanish. But these little clear-eyed pitchmen are fluent in Indian dialects, Spanish, and English and have also mastered the art of the *gringo* sale. They waited outside our restaurant for two hours, reminding us when we came out that our earlier words of "maybe later" mean "now."

"Hey, what's up with you guys, are you men of your word or not?" Pito inquires in perfect California English, his skinny body buried under brightly patterned shawls and tablecloths draped over his little shoulders. "You said later and now it's later, so what's the holdup? Come on, hurry and buy something because I have to get home and feed my hungry grandmother so she can weave more shawls."

Attempting a straight face, Brad asked the cost of one short, particularly colorful scarf. "I'm gonna reduce the price to only three dollars just for you," the little boy proudly announces, as he begins piling up his assortment of cotton artifacts onto Brad's gas tank. Brad tells him he only wants one of the three-dollar scarves, but nobody can break his ten-dollar bill.

"No problem mister, you buy three and tip me a dollar for handling the sale." The little black-haired kid with his dirty face is hilarious and Brad is ready to bring him home for sales work in California. They strike a deal on the scarves, but Brad has to come back later and buy still more genuine stuff.

His attention then focuses on me. "How about you man, wanna buy some genuine Indian stuff too? How about a nice shawl for your wife?"

"Thanks, but I don't have a wife."

"Okay, buy one for your girlfriend. Buy two cuz I know a handsome guy like you gotta have at least two girlfriends."

"No, I don't have even one girlfriend, but thanks anyway."

"Oh come on man, buy something now because later on you will have girlfriends."

"Okay how much for this shawl?"

"That's a very beautiful shawl, not phony, not made on machines in Korea like the other guys sell. This is custom made by my grandmother last week and I'm gonna give you a special one-time price of thirty dollars."

"I like the other one also, how about two for thirty dollars?"

"Oh come on man get real, I can tell you right now that's impossible, it took my grandmother a month to make that shawl."

"Yes, but the other men in the market sell them for five each."

"Yeah, only the market is closed and tomorrow you guys are gonna be too busy leaving town and won't have another chance to buy any genuine Indian stuff."

I turned to get on my bike and before I can flip the key he begins the, "Okay last price" routine, dropping from two for thirty to two for twenty-five. I go ahead and fire up the engine.

"Okay man, two for twenty but you gotta give me and my friend rides on those motorcycles."

"Deal. Hop on."

Off we sail through cobblestone streets past crowds of their friends on street corners who wave wildly as we pass, with our mini-passengers urging us to go faster. Finally, we drop them off and as the little Indian boy climbs down off the back of my bike, he says, "Hey mister, you're pretty good, maybe you could work for me someday."

MEXICO

MEXICO ES COMO MI CASA
May 5, 2002
Oaxaca, Mexico
• • • • • • • • •

Crossing the border back into Mexico is like returning to a land and people I love second only to my homeland — Mexico is like my home. Along the road north we're greeted with warm pearly smiles and roadside restaurants serving fresh, spicy meals. Sometimes we stop in places I visited last year on the way south, and so far everyone recalls *El Vikingo Loco*. When I encounter familiar faces I ask them, "Do you remember me?" They all respond with "Of course, we were wondering if you remembered us."

With plenty of time to waste, we wander San Cristobal for two days, with Brad coaxing me to lift weights in a run-down, hole-in-the-wall gym. It's been almost eight months without working out and combined with the starvation and malnutrition I experienced while a prisoner in Colombia, I am still incredibly weak. I have consumed as much protein as possible ever since being released but without hard exercise I have gained little in muscle mass. With less than half of my former strength, I foolishly charged at top speed back into my old routine and paid dearly the next several days. It hurt to breathe or laugh, and Brad seemed to enjoy watching me wince as I hobbled about.

Soon we would depart an exotic Latin world which I'd grown accustomed to and considered home. It's strange to consider that now California was the next land of unknown fate.

NORTHERN MEXICO
May 10, 2002
• • • • • • • •

When entrenched in a long-term, hardcore endeavor, somewhere inside the silence of the sweat and grimace, inner voices emerge whispering warnings of danger and trouble ahead. It's essential to listen with your gut as well as ears for certain feelings that say, "Slow down or take another route." I'm worn out on gun barrels in my face and fear this is too evident in my expression lately. I force myself to smile at teenage, machine-gun-toting Mexican soldiers peering out from oversize army helmets behind the annoyingly frequent military checkpoints. For some reason, on the return leg north, we're stopped more often than when I was heading south. One of the inspectors is fascinated with Brad's bike and asks if he can sit on it. The Canadian in him comes out, "Sure, heck, take it for a ride." I frown at Brad, holding my breath while the excited *Federale* runs a parking lot circuit and returns the bike without complication. You never know how these scenes end.

COUNTING THE MEXICAN MORNINGS LEFT
May 15, 2002
The Sonora Desert
• • • • • • • • • • •

As a rising sun pokes its blazing corona over the mountainous horizon, the blue morning sky ignites with enough warmth to swallow up whatever is left of the dwindling predawn chill. We stop for breakfast at a roadside café and shed our leathers in preparation for the 110-degree heat ahead. The deserted *autopista* encourages us to cruise an even eighty mph and before we know it, signs appear — HERMOSILLO, 50 KILOMETERS. The anticipated heat never materializes so we opt for a quick Internet email check and upload a journal entry before squeezing out two more hours of riding before dark.

It's been seven and a half months and 25,000 miles. Anticipation throbs as anxiety creases my forehead.

Three weeks before leaving on this odyssey last year, terrorists from another part of the planet delivered a cowardly blow to innocent people in New York City and Washington, D.C. Since then, I have spent most of my time in remote regions out of touch with the world, with little or no information about what's happened at home. Shortly before being taken prisoner, I heard about possibilities of invading Afghanistan in search of Osama bin Laden. There were also reports of anthrax in the U.S. mail.

After I begin reading an old *San Diego Tribune* left in a hotel room, I wonder how much my country has changed. Photos show soldiers guarding U.S. bridges and airports. As I consider the possibilities, my stomach tightens and I force myself to linger in the embrace of the Mexican countryside. The sun climbing up behind us over the horizon paints a spectacular landscape of alternating shapes and subtle colors, and the desert is wide-open for hundreds of miles. But just when we think that there is nothing that could harm us, we're nearly knocked over by the whoosh of an enormous, old rickety bus running a straight-through exhaust and sporting white-walled tires. It thunders past as though we were standing still, a metaphor of my entire last year.

The struggle is nearly over and ahead is a smooth glide to the finish line. However, this journey won't be over until we arrive safely in Palm Springs. The moment I touch my loved ones will be the final knockout blow to the ELN who tried so hard to break my spirit and rob my dignity. Only then will we have given a collective middle finger to cowardice, showing for Americans that terrorism never wins.

PALM SPRINGS, CALIFORNIA
May 20, 2002

• • • • • • • •

Friday night a handful of friends rode to Tijuana to meet and ride home with us. Later the next day, another group was waiting to join up as we crossed the magic line onto U.S. soil. CBS News coordinated with U.S. customs to open a special lane for us to slide through without having to hassle with traffic. This and the ride back to Palm Springs were filmed for a sequel to the *48 Hours* documentary.

A giant coming-home party was pleasantly heart-wrenching, with hundreds of people welcoming me home at a local nightclub. ABC News shot a live satellite broadcast for the eleven o'clock news, and we had a great time jumping up and down with tears, kisses, and bear hugs. It is beginning to feel like home, but I am still detached.

IN THE GROOVE?
May 22, 2002
Palm Springs, California

• • • • • • • • • • • • •

There's no question about it. It won't be so simple returning to my old life. When walking the streets of Palm Springs, it feels like encountering an ex-lover on the opposite bank of a river with no bridge to join us. When I left California last year I realized there might never be a homecoming. Even though plenty of strangers walk up in stores to say, "Welcome home Glen," something is sadly missing. There is an invisible wall between us. It's not just the major changes I've gone through while struggling through the last eight months, but also those of a nation that I love so deeply. I've come back to a changed America. There's a muffled alarm in the air, a fear that people are growing accustomed to, while they await the next terrorist attack that we all know is coming. For all of us, terrorism now has a new meaning.

I have always been out of step with the rest of the world, but my entire concept of life and death and what is right and wrong has now evolved even further, painfully and permanently altered by a dramatically different perspective. I've straddled the edge between two worlds for decades, and now I wonder where I belong. Maybe my home is on the road, roaming the earth.

Life on the road is simple. There are no telemarketers to annoy me, only email from people fun to write back to, with adequate time to measure our thoughts. There are no property taxes or significant bills to pay. The rules are easier and our roles as humans defined more clearly. There is no political correctness or concern about offending a particular group if I say the wrong thing or mispronounce words. People smile anyway, content that I've tried. There is only the unknown of how tomorrow will turn out.

Walking about my hometown, I find myself wanting to bellow out a big hearty *"buenos dias"* to people I meet in the street, but this would likely startle more than please. Craving a jolt of Mexico, I flip on a Spanish-speaking radio station to buff off the edge of a hesitant day. It works. The soft-spoken language pours through the speakers with those rolling Rs tickling my spirit. Sealing the windows I grin and crank the volume and laugh out loud, imagining how strange it would be to see a big tattooed Viking rocking out to the Latin top forty. I can't help it; I love the language as much as the culture and am already homesick as heck for Mexico.

Thinking maybe some tacos or enchiladas would set me straight, I give it a whirl and have a good time reminiscing with my cousin

Kjell over lunch, until the bill arrives. Twenty-seven dollars for two sterile tacos with bland beans and rice, food that wouldn't come close to a tasty meal in a Mexican roadside café with open-fire ovens and dirt floors. There is no way to imitate Mexico. You just have to go there.

While unwrapping stacks of mail and sorting through the senseless complications of life north of the border, I'm pleased to discover that there are no crises or impending catastrophes to contend with. My team has done their job superbly and it appears that life went on better without my interference. Or maybe it's not that there are no issues to gripe about; they just don't matter so much anymore. I'll deal with it *mañana*. I think I'm becoming Mexican.

Probably the most significant relief while traveling is the distinct absence of the media's brutal, overpowering influence. I definitely don't miss being told which products to buy to make me more of a man and to meet more women. The ever-offensive television vomits intelligence-insulting news shows with newscasters clucking away about the British royal family or who is having sex with whom and which movie stars have killed their spouses today. Later, on a more serious note, the international news intrudes with more lies and distortions about the Middle East.

While searching for a moment of levity, I turn on a comedy show for that old familiar tactic to slap me in the face: canned laughter. The media decides everything for us, even what is humorous and when to laugh. Maybe I'm just grumpy, but I like to decide what is funny and not leave it up to some TV executive.

They say culture shock strikes when returning home, and that certainly rings true at the moment. After being out of the influence of the media for so long, I've almost forgotten what it's like to have someone manipulate how I'm supposed think. Maybe we should take a poll today to decide how much truth we want to hear.

HOME AGAIN, HOME AGAIN
June 17, 2002

• • • • • • • •

I feel like I'm a retiring, battle-hardened travel warrior with nothing left to fear and no impending disaster to be concerned about. In this sterile world of frozen French fries and processed food, I can always turn on the TV and watch a reality show for some genuine simulated real-life adventure. When I see a cop here, there's no double-checking my stash to make sure my bribe money is in order or fear that he will rob me. I do, however, continually get stopped by police, but thus far, it has only been for a sincere handshake and a hearty "Welcome home, Glen."

When riding through the mountains to my ranch there's no more threat of being captured or murdered by guerrillas. Other than the visual impairment, driving at night in the desert is no longer a suicide run because of bandits. The only peril seems to be drunks out after midnight. Since I must cross Indian reservation land to get to my ranch, there are cattle in the roadways, but no donkeys or potholes to be concerned about. The last several miles of dirt and gravel do remind me of parts of South America, minus the mighty eighty-mile-an-hour icy winds and violent thunderstorms raging across the plains.

Southern California weather is as spectacular as ever and within an hour, a determined driver can be at the Colorado River, or Santa Monica Beach, or the Coachella Valley, or a 9,000-foot mountain peak, or best of all, Tijuana for fresh tacos and friendly conversation.

Subtract the crime and fierce weather conditions and there is not much you can't get here that you can get in Latin America except a hard time and maybe a bit more magic — well, actually a lot more magic. Maybe that's what I am missing, the peaks and valleys and flavorful challenge of survival. I already miss setting unrealistic goals, the preparation, the last-minute apprehension, and the final heart-fluttering plunge into the unknown. The only unknown in my world now is how much the insurance company will pay if something goes wrong. Is it my imagination or are we living in an overregulated society? We should be careful what we wish for.

There were weeks at a time in South America when I was uncertain if I would see the sunrise, and that's not counting the time with the ELN. Maybe a sporadic burst of authentic danger would be nice now and then — just to feel alive. Perhaps it's the threat of doom that makes me appreciate life so much. Unfortunately there doesn't seem to be any on and off switches or dials to regulate how much stark raving terror one can withstand. Then again, it is the unknowns that make life so interesting and real.

Yes, it is good to be back. But I'm still unsure where home is. My sun-scorched spirit cries out for the open road with a summer wind in my face and a map on my gas tank. The only difficulty right now is backing off the throttle for that turn up ahead to some predetermined appointment with a normal day and its predictable ending.

My heart aches to thunder down the highway, back into the unknown and unforgiving, while a persistent inner voice provocatively whispers, "I wonder what it would be like to ride around the world?"

Epilogue

THE UNTOLD STORY
• • • • • • • • • • • • •

No matter the outcome of hostage situations — freedom, murder, or disappearance — cases don't end when victims return from captivity. Even when media headlines reflect the immediate euphoria of a freed prisoner, the rest of the story quickly fades behind the next crisis as the tedious process of healing wounded minds begins. As much as home-teams pull together, when the crisis passes, often a bitter residue lingers. Despite good intentions, an adage reverberates: "There is no going home."

And today as I type these words nine years after my ordeal in Colombia, a complete story of the subsequent psychological roller coaster ride is much too personal to detail. After the temporary joy and celebration of returning home to cheering loved ones, reassembling the lives of those directly involved became a daunting task in the aftermath of a brief but punishing chaos. Compared to other kidnappings later reported in international news stories, from Iraq to Pakistan to Mexico to Colombia, my ordeal was a mere five weeks and thankfully no one chopped off my head. But those agonizing times took a painful toll on my friends and family members who anguished nightly, sleepless from worry over my fate. Staring into the darkness, wondering if I was I dead or alive, increased their awareness of how dangerous the world can be. The realities of another nation's civil war and how it affected us were further complicated during daily strategy sessions with frequent debates over how to handle publicity, deal with the FBI, and generally keep the faith.

Only those closest to me believed I was still alive, while some reluctantly accepted the rumor that I had been executed. So when news arrived that the ELN had released me on humanitarian grounds, it was as though I was returning from the dead — along with all the misunderstandings that accompany such confusion. While I was held prisoner in the chilly mountain jungles of Colombia, there were varying opinions on how to contend with our crisis, which eventually led to hurt feelings and sometimes downright fury among lifelong friends. Once the smoke cleared and I was safe at home, we soon discovered that some of those relationships would never be the same, and others would cease altogether. The damage was done and much of what occurred in my absence was kept from me, with only hints trickling out over the years about who did what. I was assured, "Glen, there are some things that you just don't need to know."

Yet as good as it felt to be back in Palm Springs, a nagging emptiness combined with a passion for Latin culture compelled me to ride south twice more for extensive journeys into Central America and Mexico. As the winds of dramatic change tugged on my soul, I was having difficulty defining the concept of home. Was it the profound intensity of time spent roaming the Andean *Altiplano* or wandering the wilds of Patagonia that created a craving for a real world stripped of false security and safety nets? Or had the ELN simply bent my mind so far out of shape I could never again be comfortable among my own kind? There were a few Internet "experts" speculating that I was experiencing Stockholm Syndrome and likened my sympathies for abused *campesinos* with being brainwashed. But none of that chatter mattered as the welcoming embrace of Latin America soothed my tormented spirit.

A single solution struck me one restless night while ceiling-gazing in Granada, Nicaragua. On the last lonely twilight in a cramped little rented apartment near the town's famous plaza, I realized that a final path home would require another extraordinary journey more challenging than the last. It was beneath the loping hum of a wobbling ceiling fan in an adobe room lined with cobwebs and rotted plumbing that I decided what to do. And to the dismay of friends and family in California, after that moment of clarity, I began loosely plotting a motorcycle ride around the globe.

When I announced soon after that in order to clear my head, I needed to return to the road for a subsequent loop around the entire planet, a few of those closest to me took big steps back. Both weary from the Colombian ordeal and wary of any future conflicts, they knew that if something went wrong again, they couldn't take the strain. They had enough "adventures of the Striking Viking" to last a lifetime.

When discussing my plan to begin the next escapade by riding across Siberia into the Gobi Desert and on to the Middle East, one friend looked at me with disgust and spoke to me for what turned out to be the last time — "Glen, you are one selfish jerk." Worst of all, I knew he was right. But I still needed to go.

Realizing that I was determined to set out again no matter what, other friends sighed with silent but similar disappointment while half-heartedly egging me on. But as my departure date neared, in a deepening gloom of hand wringing and forced smiles, chasms in once rock-solid relationships widened. Only my brother Brad totally understood and accepted the new mission — yet I suspect his first choice would have been for my healing process to transpire on relatively safer North American highways. As one of the most psychologically sound men I know, Brad confided in me that he had only cried twice as a grown man, once on the day when he heard I was captured in Colombia, and the other on the day when I was freed. Nonetheless, he promised to, and did in fact, temporarily join me twice as I subsequently toured the developing world from Siberia to Africa by way of Asia. Riding mostly solo by motorcycle over 52,000 miles of often very difficult terrain proved to be as enlightening as it was demanding while I met fellow inhabitants of the planet, shaking their hands and booming a hearty "Howdy from California!"

But closure on the experience of captivity is proving to be elusive. Once I returned from that colorful journey around the earth through fifty-seven developing countries, living back in sunny southern California still seemed too awkward. Within weeks of returning from that odyssey, I again rode south of the border to resettle in Mazatlán, Mexico, for the next three years. It was there that I finished writing my second book.

Still, to settle my mind completely, I need to know exactly what my government did or did not do on my behalf while I was held prisoner in Colombia. And thus far, the FBI report on those events is a nationally guarded secret. Over the years, my requests filed under the Freedom of Information Act were denied, as were my follow-up appeals; Congresswoman Mary Bono Mack and U.S. Senator Dianne Feinstein were both unsuccessful in pleading with the government to release information. No matter who pitched who on my behalf, each plea was met by stonewalling bureaucrats refusing to cooperate, stating reasons of national security. When government agencies rally so hard for secrecy, an obvious question arises — what are they hiding?

That situation may change someday but in the meantime, life goes on and I am convinced that living well is the best revenge. And now more than ever, an effective way for average world citizens to demoralize terrorists gangs like Hezbollah and the ELN is by refusing to be afraid and, more importantly, refusing to hate. Al-Qaeda can claim victory if they are able to turn a free people against each other so much that they eventually strangle themselves in panic legislation, reversing freedoms earned through bloodshed, and depleting national treasure. Maybe the answer is simple: when the average people of the planet refuse to hate, terrorism fails and freedom prevails as we reach out to one another.

Being born within the specific geographic coordinates designating history's strongest economy backed by a powerful military has assured me a life of relative comfort. Yet it's puzzling that to this day I feel so connected, and most often more comfortable, traveling among the stark and often tragic realities of the developing world. Was this a predetermined path illuminated by an unfortunate incident in a remote Colombian wilderness that has taken me full circle? When life's silent tragedies unfold before the eyes of international travelers it is a common reaction to want to alleviate the suffering and ultimately remedy the future. But how to alleviate that suffering? Solutions are debatable.

For a lone motorcyclist roaming strange lands during the past decade, long hours in the saddle witnessing the surrounding pathetic realities have made for long evenings of introspection and pondering the fate of humanity. From dusty fleabag hotels in crumbling capital cities, can tapping out journals on a glowing laptop spark an awareness in those more powerful than me to take a long serious look at our future? Will this modern era of mass communication and lightning-fast Internet provide a platform for history to finally teach us something? And what would those lessons suggest we do?

Is the answer in rallying the exploited to gather arms against tyranny? Or should those from wealthy countries invest in relief efforts? Or perhaps provide means to educate the impoverished so that one day they are better able to govern themselves and hopefully better control their own destiny? Is eliminating the causes of war too lofty a goal for the individual? Or can the collective might of millions focused on positive thought reverse the course of humanity's demise? A more important question is whether we continue to turn our backs in self-absorption or roll up our sleeves and get to work? As human beings should we reconsider our responsibilities to those less fortunate? In terms of where the world is heading, should we at least consider the cup half full, and make a communal effort to do the right thing? In the meantime, if you bought this book, know that one hundred percent of the royalties have been donated to international aid organizations dedicated to improving education in the developing world.

All the best,
Glen Heggstad

Chief of FOIA & Privacy Act Section   June 16, 2003
Federal Bureau of Investigation
935 Pennsylvania Ave
Washington DC 20535

Re: Freedom of Information Act Request and Privacy Act Request

Dear Staff,

This is a request under the Freedom of Information Act, 5 U.S.C. Sec. 552.

November 6, 2001, while en route to Argentina from my home in Palm Springs, California on my
motorcycle I was kidnaped by the terrorist group, ELN in Colombia outside Medellin. I was
released approximately five weeks later and picked up by a team of FBI agents in Medellin and
flown back to Bogota. They were very helpful to me throughout my ordeal but when I asked for a
copy of their reports, I was told to file a request under the FOIA. Your cooperation would be
greatly appreciated and help me to obtain closure on my ordeal.

I request a copy of the following documents: All records and reports regarding my kidnaping in
Colombia on or about November and December of 2001 and any subsequent data kept on me
since. Please provide this to me: Glen Paul Heggstad. Social Security # ███████ Current
passport # 70189523█ issued in Bogota, Colombia 12/10/01

In order to help determine my status to assess fees, you should know that I am an individual
seeking information for personal use and not for a commercial use.

I am aware that I am entitled to make this request under the Freedom of Information Act, and if
your agency response is not satisfactory, I am prepared to make an administrative appeal. Please
indicate to me the name of the official to whom such an appeal should be addressed.

I am aware that if my request is denied I am entitled to know the grounds for this denial.

I am aware that while the law allows your agency to withhold specified categories of exempted
information, you are required by law to release any segregable portions that are left after the
exempted material has been deleted from the data I am seeking.

I am willing to pay fees for this request up to a maximum of $100.00. If you estimate that the fees
will exceed this limit, please inform me first.

Sincerely,

Glen P. Heggstad

U.S. Department of Justice

Office of Information and Privacy

Telephone: (202) 514-3642   _Washington, D.C. 20530_

JAN 28 2004

Mr. Glen P. Heggstad   Re: Appeal No. 03-3309
███████████████████   Request No. 981173
Palm Springs, CA ████   RLH:ADW:JYC

Dear Mr. Heggstad:

     You appealed from the action of the Headquarters Office
of the Federal Bureau of Investigation on your request for
access to records concerning you.

     After carefully considering your appeal, I have decided
to affirm the FBI's action on your request.

     You are the subject of two Miami Field Office main files
entitled Hostage Taking and Administrative Matters. These
files were processed at the FBI Headquarters Office.

     These records are exempt from the access provision of the
Privacy Act of 1974 pursuant to 5 U.S.C. § 552a(j)(2). See
28 C.F.R. § 16.96(a) (2003). Because these records are not
available to you under the Privacy Act, your request has been
reviewed under the Freedom of Information Act in order to
afford you the greatest possible access to the records you
requested.

     The FBI properly withheld certain information that is
protected from disclosure under the FOIA pursuant to:

     5 U.S.C. § 552(b)(7)(A), which concerns records or
     information compiled for law enforcement purposes, the
     release of which could reasonably be expected to
     interfere with enforcement proceedings; and

     5 U.S.C. § 552(b)(7)(C), which concerns records or
     information compiled for law enforcement purposes, the
     release of which could reasonably be expected to
     constitute an unwarranted invasion of the personal
     privacy of third parties (including, in this instance,
     those of investigative interest to the FBI).

May 17, 2004

Dear Congresswoman Bono,

Two years ago, while on a motorcycle ride to Argentina, I was taken prisoner by a terrorist army known as the ELN. This occurred on the highway outside Medellin, Colombia November 6, 2001. After five weeks, I was freed through the Red Cross and later flown back to Bogota on an embassy plane escorted by FBI agents.

I maintained contact with them after being released but when I asked for a copy of the official report, they denied me. They stated it was policy to direct me to file for this under the Freedom of Information Act. Enclosed are copies of correspondence with the appropriate agency.

As you can see, I am getting nowhere and feel as a tax paying American citizen, I am entitled to all information relating to my case. This nonsense about "National Security" is an overused excuse by the government *we the people* are supposed to trust. I am not requesting anything that any other person would want in similar circumstances.

Frankly, I have never asked my government for anything. I just work and pay my taxes and try to mind my own business. Now, when I request this report, there is a bunch of secrecy. This kind of secrecy usually means someone did something somewhere they are ashamed of or don't want to own up to.

Thank you for your time and I would appreciate any help in this matter.

Sincerely yours,

Kean P. Heggstad

PS
I will be riding my motorcycle around the world as of June 20,2004 until 2006. The best way to reach me will be through email. locovikingman@yahoo.com

U.S. Department of Justice

Federal Bureau of Investigation

Washington, D. C. 20535-0001

June 21, 2004

Honorable Mary Bono
Member of Congress
Suite 9
707 East Tahquitz Canyon Way
Palm Springs, CA 92262

Dear Congresswoman Bono:

Your facsimile dated May 24, 2004, directed to Ms. Eleni Kalisch of our Congressional Affairs Office, concerning the Freedom of Information and Privacy Acts (FOIPA) request of your constituent, Mr. Glen Paul Heggstad, has been referred to me for response.

In response to Mr. Heggstad's FOIPA request, a search of the central records indices at FBI Headquarters revealed that Mr. Heggstad's name was referenced as a victim in two Miami Field Office files captioned "Hostage Taking and Administrative Matters." He was advised the material in these files was being withheld in their entirety pursuant to Title 5, United States Code, Sections 552 and 552a, subsections (j)(2), (b)(7)(A) and (b)(7)(C). Release of these records could reasonably be expected to interfere with enforcement proceedings and would constitute an unwarranted invasion of personal privacy. In response to Mr. Heggstad's appeal to the Office of Information and Privacy, Department of Justice, he was advised by letter dated January 28, 2004, that the information was not appropriate for discretionary release; therefore, the initial action taken by the FBI was affirmed.

On June 10, 2004, our Miami Field Office was contacted regarding the current status of these cases. The files remain in pending status due to outstanding investigative leads and release of these records could interfere with enforcement proceedings. I certainly understand Mr. Heggstad's desire to see documents relating to his ordeal; however, we are compelled to protect the integrity of this investigation and cannot make them available at this time.

Sincerely yours,

William L. Hooton

William L. Hooton
Assistant Director
Records Management Division

JUN 30 2004

Acknowledgments

I would like to thank the following people for their undying loyalty and support:

Tim and Sherry Bernard
Mike and Sue Brown
John and Michele Cockrell
Chuck and Georgia Decker
Peter Doyle
Tex and Pam Earnhardt
Clifford and Dale Fischer
Joe Gallagher
Loren and Kathryn Gallagher
Dr. David Gansei
Dean Garner
Andy Goldfine
Luis Gonzales
Kjell Hegstad
Big Don and
    Brandon Hinshaw

Brian Hixson
Dennis Hof
Al Jesse
Patrick Larkin
Daniel McCown
Anthony Montanona
Brad and Wanda Neste
Whitney Parsons
Mark Pfenning
Dan Rather
Chad Rivera
Ricardo Rocco
Donal Rodarte
Sue Salvatore
Hushang Shahidi
Jimmy Weems

All royalties from Glen Heggstad's projects are donated to international aid organizations.

For more photos and information, please visit
www.strikingviking.net
Photo gallery images are available in high-resolution
eight–mega pixel format.

Contact Glen:
locovikingman@yahoo.com